D0451161

THE POLITICS OF CLIMATE CHANGE

Books by Anthony Giddens:
Capitalism and Modern Social Theory
Politics and Sociology in the Thought of Max Weber
The Class Structure of the Advanced Societies
New Rules of Sociological Method
Studies in Social and Political Theory
Emile Durkheim
Central Problems in Social Theory
A Contemporary Critique of Historical Materialism
Sociology: A Brief but Critical Introduction
Profiles and Critiques in Social Theory
The Constitution of Society
The Nation-State and Violence
Durkheim on Politics and the State
Social Theory and Modern Sociology
Sociology Sixth Edition
The Consequences of Modernity
Modernity and Self-Identity
The Transformation of Intimacy
Beyond Left and Right
Reflexive Modernization (with Ulrich Beck and Scott Lash)
Politics, Sociology and Social Theory
In Defence of Sociology
The Third Way
Runaway World
The Third Way and its Critics
Where Now for New Labour?
Europe in the Global Age
Over to You, Mr Brown

Edited Works:
Emile Durkheim: Selected Writings
Positivism and Sociology
Elites and Power In British Society (with Philip Stanworth)
Classes, Conflict and Power
Classes and the Division of Labour
Social Theory Today
Human Societies
On the Edge: Living with Global Capitalism (with Will Hutton)
The Global Third Way Debate
The Progressive Manifesto
The New Egalitarianism (with Patrick Diamond)
Global Europe, Social Europe (with Patrick Diamond and Roger Liddle)

THE POLITICS OF CLIMATE CHANGE

Anthony Giddens

polity

Copyright © Anthony Giddens 2009

The right of Anthony Giddens to be identified as Author of this Work has been asserted in accordance with the UK Copyright, Designs and Patents Act 1988.

First published in 2009 by Polity Press
Reprinted 2009 (five times)

Polity Press
65 Bridge Street
Cambridge CB2 1UR, UK

Polity Press
350 Main Street
Malden, MA 02148, USA

All rights reserved. Except for the quotation of short passages for the purpose of criticism and review, no part of this publication may be reproduced, stored in a retrieval system, or transmitted, in any form or by any means, electronic, mechanical, photocopying, recording or otherwise, without the prior permission of the publisher.

ISBN-13: 978-0-7456-4692-3
ISBN-13: 978-0-7456-4693-0 (pb)

A catalogue record for this book is available from the British Library.

Typeset in 11 on 13pt Palatino
by Servis Filmsetting Ltd, Stockport, Cheshire
Printed and bound in Great Britain by the MPG Books Group

The publisher has used its best endeavours to ensure that the URLs for external websites referred to in this book are correct and active at the time of going to press. However, the publisher has no responsibility for the websites and can make no guarantee that a site will remain live or that the content is or will remain appropriate.

Every effort has been made to trace all copyright holders, but if any have been inadvertently overlooked the publishers will be pleased to include any necessary credits in any subsequent reprint or edition.

For further information on Polity, visit our website: www.politybooks.com

CONTENTS

ACKNOWLEDGEMENTS

This book grew out of my involvement in a project organized under the auspices of the think-tank Policy Network and the Centre for the Study of Global Governance at the London School of Economics. I should like to thank my colleagues in both institutions for their help and advice during the writing process. My gratitude is due in particular to Roger Liddle, Olaf Cramme, Simon Latham and Jade Groves at Policy Network; and to David Held at the Centre. Anne de Sayrah helped the project in more ways than I can count. Karen Birdsall did a marvellous job checking footnotes and assembling the bibliography. Joe Livesey carefully and skilfully checked over the figures in some of the chapters. Olaf Corry provided some important feedback on a draft manuscript. I owe an especially large debt to Hugh Compston, who commented in a meticulous way on an early version of the book; and to Johanna Juselius, who did the same at a later point. Victor Philip Dahdaleh generously provided the funding for the collective project, so a big vote of thanks to him. I owe a great debt to everyone at Polity Press, including especially John Thompson, Gill Motley (as always), Sarah Lambert and Emma Hutchinson. I would like to thank Emma in particular for her attention to detail and for the amount of work she put into the project. Sarah Dancy did a great job with the copy-editing and I'm most grateful. She is a delight to work with. Finally, my thanks are due as always to Alena for her constant support and encouragement, and for her insouciance on the days when the whole project looked just too difficult. I dedicate the work to Indie and Matilda, definitely members of the younger generation, in the hope that it might contribute a little to making the world in which they will grow up less daunting.

INTRODUCTION

This is a book about nightmares, catastrophes – and dreams. It is also about the everyday, the routines that give our lives continuity and substance. It is about SUVs – Sports Utility Vehicles, or 4x4s. The book is a prolonged enquiry into a single question: why does anyone, anyone at all, for even a single day longer, continue to drive an SUV? For their drivers have to be aware that they are contributing to a crisis of epic proportions concerning the world's climate. On the face of things, what could be more disturbing than the possibility that they are helping to undermine the very basis of human civilization?

In case it isn't obvious, I hasten to add that SUVs are a metaphor. If I can put it this way, we are all SUV drivers, because so few of us are geared up to the profundity of the threats we face. For most people there is a gulf between the familiar preoccupations of everyday life and an abstract, even if apocalyptic, future of climate chaos. Almost everyone across the world must have heard the phrase 'climate change' and know at least a bit about what it means. It refers to the fact that the greenhouse gas emissions produced by modern industry are causing the earth's climate to warm up, with potentially devastating consequences for the future. Yet the vast majority are doing very little, if anything at all, to alter their daily habits, even though those habits are the source of the dangers that climate change has in store for us.

It is not as if climate change is creeping up on us unawares. On the contrary, large numbers of books have been written about it and its likely consequences. Serious worries about the warming of the earth's climate were expressed for a quarter of a century or more without making much of an impact. Within the past few years the issue has jumped to the forefront of discussion and debate, not just in this or that country but across the world. Yet, as collective humanity, we are only just beginning to take the steps needed to respond to the threats that we and succeeding generations are confronting. Global warming is a problem unlike any other, however, both because of its scale and because it is mainly about the future. Many have said that to cope with it we will need to mobilize on a level comparable to fighting a war; but in this case there are no enemies to identify and confront. We are dealing with dangers that seem abstract and elusive, however potentially devastating they may be.

No matter how much we are told about the threats, it is hard to face up to them, because they feel somehow unreal – and, in the meantime, there is a life to be lived, with all its pleasures and pressures. The politics of climate change has to cope with what I call 'Giddens's paradox'. It states that, since the dangers posed by global warming aren't tangible, immediate or visible in the course of day-to-day life, however awesome they appear, many will sit on their hands and do nothing of a concrete nature about them. Yet waiting until they become visible and acute before being stirred to serious action will, by definition, be too late.

Giddens's paradox affects almost every aspect of current reactions to climate change. It is the reason why, for many citizens, climate change is a back-of-the-mind issue rather than a front-of-the-mind one. Attitude surveys show that most of the public accept that global warming is a major threat; yet only a few are willing to alter their lives in any significant way as a result. Among elites, climate change lends itself to gestural politics – grandiose-sounding plans largely empty of content.

What social psychologists call 'future discounting' further accentuates Giddens's paradox – more accurately, one could say it is a sub-category of it. People find it hard to give the same level of reality to the future as they do to the present. Thus a small reward offered now will normally be taken in preference to a much larger one offered at some remove. The same principle applies to risks. Why do many young people take up smoking even though they are well aware that, as it now says on cigarette packets, 'smoking kills'? At least part of the reason is that, for a teenager, it is almost impossible to imagine being 40, the age at which the real dangers start to take hold and become life-threatening.

Giddens's paradox is at the centre of a range of other influences that tend to paralyse or inhibit action. Think back to the SUV. In the US, lots of people drive them, partly because, under the presidency of George W. Bush, no attempt was made to impose the taxes on gas-guzzling vehicles that some other countries have levied. The large motor-vehicle companies, not just in America but to some extent elsewhere as well, continued to pour them forth and had a vested interest in so doing. And their sales had a certain justifiable rationale. SUVs are valuable in rough terrain. People who use them in cities often do so because of a sense of style, but also because they offer more protection in accidents than smaller vehicles do. And not all SUV drivers are macho men by any means. Women sometimes drive them, because of the sense of security they provide.

People carry on driving SUVs for other reasons too. There is a high level of agreement among scientists that climate change is real and dangerous, and that it is caused by human activity. A small minority of scientists, however – the climate change 'sceptics' – dispute these claims, and they get a good deal of attention in the media. Our driver can always say, 'it's not proven, is it?' if anyone were to suggest that he should change his profligate ways. Another response might be: 'I'm not going to change unless others do', and he could point out that some drive even bigger gas-guzzlers, like Bentleys or Ferraris. Yet another reaction could be: 'Nothing that I so, as a single individual, will make any difference'. Or else he could say, 'I'll get round to it sometime', because one shouldn't underestimate the sheer force of habit. I would suggest that even the most sophisticated and determined environmentalist – who owns no car at all – struggles with the fact that, under the shadow of future cataclysm, there is a life to be lived within the constraints of the here-and-now.

As for SUVs, so for the world: there is a long way to go before rhetoric becomes reality. Politicians have woken up to the scale and urgency of the problem and many countries have recently introduced ambitious climate change policies. Over the past few years, a threshold has been crossed: most political leaders are now well aware of the hazards posed by climate change and the need to respond to them. Yet this is just the first wave – the bringing of the issue onto the political agenda. The second wave must involve embedding it in our institutions and in the everyday concerns of citizens, and here, for reasons just mentioned, there is a great deal of work to do. The international community is on board, at least in principle. Negotiations aimed at limiting global warming have taken place at meetings organized by the United Nations, starting in Rio in 1992, moving on to Kyoto in 1997 and then to Bali in 2007, in an attempt to get global reductions in greenhouse gas emissions. They are still continuing, but have produced little in the way of concrete results so far.

Much of this book concentrates on climate change policy in the industrial countries. It is these countries that pumped most of the emissions into the atmosphere in the first place, and they have to take prime responsibility for controlling them in the near future. They must take the lead in reducing emissions, moving towards a low-carbon economy and making the social reforms with which these changes will have to be integrated. If they can't do these things, no one else will.

I want to make the somewhat startling assertion that, at present, *we have no politics of climate change*. In other words, we do not have a developed analysis of the political innovations that have to be made if our aspirations to limit global warming are to become real. It is a strange and indefensible absence, which I have written this book to try to repair. My approach is grounded in realism. There are many who say that coping with climate change is too difficult a problem to be dealt with within the confines of orthodox politics. Up to a point I agree with them, since quite profound changes will be required in our established ways of political thinking. Yet we have to work with the institutions that already exist and in ways that respect parliamentary democracy.

The state will be an all-important actor, since so many powers remain in its hands, whether one talks of domestic or of international policy. There is no way of forcing states to sign up to international agreements; and even if they choose to do so, implementing whatever is agreed will largely be the responsibility of each individual state. Emissions trading markets can only work if the price of carbon is capped, and at a demanding level, a decision that has to be made and implemented politically. Technological advance will be vital to our chances of cutting greenhouse gas emissions, but support from the state will be necessary to get it off the ground. The one major supra-national entity that exists, the European Union, is heavily dependent on decisions taken by its member nations, since its control over them is quite limited.

Markets have a much bigger role to play in mitigating climate change than simply in the area of emissions trading. There are many fields where market forces can produce results that no other agency or framework could manage. In principle, where a price can be put on an environmental good without affronting other values, it should be done, since competition will then create increased efficiency whenever that good is exchanged. However, active state intervention is once again called for. The environmental costs entailed by economic processes often form what economists call 'externalities' – they are not paid for by those who incur them. The aim of public policy should be to make sure that, wherever possible, such costs are internalized – that is, brought into the marketplace.

'The state', of course, comprises a diversity of levels, including regional, city and local government. In a global era, it operates within the context of what political scientists call multilayered governance, stretching upwards into the international arena and downwards to regions, cities and localities. To emphasize the importance of the state to climate change policy is not to argue for a reversion to top-down government. On the contrary, the most dramatic initiatives are likely to bubble up from the actions of far-sighted individuals and from the energy of civil society. States will have to work with a variety of other agencies and bodies, as well as with other countries and international organizations if they are to be effective.

One can't discuss the politics of climate change without mentioning the green movement, which has been a leading influence on environmental politics for many years. It has had a major impact in forcing the issue of climate change onto the political agenda. 'Going green' has become more or less synonymous with endeavours to limit climate change. Yet there are big problems. The green movement has its origins in the hostile emotions that industrialism aroused among the early conservationists. Especially in its latter-day development in Germany in the 1970s and 1980s, the greens defined themselves in opposition to orthodox politics. Neither position is especially helpful to the task of integrating environmental concerns into our established political institutions. Just what is and what is not valuable in green political philosophies has to be sorted out.

It isn't possible – or so I shall argue – to endorse any approach which tries in some sense to 'return to nature'. Conservationism may be a defensible value, but it has nothing intrinsically to do with combating global warming. Indeed, it may even hamper our efforts. As a result of the advance of science and technology, we have long since crossed the boundaries which used to separate us from the natural world. More of the same will be needed, not less, if we are seriously to confront problems of climate change. Partly for this reason, I reject one of the core ideas of the green movement – the precautionary principle: 'Don't interfere with nature.' Moreover, in seeking to stem climate change, no matter what is often said, we are not trying to 'save the planet', which will survive whatever we may do. The point is to preserve, and if possible enhance, a decent way of life for human beings on the earth.

The word 'green' is in such widespread use that I have no hope of dislodging it. But it is now more of a problem rather than any help when it comes to developing policies to cope with climate change. I shall avoid using the term in what follows.

A whole range of questions has to be asked and answered. I list only a few briefly here. Later in the book, I try to respond to all of them, no doubt with varying degrees of success.

To cope with global warming, a long-term perspective must be introduced into politics. There has to be some sort of forward *planning*. 'Planning' is not a word with particularly pleasant connotations, since it conjures up images of authoritarianism on the one hand and ineptness on the other. State planning fell out of favour partly because it was oppressive and partly because it didn't work. If there is to be a return to such an endeavour, what form should it take?

And then there is the issue of coping with *risk* and *uncertainty*. Climate change politics is all about risk and how to manage it, and the notion appears on almost every page of this volume. We can't know the future: the philosopher Karl Popper used to say that if we could, it wouldn't be the future. The long-term thinking needed to counter climate change has to operate against the backdrop of uncertainty. It is often possible to assign probabilities to future events, yet there are many contexts where existing knowledge is stretched thin and large areas of uncertainty loom. What political strategies are needed to confront this range of problems?

To be able to mitigate climate change, members of the public have to be on board. Most at the moment are not. How can Giddens's paradox be unlocked? Should people be more scared than currently they are? Yes, but it doesn't follow that fear is the best motivator to get people to respond. Moreover, there are other risks that have to be faced up to, which intersect with those created by climate change – for example, pandemics, international terrorism and the spread of nuclear weapons.

In democratic countries governments come and go. Moreover, in real-life contexts many issues jostle for attention, including immediate questions of the day, which at the time may seem overwhelmingly important. In such circumstances, how is continuity of climate change policy to be maintained? Climate change, I shall argue, is not a left–right issue. There should be no more talk of 'green being the new red'. A cross-party framework of some kind has to be forged to develop a politics of the long term, but how? Countering climate change will cost money – where will it come from? Countries that are in the vanguard of climate change policy, as the developed countries have to be, could face problems of competitiveness. Their industries could be hampered by having to compete with goods that can be made more cheaply elsewhere where there are no environmental taxes or regulatory restrictions. How big a problem is this likely to be? Certainly, many business firms and employers' groups have used it as a basis for dragging their heels as far as climate change initiatives are concerned.

Finally, there are many difficult questions surrounding technology. Investment in renewable energy resources is crucial in countering climate change. Yet those resources won't develop in some sort of automatic way, nor will they be stimulated by the operation of market forces alone. The state has to subsidize them, in order for them to be competitive against fossil fuels and to protect investment in the face of the fluctuations to which the prices of oil and natural gas are subject. Technological change can only be predicted to a limited degree. How should governments decide which technologies to back? How can they cope with the fact that the most radical technological innovations – such as the internet – are often not foreseen by anybody?

To develop a politics of climate change, new concepts are needed and I introduce quite a large number in the book. One is the idea of the *ensuring state*. As far as climate change is concerned, the state has to act as a facilitator, an enabler – it has to help stimulate and support the diversity of groups in society that will drive policy onwards. Yet it can't be only an enabling body, since it has to ensure that definite outcomes are achieved – most notably a progressive reduction in carbon emissions. An ensuring state is one that has the capacity to produce definite outcomes, upon which not only can its own citizens rely, but so too can the leaders of other states.

Two other basic concepts are those of *political* and *economic convergence*. The first refers to how far climate change policy overlaps in a positive way with other values and political goals. Political convergence is crucial to how far climate change policy becomes innovative and energetic, but also to whether it receives widespread public support. For instance, lessening dependence upon the car (all cars), improving public transport and upgrading the quality of the built environment all converge with the objective of reducing carbon emissions. There are much more profound convergences as well. In the developed countries, we can no longer equate progress with economic growth. Above a certain level of affluence, growth no longer correlates highly with wider criteria of welfare.

Placing such a notion of welfare at the forefront might mesh very closely with climate change goals. Economic growth elevates emissions; what is the point of making a fetish of growth if in some large part it diminishes rather than promotes welfare? Tackling climate change, I shall try to show, provides the opportunity to develop a range of other political goals. At the same time, those goals offer the chance to push forward the climate change agenda.

Economic convergence concerns how far economic and technological innovations that are developed to combat global warming also generate competitive advantage to those who deploy them. I have mentioned earlier that the aim of reducing emissions might conflict with the competitiveness of businesses, but could that relationship perhaps be turned around? We might be moving rapidly into a situation in which firms that neglect environmental goals actually lose out in terms of competitiveness, or will do soon in the future. The greater the level of economic convergence, the better our chances of success in limiting climate change. It is essential that politicians and business leaders seize, and broaden, the opportunities offered, as many are now trying to do. By far the most important area of political and economic convergence is the overlap between climate change and energy security, on which more below. Through coping with the latter, we are most likely to be able to come to terms with the former.

To these notions I add that of the *development imperative*. The poorer nations have contributed only marginally to global warming; they must have the chance to develop, even if such a process raises emissions, for a period quite steeply. Development is imperative not simply for moral reasons. The consequences of climate change will worsen the enormous tensions that already derive from global inequalities, with implications for the world as a whole. Through technology transfer and other means, it should be possible for the developing countries to avoid a wholesale recapitulation of the path followed earlier by the industrial ones, but essentially a bargain between the more and less developed parts of the world has to be struck.

Like climate change, energy has suddenly come into the limelight as a fundamental problem for many nations and for the world as a whole. The underlying causes are to some degree the same. The energy needs of the industrial countries have created most of the emissions that are causing global warming. The rapid economic growth of developing nations, especially China, given its immense population size, is putting further strain on available energy sources, as well as increasing the level of greenhouse gases in the atmosphere. Responding to climate change has to be closely integrated with questions of energy security. It has become conventional to say so these days, but I have been struck by how loosely connected in most writings they actually are.

At what point will the world begin to run out of oil and gas, the energy sources upon which our civilization currently depends? There is an intense discussion about when world oil and gas supplies will peak – in other words, when half or more of them will have been consumed. If the peak in world oil and gas supplies is in fact approaching, then serious problems loom. Our SUV driver is there in the midst of them again, of course. In 2008, sales of the vehicles started to plummet. Why? It wasn't because of climate change, but because of the price of oil, which at that point was rising steeply in the face of worries about supply. Modern society is not only very heavily based upon oil in so far as energy is concerned, but also because oil figures in so many of the manufactured goods which figure in people's lives. Some 90 per cent of the goods in the shops involve the use of oil in one way or another.

We are currently living in a civilization that, as far as we can determine future risk, looks unsustainable. It isn't surprising that the past few years have seen the emergence of a doomsday literature, centred on the likelihood of catastrophe. Other civilizations have come and gone; why should ours be sacrosanct?

Yet risk is risk – the other side of danger is always opportunity. A lot of policy mistakes are being made at the moment. Most prescriptions about how to cope with climate change are negative. They are about saving, cutting back, retreating, retrenchment. Many are important. For instance, driving more economical cars, cutting back on air travel, reducing domestic energy bills, walking more often, or taking fewer baths are all small actions that can add up to a big difference in terms of reducing emissions.

Yet because of Giddens's paradox, no approach based mainly upon deprivation is going to work. We must create a positive model of a low-carbon future – and, moreover, one that connects with ordinary, everyday life in the present. There is no such model at the moment and we have to edge our way towards it. It won't be a green vision, but one driven by political, social and economic thinking. It can't be a utopia, but utopian strands will be involved, since they supply ideals to be striven for. A mixture of the idealistic and the hardheaded is required. For instance, lifestyle changes that serve to lower emissions will have direct economic implications. If they help generate more net jobs, or better jobs, than those currently available, they will have immediate and pragmatic value.

Energetic leadership on the part of businesses, NGOs and citizens will be needed to pursue such goals; so also will the development of new forms of mutual action and collaboration, where necessary making use of the full panoply of modern networked communications. Governments should have more ambitious aims alongside targets. For example, there could be competitions to promote new ideas or technologies, coupled perhaps to public recognition and rewards for those who make breakthrough contributions.

I don't want to sound panglossian. Quite to the contrary – some policies will have to have a hard edge to them; many will be unpopular and actively resisted. Powerful interests often stand in the way of reform and have to be faced down. My point is that even hard-edged constraints, if handled properly, can – and in fact almost always do – generate new opportunities. We can anticipate, and should do our best to encourage, a surge of technological innovation in response to both climate change and energy security. Without such innovation, it is impossible to see how we can break our dependency upon oil, gas and coal, the major sources of environmental pollution. A turn to renewable sources of energy is essential, and it has to be on a very large scale. Yet research shows that technological change can take years to percolate through the whole economy and society. No quick fix is available to deal with the problems we face – it's going to be a slog, even with the breakthroughs we need, and in fact must have.

The prize is huge. There is another world waiting for us out there if we can find our way to it. It is one where not only climate change has been held at bay, but where oil has lost its capacity to determine the shape of world politics.

Summarizing some of the key themes I discuss in the book, my advice to policy-makers would be as follows:

1 Promote political and economic convergence wherever possible and do so in an active way. It is important, for example, to cultivate an advance guard of entrepreneurs who will maximize the economic advantages of enlightened environmental policy. Work with what I call climate change positives – as has aptly been said, Martin Luther King didn't stir people to action by proclaiming, 'I have a nightmare!'. Fear and anxiety are not necessarily good motivators, especially with risks perceived as abstract ones, or dangers that are seen as some way off. Moreover, the risks from climate change, as the public experiences them, constitute only one set of worries among others.

2 Look first and foremost to embed a concern with climate change into people's everyday lives, while recognizing the formidable problems involved in doing so. Indirect means may sometimes be the best way. For instance, the public may be more responsive to a drive for energy efficiency than to warnings about the dangers of climate change. Don't wrangle too much about targets. What matters at this point is the how of climate change policy. Plan ahead, but remember that the short term is the key to the long term. Target-setting can be an excuse for inaction rather than the reverse. Don't place too much faith in carbon markets. The point is not only that their level of likely success at present is difficult to evaluate, but that they can easily become a political cop-out. They sound painless even if they are not. Carbon taxes are the way to go, but they must not be introduced piecemeal. A full-scale audit of the fiscal system is needed.

3 Avoid making political capital out of global warming. The temptation to do so may be great, especially when a

government or party is under pressure. If possible, establish an agreement with major party rivals to ensure continuity of climate change policy. Feed a concern with climate change through all branches of government and work to produce consistency in different political areas. It is no good introducing progressive environmental policies and then subverting them through decisions taken elsewhere. Don't neglect issues of social justice. Poorer people are more likely to be affected by the consequences of changes affecting the climate unless policy is specifically directed to countering those influences.

4 Set up detailed risk assessment procedures, stretching into the long term, since the implications of climate change policy are complex. We have to construct a future in which renewable sources will comprise the bulk of energy use. It will be a far-reaching transition indeed, with a whole raft of complex social and economic effects. Cooperate with other countries, regions or cities in an intensive and continuing way, with as wide a global spread as possible. Season policy with a dash of utopian thinking. Why? Because, however it happens, we are working our way towards a form of society that eventually will be quite different from the one in which we live today. We have to chance our arm.

In the three concluding chapters, I move the discussion onto more of an international level. Because of the volume of emissions already in the air, no matter how successful we might or might not be from this moment on, we will have to face some consequences of climate change and adapt to them as best we can. 'Adaptation' cannot mean just coping with such changes once they have occurred. As far as possible we have to prepare beforehand – adaptation must be proactive. It has to draw on the same resources of ingenuity as our attempts to mitigate climate change. We must prepare now to face hazards (but also to grasp opportunities) some way down the line. All countries will be affected, but the poorer nations will suffer more than the developed ones. The rich world has an obligation to help.

There is a clear imbalance between the literatures of energy security and of climate change. Analyses of energy security concentrate – and rightly so – upon the tensions, interests and divisions that characterize global politics. In discussions of climate change, by contrast, geopolitics appears as a shadowy presence in the background when negotiations about emissions reductions are carried out. That balance needs redressing. Just as we do not have a developed politics of climate change, we lack a geopolitics of it too. What institutions, mechanisms or international relationships are likely, in the real world, to deliver on climate change goals? Attempts to forge international agreements to limit carbon emissions have been deeply influenced by geopolitical considerations, but these have rarely been brought into the open. Most discussions focus on the details of negotiations, or are about the likely geopolitical fall-out from climate change. What is missing is analysis of the geopolitical influences that affect the decisions made by political leaders.

As crucial as national politics will be in responding to climate change, effective response has to be multilateral – it must involve nations working together, even countries whose interests in other respects might seem opposed. The European Union is an inherently multilateral organization, and has striven to take a leadership position in developing such a response. I am a committed pro-European, and I hope its endeavours will meet with success. However, it is going to be difficult. The EU's programmes will work only if its member-states themselves manage to make the structural changes I analyse in this book. For reasons I explain, I don't believe the post-Bali international discussions are likely to produce much in the way of concrete results either, although I hope I am wrong.

Other forms of collaboration will have to be pioneered to complement these discussions. For example, the developed countries should explore ways of direct bilateral cooperation with one another, to forge common policies and share the fruits of technological advance. In terms of relations of power, the future of the world's climate lies in some large degree in the hands of two nations alone – the US and China – since they contribute between them such a high proportion of the world's greenhouse gas emissions. Both are restlessly scouring the world for energy supplies to fuel their economies. Will they enter into a struggle for resources, or can they learn to cooperate? A great deal rides on the answer. A Gestalt switch is needed in the attitudes of the US government to climate change, which President Obama has promised to deliver.

'Yes we can!', he says, referring to America's capacity for renewal. One shouldn't forget that his predecessor made much the same claim, even if in quite a different way – former leader George W. Bush believed that the US was so powerful that it could ride roughshod over the rest of the world should it so choose. 'No you can't!' was the response, and it was a rude awakening. America will be able to lead only through collaboration with other nations and the world community as a whole, only through an awareness of the limitations of its power. That humility of which Bush spoke but never acted upon should be the basis of America's role in the world as the country comes back to multilateralism.

Of course, the impact of world economic slowdown on all this will be considerable. In the wake of the crisis in financial markets of 2008, the state has made something of a comeback. The period of freewheeling deregulation is over. However, a return to the state absolutely must not mean a reversion to the past. We won't find the answers that way. Quite the contrary: we have to find a new role for government and for market-based mechanisms too.

At the time of writing, financial markets are under a black cloud; but they will have a fundamental role in the struggle against global warming, in the context of appropriate legislation. As in all other areas of climate change policy, such legislation should be enabling rather than prohibitive, and promote new government and market-based partnerships. Complex financial instruments have suddenly gone out of fashion, blamed for market collapse. Yet we will need them, because, properly regulated, they are actually sometimes the key to long-term investment rather a force against it. For instance, a lot of ingenuity will be required to provide insurance cover against extreme weather events, even given the advance of global warming thus far. Private insurers will be needed to supply most of the necessary finance, since, given its many other obligations, the state can only be the insurer of last resort.

The end of the era of deregulation means that government is going to have a lead role in designing economic reconstruction following recession. The chance will exist to promote large-scale investment in new enterprises and technologies geared to a low-carbon future. What is important is that the right structures be set up for the next 20 years and beyond.

Much is being written about the possibility of instituting a 'Climate Change New Deal', designed to combine recovery from recession with large-scale investment in renewable energy sources. I am sympathetic to the idea, but it has to be done carefully and with due attention paid to more enduring remedies. In the meantime, there may be a difficult path to tread. Rising unemployment coupled to the steep drop in the price of oil that has occurred reintroduces temptations that could be difficult to resist. If lower prices are simply passed onto the consumer, they may aid recovery, but will reintroduce bad habits. Our driver will be back in his SUV with little reason to dispose of it. Yet the price of oil is certain to rise steeply again as soon as the world shows signs of moving out of recession. The worst outcome of all would be if climate change were simply put on the back burner until recovery occurs, and this we must bend all our efforts to prevent.

This is not a book about climate change, but about the politics of climate change. In the opening chapters I offer only a minimalist account of the debate about global warming. Many detailed discussions are available to the reader elsewhere.[1] I shall spend rather more time, in fact, upon energy security, to make up for the fact that the two are not usually discussed together.

1

CLIMATE CHANGE, RISK AND DANGER

Our understanding of the greenhouse effect, the origin of global warming in current times, dates back to the work of the French scientist Jean-Baptiste Joseph Fourier in the early part of the nineteenth century. Energy reaches the earth from the sun in the shape of sunlight; it is absorbed and is radiated back into space as infrared glow. When Fourier calculated the differential between the energy coming in and that going out as infrared radiation, he found that the planet should, in theory, be frozen. He concluded that the atmosphere acts like a mantle, keeping a proportion of the heat in – and thus making the planet liveable for humans, animals and plant life. Fourier speculated that carbon dioxide (CO_2) could act as a blanket in the atmosphere, trapping heat and causing surface temperatures to increase.

Later observers, most notably John Tyndall, a scientist working at the Royal Institution in London, worked out just which atmospheric elements trap infrared. The gases that make up most of the atmosphere, nitrogen and oxygen, offer no barrier to heat loss. Those producing what came to be called the greenhouse effect, such as water vapour, CO_2 or methane, are only present in relatively small amounts. Scientists use the calculation of 'parts per million' (ppm) to measure the level of greenhouse gases in the air, since the percentage figures are so small. One ppm is equivalent to 0.0001 per cent. It is because a tiny proportion makes such a large impact that greenhouse gases created by human industry can have profound effects on the climate (CO_2 makes up less than 0.04 per cent of the composition of the air, and the other greenhouse gases even less). Since CO_2 is the most important greenhouse gas in terms of volume, it is sometimes used as a standard of measurement when assessing emissions. The notion of 'CO_2 equivalent' is also often employed. It is the amount of CO_2 emission that would be involved to produce the same output as all the greenhouse gases combined. It is usually written as CO_2e.

Over the past 150 years or so, greenhouse gases in the atmosphere have progressively increased with the expansion of industrial production. The average world temperature has increased by 0.74 degrees since 1901. We know from geological studies that world temperatures have fluctuated in the past, and that such fluctuations correlate with CO_2 content in the air. The evidence shows, however, that at no time during the past 650,000 years has the CO_2 content of the air been as high as it is today. It has always been below 290ppm. By early 2008, it had reached 387ppm and is currently rising by some 2ppm each year.

The growth rate for 2007 was 2.14ppm, as measured by scientists at the Mauna Loa observatory in Hawaii. It was the fourth year out of the previous six to see a rise of more than 2ppm. This increase was considerably higher than scientists at the observatory had expected. It could indicate that the natural sinks of the earth are losing their capacity to absorb greenhouse gases. Most climate change models assume that some half of future emissions will be soaked up by forests and oceans, but this assumption may be too optimistic. Because CO_2 and most other greenhouse gases, once there, stay in the atmosphere a long time, and temperature takes some while to build up, an average surface warming of at least 2 °C, possibly more, may now be unavoidable, even were emissions to be cut back immediately – which of course won't happen.

Warming is greater over land areas than over the oceans, and is higher at northern latitudes than elsewhere. Very recent studies show that the temperatures of the oceans are rising several times faster than was thought likely a few years ago. Higher temperatures produce more acidity in the water, which

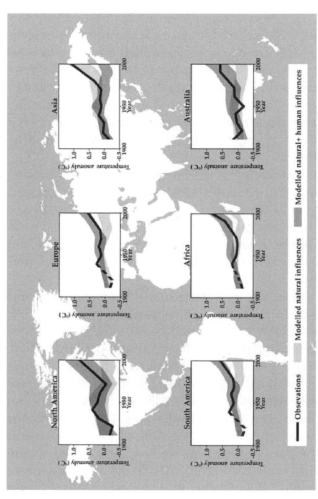

Average annual temperatures are rising on every inhabited continent. Computer studies indicate that the patterns seen can only be explained if they incorporate human-induced increases in greenhouse gases.

Figure 1.1 Rising temperatures

Source: Adapted from *Climate Change 2007: The Physical Science Basis.* Working Group I Contribution to the Fourth Assessment Report of the Intergovernmental Panel on Climate Change. Figure SPM.4. Cambridge University Press.

could seriously threaten marine life. Warmer seas release more CO_2, accelerating the global warming effect. As measured over the period from 1982 to 2006, temperatures rose most in the Baltic Sea (1.35 °C), the North Sea (1.3 °C) and the South China Sea (1.22 °C).

Satellite data, available since 1978, show that the annual average Arctic sea ice coverage is shrinking by nearly 3 per cent per decade, with larger decreases in the summer of over 7 per cent. The Arctic ice-cap is less than half the size it was 50 years ago. Over that time, average temperatures in the Arctic region have increased by about seven degrees, a result of a specific feedback cycle that exists there. The sun's rays strike the Arctic at a sharper angle than elsewhere over the summer, at a time when the ice is giving way to open water, which absorbs more solar radiation.

Some of the forecasting models presented at the annual meeting of the American Geophysical Union in 2007 suggested that the Arctic could be ice-free in the summer by as early as 2030.[1] Commercial trans-Arctic voyages could then be initiated. It would be possible to go from Northern Europe to East Asia or the north-west coast of the US avoiding the Suez and Panama Canals.

Mountain glaciers are retreating in both hemispheres and snow cover is less than, on average, it once was. Sea levels rose over the course of the twentieth century, although there is considerable controversy among scientists about just how much. Warming is likely to intensify the risk of drought in some parts of the world and lead to increased rainfall in others. Evidence indicates that the atmosphere holds more water vapour than used to be the case even a few decades ago, a major influence over unstable weather patterns, including tropical storms and floods. Over the past 40 years, westerly winds have become stronger. Tropical cyclones in the Atlantic have become more frequent and more intense over that period, probably as a result of warming.

The most authoritative body monitoring climate change and its implications is the Intergovernmental Panel on Climate Change of the UN (IPCC), first established in 1988. It has had an enormous impact upon world thinking about global warming. Its declared aims are to gather together as much scientific data about climatic conditions as possible, subject it to rigorous review, and reach overall conclusions on the state of scientific opinion. In several authoritative reports it has mapped the changing world climate in detail, showing that the potential consequences range from the worrying to the disastrous. In the fourth of such reports, published in 2007, the IPCC says 'warming of the climate system is unequivocal'. It is the only part of the document where such a term is used. All the rest is couched in terms of probabilities. There is a '90 per cent probability' that observed warming is the result of human activity through the introduction of greenhouse gases into the atmosphere, these coming from the consumption of fossil fuels in industrial production and travel, and from new forms of land use and agriculture.[2] Records of global surface temperature date back to 1850. Since that date, 11 of the hottest years have occurred during the past 13. Observations from all parts of the world show progressive increases in average air and sea temperatures.

The IPCC assesses the implications of climate change in terms of a number of different possible scenarios for the period up to the end of the current century. There are six different scenario groups – in other words, future possibilities – depending upon factors such as levels of economic growth, resource scarcities, population increase, the expansion of low-carbon technologies and the intensifying of regional inequalities. Under the most favourable scenario, global warming will still occur, within a range of between 1.1 and 2.9 °C. Sea levels will rise between 18 and 38 centimetres by the end of the century. If, on the other hand, the world continues to run, as is the case now, on oil, gas and coal, and to strive for high levels of economic growth, world temperatures could increase by more than 6 °C by 2100. In these circumstances, the sea level might rise by between 26 and 50 centimetres.

The 'most probable' scenario distinguished by the IPCC, in which fossil fuels are quite widely used, but are balanced by cleaner forms of energy generation, and where population growth is brought under control, is still worrying. In this scenario, temperatures could rise by more than 4 °C, with an increase of 48 centimetres in sea levels. There would probably be a decrease in rainfall of 20 per cent in sub-tropical areas, while more rain would fall in the northern and southern latitudes.

The IPCC and the European Commission have both stated that the aim of emissions control policy should be to limit global warming to 2 °C, and that to have even a 50:50 chance of achieving this outcome, atmospheric concentrations of greenhouse gases must be stabilized at 450 CO_2e. However, given the existing build-up of emissions, some regard this target as already impossible to achieve.

The effects of climate change are probably already being felt. The 2007 report of the IPCC states that we can assert with 'High Confidence' (an 8 in 10 chance or above of being correct) that global warming has led to more and larger glacial lakes, faster rates of melting in permafrost areas in Western Siberia and elsewhere, changes in some Arctic and Antarctic eco-systems, increased and earlier run-off from glacier and snow-fed rivers, earlier spring times in northern areas and a movement of some plant and animal species towards the poles.[3]

The IPCC says that resource-based wars could dominate the current century; coastal cities could become flooded, provoking mass destitution and mass migration, and the same could happen as drier areas become more arid. Given their location and lack of resources, the poorer parts of the world will be more seriously affected than the developed countries. Yet the latter will have their share of problems, including more and more episodes of violent weather. The United States, for example, has greater extremes of weather than most other parts of the world and these are likely to intensify further.

The sceptics and their critics

Scenarios are about future possibilities, so it is not surprising that there are those who question them, or who object to the very thesis that current processes of global warming are produced by human activity at all. Since the *sceptics* are in a minority, they see themselves not only as questioning a broad scientific consensus, but as tilting against a whole industry that has grown up around it.

Fred Singer and Dennis Avery, for example, advance the thesis that 'modern warming is moderate and not man-made'.[4] Their view, they complain, does not get much of a hearing, because of the attention that surrounds the claims made by the IPCC. 'A public relations campaign of staggering dimensions', they say, 'is being carried forward to convince us that global warming is man-made and a crisis ... environmental advocacy groups, government agencies, and even the media have spared no expense in spreading [the] dire message.'[5]

For them, there is nothing new about the increasing temperatures observed today. The world's climate has always been in flux. A moderate but irregular 1,500-year climate change cycle, driven by shifts in sun-spot variations, is well documented by the work of geologists. We are in the warming phase of just such a cycle at the moment. The chief worry we should have for the long-term future is, in fact, a coming ice age, as our relatively mild period draws to a close.

Other climate change sceptics take a somewhat different tack, while also emphasizing that heretical views don't get much of a hearing, let alone research funding. Patrick Michaels, for instance, claims that the findings and projections of the IPCC are intrinsically flawed.[6] Too many individuals and groups, he says, have a stake in predicting disasters and cataclysms to come. Only about a third of those producing the IPCC documentation are in fact scientists; the majority are government bureaucrats. Facts and findings that don't fit the main storyline are suppressed or ignored.

The Danish author Bjørn Lomborg is often lumped with the sceptics, and indeed entitled his first book on climate change *The Skeptical Environmentalist*.[7] His is an unusual form of scepticism, however. He accepts that global warming is happening and that human activity has brought it about. What is much more debatable, he says, 'is whether hysteria and headlong spending on extravagant CO_2-cutting programmes at an unprecedented price is the only possible response'.[8] Lomborg questions the idea that climate change risks must inevitably take precedence over all others. For the moment, world poverty, the spread of AIDS and nuclear weapons pose greater problems.

Other authors, writing about risk more generally rather than only about global warming, have suggested that we live in an 'age of scares', of which climate change is one. Our worries and anxieties, as Christopher Booker and Richard North put it, mark the emergence of a 'new age of superstition', resembling episodes of mass hysteria in the past, such as the witch-hunts of the post-mediaeval period. Scares, nearly all of which have turned out to be unfounded, have become part of our everyday lives, 'from mysterious and deadly new viruses and bacteria in our food, or floating about in the environment, to toxic substances in our homes and workplaces; all culminating in the ultimate apocalyptic visions conjured up by the fear of global warming'.[9]

Should one pay any attention to what the sceptics say, given that they are a small, albeit vocal, minority? Many scientists believe their writings are irresponsible, since they convey to the public that there is extensive space for doubt about the origins, and probable consequences, of warming when in fact there is little. There was a furore when Channel 4 TV in the UK produced a documentary in March 2007 called *The Great Global Warming Swindle*, which featured several of the most prominent sceptics.

Yet the sceptics do deserve and must receive a hearing. Scepticism is the life-blood of science and just as important in policy-making. It is right that whatever claims are made about climate change and its consequences are examined with a critical, even hostile, eye and in a continuing fashion. There is no doubt that 'big science' can attain a momentum of its own. The IPCC is not simply a scientific body, but a political and bureaucratic one. The sceptics are right to say that in the media, and sometimes in the speeches of politicians, climate change is now often invoked as though it explains every weather episode: 'Whenever there was any kind of unusual weather event, heatwaves, storms, droughts or floods, some broadcaster could be relied upon to describe it as "further confirmation of climate change".'[10]

However the sceptics do not have a monopoly on critical scrutiny. Critical self-examination is the obligation of every scientist and researcher. The fact that the findings of the IPCC are almost always expressed in terms of probabilities and possibilities gives due recognition to the many uncertainties that exist, as well as gaps in our knowledge. Moreover, the scientists contributing research findings to the IPCC have many differences among themselves about the progression of global warming and its likely consequences.

Risk and uncertainty cut two ways. The sceptics say the risks are exaggerated, but it is quite possible to make the opposite case. There are some who say we have underestimated both the extent and the imminence of the dangers posed by climate change. They argue that the IPCC is in fact something of a conservative organization, which is reserved in its judgements exactly because it has to cover a wide constituency of scientific opinion.

Fred Pearce, a writer for the *New Scientist*, says that the world's climate does not go in for gradual change, as the past history of climatic variation shows. The climate (as the sceptics also argue) has undergone all sorts of changes in the past, long before human beings appeared on the scene and well before the advent of modern industrial production. However, Pearce draws quite a different conclusion from this observation to that of the sceptics. Transitions from one climatic condition to another are often very abrupt, and climate change in our era, he argues, will probably be the same. We can make a distinction, he says, between Type 1 and Type 2 processes of climate change. Type 1 changes evolve slowly and follow the trajectories outlined in most of the scenarios of the IPCC. Type 2 change is radical and sharp – it comes about when a tipping point is reached, which triggers a sudden lurch from one type of system to another. Such change does not form part of the usual models for calculating climate change risk.[11]

The potential for Type 2 change today, Pearce says, is large. Some areas that were widely thought to be stable may in fact be dynamic and volatile – they include the ice sheets covering Greenland and Antarctica, the frozen peat bogs in Western Siberia, the Amazon rainforest and the weather pattern known as El Niño.

The IPCC has suggested that, should the world warm any more than 3 °C, the Greenland ice pack could start to melt, a process which, once it gets under way, would be impossible to reverse. The IPCC sees this possibility as one for the distant future. Some specialists in glacial studies, however, as Pearce points out, warn that such a process could happen much faster. As warming proceeds, and in conjunction with certain natural processes, lakes form at the tops of the glaciers. These set up water flows which drain down crevasses in the ice and, at the same time, widen them so that, instead of water taking many years to reach the bottom of the glaciers, it can do so almost instantaneously. The result, it is argued, might be the fracturing of large areas of ice, with profoundly destabilizing consequences. Were such effects to become generalized, large-scale melting could take place in a matter even of a decade.

The vast area of peat bog stretching from Western Siberia through northern Scandinavia, Canada and Alaska is covered by solid and seemingly permanent frost, but it has begun to thaw, a phenomenon 'that makes even the soberest scientists afraid'.[12] The Arctic permafrost holds down very large amounts of decayed vegetation, packed with carbon. As the frost melts, the leaves, roots and mosses beneath it start to decay, and release not only CO_2, but also methane. Methane is many times more potent a greenhouse gas than CO_2. One of the problems is that, so far, there have been relatively few studies of just how far these processes are advancing, largely because of difficulties of access to Siberia on the part of non-Russian scientists. One estimate is that the release of methane occurring from the West Siberian peat bogs is already equivalent to more than the greenhouses gases emitted by the United States in a single year.

And then there is El Niño, linked to the so-called 'Southern Oscillation'.[13] The term refers to unusually warm ocean conditions that can develop in the Pacific Ocean along the Western coasts of Ecuador and Peru. 'El Niño' means 'boy child' in Spanish, referring to the infant Jesus Christ. The name came from the fact that the phenomenon normally develops during the Christmas season. It happens every three to five years and can have a major effect on global climatic conditions. As El Niño moves across the world, following a path along the equator, disruptive weather follows in its wake, causing storms and heavy rainfall in some areas and droughts in others. After some 12–18 months it usually abruptly goes into reverse, causing unusually cold ocean temperatures in the equatorial Pacific, which also have disruptive effects upon weather conditions (moving this way around, it is known as La Niña).

Little is known about the long-term history of El Niño, but in recent years it has occurred more often, and with increasingly severe consequences. As with so many other climatic changes, we do not know how far global warming is playing a part. El Niño may act to moderate warming, but – at least as likely – could serve to accentuate turbulent weather conditions.

James Hansen, head of the NASA Goddard Institute for Space Studies, is one of the most influential authors to argue that the dangers from advancing temperatures have been under-estimated. It is a theme he has pursued for more than 20 years. He says that the goal of confining global warming to 2 °C, already very difficult to achieve, is not enough to prevent the dangerous consequences. The safe level of atmospheric carbon dioxide is 350ppm – below that which already exists.[14]

The authors who write about tipping points in climate change are not eccentrics, but mostly those who once believed that the effects of climate change would be un-dramatic and long drawn out. Fred Pearce, for example, like Lomborg, describes himself as a 'sceptical environmentalist' – by which he means someone who thoroughly investigates suspect claims wherever they are made. He recognizes that there are few or no certainties in climate change. The thresholds that he and others identify are sometimes called wild cards in the climate change pack.[15]

The three different positions referred to above tend to be linked to varying views of the earth and the impact of human beings on it. According to the sceptics, the earth is robust, and nothing that we do is likely to have any major impact upon it. To those closer to the mainstream, on the other hand, the earth – or at least its eco-systems – is fragile and has to be protected from the damaging intrusions we are making into it. Then there are writers like Pearce, who see the earth more as a wild beast, ready and able to react violently and precipitously once it is sufficiently roused. As Pearce puts it: 'She is strong and packs a serious counter-punch. . . . Nature's revenge for man-made global warming will very probably unleash unstoppable planetary forces. And they will be sudden and violent.'[16]

Gee-gees

Climate change comes with a doomsday literature attached. History has seen the rise and fall of many civilizations. According to the anthropologist Jared Diamond, civilizations become threatened with collapse when they burst the bounds of their environmental sustainability.[17]

A microcosmic example is what happened on Easter Island in the Pacific. The island once had a luxurious ecosystem, and was able to support a developed, monarchical civilization. However, over time the status of the kings came to be marked by the size of the statues they were able to build, constructions that consumed substantial natural resources, including a large amount of timber. Any monarch who tried to halt the process would be outflanked by others who would then continue the tradition. The outcome was the deforestation of the island, as the environment became barren and inhospitable. 'The overall picture for Easter is the most extreme example of forest destruction in the Pacific, and among the most extreme in the world – the whole forest gone, and all of its tree species extinct.'[18]

The possible parallels with our own civilization, on a much grander scale, are not difficult to spot. Diamond calls them 'chillingly obvious':

> Thanks to globalization, international trade, jet planes, and the internet, all countries on earth today share resources and affect each other, just as did Easter Island's dozen clans. Polynesian Easter Island was isolated in the Pacific Ocean as the earth is today in space. When the Easter Islanders got into difficulties, there was nowhere to which they could flee, nor to which they could turn to for help; nor could us modern Earthlings have recourse elsewhere if our troubles increase.[19]

Global warming, other authors point out, is not the only danger created by humans that could wreak havoc with our way of life. Other threats come from nuclear proliferation, which could at some point converge with tensions initiated by global warming; from self-reproducing nanotechnology, particles of which could get through the skin, into the blood-stream and from there be carried to the brain; from a food crisis, producing levels of starvation and mass migration on a massive scale; or from runaway population growth.[20] In *Our Final Century*, the distinguished scientist Martin Rees speaks seriously of the possibility that we – the human race – might not survive the twenty-first century, because of the quantity of dangers built up through our diverse interventions into (what used to be) nature.[21]

Some such 'doomsday books' concentrate on potential catastrophes in which human activities play little or no part. These happenings are extremely infrequent, but, by scientists, they 'are now very much regarded as part of the compendium of hazards that we have to consider' when thinking of the earth's vulnerabilities.[22] They have been labelled Global Geophysical Events – GGEs or, such is the human propensity for playfulness, 'gee-gees'. Gee-gees are catastrophes of sufficient scale either to impinge on the whole planet, or to cause regional devastation of such strength that it could severely damage the social fabric or the economy of the world as a whole.

An ocean-wide giant tsunami is one such catastrophe. The tsunami that occurred in December 2004 killed an estimated quarter of a million people, spread out in areas far from the source itself. The waves produced by the tsunami were mostly less than 10 metres high. Should a giant tsunami occur, it could generate waves several times larger. Such an event could be brought about – among several possibilities – by the eruption of the Cumbre Vieja volcano on La Palma, one of the Canary Islands. Scientists have been monitoring the volcano for some time; it has a series of long fractures along its seaboard side, the result of an eruption in 1949. In a further such eruption, the entire flank of the volcano could become violently thrust into the sea, triggering a mega-tsunami that would race across the Atlantic.

Another gee-gee would be an earthquake that strikes in the middle of a major population centre. Tokyo is a case in point. The city experiences constant tremors, although the last time there was a big earthquake was in 1923. In shaking that lasted only about a minute, 360,000 buildings were destroyed in Tokyo and its twin city of Yokohama. More than 70 per cent of the inhabitants of Tokyo and 85 per cent in Yokohama lost their homes. In all, more than 100,000 people died in the disaster.[23]

Three times as many people live in the Greater Tokyo area now than in the 1920s – over a quarter of the population of the country. Homes and workplaces are more solidly built than they used to be, but, because of the population density, another big earthquake would be likely to result in as many or more people being killed than perished 80 years ago. The property damage likely to be incurred is considerably greater than it was then, because the society is so much wealthier. A study funded by the insurance company Swiss Re calculated that the cost of the damage would be around $4.3 trillion.

The possibility that the earth might be struck by a large asteroid or comet is a third gee-gee. It is only over the past 20 years or so, as a reult of advances in satellite and infra-red mapping, that the progress of foreign bodies through space has been able to be accurately mapped and monitored. An 11-point scale – the Torino scale, so-called because it was established in a conference held in that city – is used to assess the likelihood of newly discovered asteroids and comets posing a threat to the earth. Some 3,000 small rocks do in fact hit the earth every day, the large majority of which burn up in the atmosphere. About 100 get through and hit the ground as meteorites. Asteroids and comets are gigantic by comparison. If it were to collide with the earth, an asteroid one kilometre in diameter would generate an explosion equivalent to 60,000 Hiroshima bombs. Such an event is not quite as far beyond the bounds of possibility as one might imagine. On 13 January 2004, according to some calculations, for several hours asteroid AL00667 had a one in four chance of striking the earth. It measured 30 metres in diameter and would have had the capacity utterly to destroy a major population centre.

Why mention gee-gees in a book about climate change? There are several reasons. In the first place, awareness of such hazards contributes to the fears that tend to swill around in our consciousness today. Bill McGuire, whose work I have used extensively in the preceding few paragraphs, has written a string of doomsday books, including *Apocalypse*, *Raging Planet* and *A Guide to the End of the World*, before producing his most recent one, *Surviving Armaggedon*. These are all based on the latest and most advanced scientific findings and research capabilities. We simply know more about the hazards described than we did even a decade ago.

Second, some gee-gees could intersect with dangers arising from climate change. For instance, tsunamis could become more lethal if ocean water levels were to rise significantly, making coastal cities more exposed than they had been before.

Third, some of the strategies that have been suggested to reduce threats from gee-gees could in principle be relevant when it comes to controlling climate change. At first sight, it might look as if nothing could possibly be done to influence them. However, scientists have some of the gee-gees in their sights. The National American Space Agency (NASA) is testing methods of altering the trajectory of a threatening asteroid, for example. It would take only a small nudge to deflect it from its path, and the further away the asteroid is when this is done, the smaller the deflection would have to be. One possibility being looked at is that a rocket motor could be landed on the asteroid, which, when activated, would provide the necessary thrust. Large-scale engineering has also been proposed to limit global warming, such as suspending giant mirrors in space to reflect back a proportion of the sun's rays. (See below, pp. 136–7.)

Enter the optimists

Discussing why doomsday thinking is apparently so prevalent today, Frank Furedi, who has written widely on risk and danger, argues that it is partly because of cultural change that has taken place over the past two or three decades. We have become preoccupied with safety and therefore tend to see threats everywhere – which translate into feelings of apprehension and powerlessness. Furedi sees writers on climate change as having a key role in getting all this under way – they are writing the pre-history of disasters and catastrophes to come, stoking up anxieties that invade other areas of life. Our current feelings of vulnerability are, he says, 'unprecedented'. They stand behind our – largely irrational – 'attitude of pessimism, dread and foreboding' towards the future.[24] Furedi joins those critics of doomsday thinking who say, as one of them puts it after a lengthy survey of risk, 'There's never been a better time to be alive.'[25]

One such critic, Dan Gardner, offers a cogent analysis of some of the incoherent or inconsistent views that the public have about risk. People tend to worry much more about some risks than about others, even though the probability of their occurrence is lower. For instance, after 9:11 many people in America for a while gave up flying in favour of driving. In fact, driving is more dangerous to life and limb than flying. Many more people die on the roads each year in the US than were killed in the attack on the Twin Towers. If terrorists were to hijack and crash one passenger jet every week in the US, a person's risk of dying that way would be a fraction of the risk of being killed in a car journey covering the same mileage.[26]

Risk perception, Gardner goes on to show, is influenced by many factors, including especially the ways in which messages are framed. For instance, in one experiment people were asked to imagine they were patients with lung cancer who had to decide whether to opt for surgery or for radiation treatment. They were divided into two groups. One group was informed that they would have a 68 per cent chance of being alive a year after surgery. The other was told that there was a 32 per cent chance of dying before that date. Of the first group, 44 per cent chose surgery over radiation; the proportion making that choice in the second group was only 18 per cent. Similar results have been found in many other similar studies.

Public perceptions of risk are quite often at odds with reality, for example in the area of crime. Gardner cites the instance of the wave of anxiety about child abduction which swept through the US in the 1980s. In response, the government commissioned research to find out the extent of the problem. The total number of cases each year in which children under the age of 14 were abducted by a stranger turned out to be 90, giving an annual risk factor of 1 in 608,696. More than 2,000 children die every year in the US in car accidents – a proportion of whom were not wearing seat-belts, a simple enough precaution to take. The extent of public agitation about abduction bore no real relation to the risk factor, compared to the relatively relaxed attitudes people hold towards other dangers.[27]

Most of those who have studied the evolution of contemporary attitudes surrounding risk trace the beginnings of a preoccupation with safety, and a stoking up of fears, to the 1970s – the time at which, as has often been pointed out, the expansion of electronic media really got under way. Are the two trends causally connected? It would be difficult to deny some kind of relationship, especially given the core precept of media presentation, that 'bad news is good news'. There is a great deal of research demonstrating that the media give far more coverage to dramatic and/or violent causes of death than to more mundane ones, thus conveying a false impression of risk to the public.[28] Even when serious crime rates are going down, the public can come to believe that they are in fact going up.

The reporting of risk, studies show, rarely puts risk calculations in context. Thus a newspaper might report that the number of people murdered over the past 10 years in London has increased by a quarter, giving the impression there is mayhem on the streets. Yet since the overall numbers are so low, amounting to fewer than 30 a year, the true level of risk of dying in such a way is 0.0001 per cent; with the rise in question, the risk would still be absolutely minimal for each member of the public.[29] The media are one of the main filters through which scientific findings and discussions are disseminated and there have been many instances when sensationalist reporting displaces caution.

The political management of risk has to tread a difficult path between alarmism and reassurance. I don't think we should take doomsday thinking at face value. Rather, we should see it as a set of cautionary tales. It is about what could go wrong if we aren't on our guard and if we don't take appropriate remedial action. The dangers that Martin Rees talks about, for example, are on the border between risk and uncertainty – it is difficult to attach more than extremely loose probabilities to them.[30] In the case of new-style risks – those related to the advance of science and technology – we struggle to decide how seriously to take them, because of the way they shade off into uncertainty.

It is hard to keep a given risk – including global warming – in the public consciousness in the context of other perceived dangers that come and go. The phenomenon of attention fatigue has been well documented in research studies. Already, opinion polls reveal that, even when they accept the risks of global warming as real, some respondents report that they get fed up with hearing so much about it. That reaction is also coupled to an inclination just to 'forget about it all and get on with ordinary life'. There is a similar reaction to perceived alarmism – 'if the situation is as bad as you say, we might as well just give up worrying'.

All the above factors are relevant when we consider what the response in public policy should be to those who claim that climate change is advancing more quickly than the majority of scientists think. We should be careful about what the implications of such views are for practical action. How does Pearce know that 'nature will take revenge' for our influence on the climate? What is the force of 'very probably'?[31] Concentrating on worst-case scenarios is rarely, if ever, the best way to deal with risks. On the contrary, it can provoke exaggerated reactions which paralyse policy rather than furthering it.

Some of the 'competing risks' in world society which Lomborg quite rightly says we also have to focus on are every bit as dangerous as climate change if we only take worst-case possibilities. Failure to contain the spread of nuclear weapons, for example, could lead to conflicts in which millions could die. I don't believe it would be appropriate to respond with a panic stations call. 'There's never been a better time to be alive' – it may not be literally true, certainly for large numbers of people in the world, but it is a sentiment to be taken seriously. We have an obligation to take as balanced and nuanced assessment of risk as possible, an issue I shall come back to later.

In the next chapter, I move on to another set of risks – those connected with energy security. At first sight, they have quite a different feel and texture from those connected to climate change. A short historical perspective is needed to introduce them. Who says oil says geopolitics. Maintaining a constant flow of oil has been, and remains, one of the main objects of the foreign policy of the developed countries over the past 60 or 70 years. For a long while, guaranteeing supply seemed wholly a political problem. It used to be thought that there was sufficient oil to go round to meet the world's need for many decades into the future, so long as the producers continued to supply it. This assumption is now in serious doubt.

2

RUNNING OUT, RUNNING DOWN?

Oil, gas and coal, the three dominant energy sources in the world, are all fossil fuels, producing greenhouse gases on the large scale. Reducing our dependence on them, or (most notably in the case of coal) making them far cleaner environmentally than they are at the moment, is imperative for mitigating climate change. The technologies required both to reduce our vulnerability to energy shortfalls and to reduce carbon emissions are one and the same; they include wind, wave and solar energy, hydroelectricity and thermal power. Lifestyle change is likely to be of key importance in both spheres, particularly when directed at curbing profligate habits of energy use.

The industrial revolution in its country of origin, Britain, was fuelled by coal – or, more accurately, by the scientific and technological discoveries which turned coal into a dynamic energy source. The changeover from burning wood – previously the prime energy source – was not easy, since it meant a transformation of habits. By the mid-seventeenth century wood was running out as a source of fuel; but many initially detested the sooty coal that came to replace it, and which, in the end, actually helped create a whole new way of life based on cities and machine production.

The turn to coal ushered in the world we now inhabit, in which the energy of the individual citizen or worker is of trivial importance compared to that produced from inanimate resources. As Richard Heinberg has observed in relation to the US:

> If we were to add together the power of all the fuel-fed machines that we rely on to light and heat our homes, transport us, and otherwise keep us in the style to which we have become accustomed, and then compare that total with the amount of power that can be generated by the human body, we would find that each American has the equivalent of over 150 'energy slaves' working for us twenty-four hours a day.[1]

Oil has never replaced coal, but it began to mount a challenge to coal's dominance from the turn of the twentieth century onwards. For a while, in the early part of that century, the US was the biggest oil producer in the world and for a long period was largely self-sufficient in oil. During much of that time the US was an anti-imperial power, with quite a different philosophy from the dominant imperial formation, the British Empire; for instance, the US opposed the Franco-British intervention in Suez in 1957, partly on strategic grounds, but also on moral ones. Of course, these roles were later reversed, as the US came to see the Middle East as more and more vital to its interests. Yet it is worth restating the obvious – the history of oil is the history of imperialism, in one guise or another.

Britain's oil derived mostly from its colonies in the Middle East, where it set the conditions of the relationship. The Anglo-Iranian oil company (later to become BP, aka 'Bloody Persians', 'British Petroleum' or, under the leadership of CEO John Browne more recently, 'Beyond Petroleum') was set up under a one-sided arrangement of 'concessions' – a system adopted also by US corporations. The country that needed the oil provided the expertise and technology to locate and extract it; the one that owned the oil was paid in terms of the volume extracted. The colonial or ex-colonial countries thus became 'rentier' states – income flowed into them without corresponding processes of economic development. Even within the oil industry itself, expertise was rarely shared with the host nations. These phenomena are at the origins of the much-discussed 'curse of oil' that afflicts so many oil-based states around the world, and to which I will return in the concluding chapter. The often vast wealth generated by the presence of oil and other mineral resources either is transported abroad, or ends up in the hands of local elites. It is not accidental that oil and gas resources are so widely concentrated in countries which are intrinsically authoritarian and corrupt.

OPEC, the Organization of the Petroleum Exporting Countries, was set up by the producing nations to act as a counter-balance to the influence of the oil corporations. It was followed over the years by the widespread and progressive take-over of oil assets by state-owned companies in those nations. OPEC was founded in 1960 and for some while there were no major shocks affecting energy prices or world supply. However, the leaders of OPEC were outraged by the support given by the US and other Western countries to Israel in the Arab-Israeli war of 1973. Oil exports to the US, Britain and some other states were blocked, while OPEC raised the price of oil by 70 per cent, precipitating economic recession in the industrial countries.

I mention these well-known episodes because they bring home how close the connections at some points between international politics and energy security are (and will continue to be); and also because they serve as a reminder that whether or not the oil will flow does not depend upon the assessment of resources alone, but on how those resources intersect with geopolitics.

French emissions of greenhouse gases are markedly lower today than they might otherwise have been because, following the oil crisis provoked by OPEC's actions, France took the decision to become more independent of world energy markets and invested heavily in nuclear power. Japan also took note and introduced policies to regulate energy use and promote energy conservation. Today it is among the most energy-efficient of the industrial countries and is in the vanguard of clean energy technology, for instance in the car industry. Its emissions are relatively high, however, because of its dependence upon coal for electricity production. Sweden instituted a range of energy-saving policies and started to reduce its oil dependency, a process that is still continuing. Far more waste is currently recycled in Japan and Sweden than in most other industrial countries. Having no indigenous resources of its own in the 1970s, Denmark took fright and initiated measures to transfer parts of its electricity production to renewable energy sources, particularly wind-power. At the same time, Brazil made the decision to invest in bio-fuels and now has a higher proportion of motor transport running off them than any other country, although the environmental benefits are dubious because of the deforestation involved.

The US was also obliged to react. Its responses included considering plans to invade Saudi Arabia, but also, more realistically, introducing measures to conserve energy, in the shape of the Energy Policy Conservation Act.[2] It was a significant intervention, because it showed that the wasteful energy habits of American consumers could be curbed if the impetus was strong enough. The aim of one section of the Act was to double the energy efficiency of new cars within 10 years. The target wasn't reached, but major improvements were nevertheless achieved. However, as the sense of crisis receded, fuel consumption rose again, soon to become lower per mile travelled than it had been before.

Peak oil

The debate about the limits of the world's fossil fuel resources is of great consequence for climate change policy. In 1956 the American geologist Marion King Hubbert made the now famous prediction that indigenous oil production in the US would peak in 1970 – a prediction that was widely rejected early on, but which turned out to be valid, even though the actual level of oil production was still going up in 1970. Peak oil calculations depend upon assessments of what in the oil industry is known as the 'ultimate reserves' a given country or oilfield has. It does not refer to how much oil exists, but to how much can ever be extracted – usually a much smaller amount.[3]

The controversies surrounding peak oil are as intense as those concerned with global warming, and the two debates in fact closely resemble one another. There are those who believe that there is plenty of oil and gas to go round. They do not accept that we should be worried about future sources of supply. In their view there are sufficient resources to last for a long while, even given the rising levels of economic growth of the large developing countries and even given the growing world population. David Howell and Carol Nakhle, for example, argue that there is enough of the 'known, relatively easy-to-extract stuff' to last for at least another 40 years. More reserves, they continue, are certain to be found. Under the melting ice of the Arctic, 'billions of tonnes of oil and billions of cubic metres of gas lie waiting'. New oilfields are available for exploration in Alaska, off the coast of Africa and offshore in Brazil. Even in the much-explored Middle East, a possible further cornucopia awaits.[4]

Such authors are the functional equivalents of the climate change sceptics – they are saying, 'Crisis, what crisis?' Mainstream opinion is less sanguine, or at least has become so over the past few years, and is represented by the bulk of industry analysts and the official publications of the major oil countries. It holds that there may be enough oil (and even more gas) to continue to expand levels of production for some while. However, no one knows, almost by definition, how much there is in as yet unexplored fields or what the difficulties of recovering it may be. The International Energy Agency (IEA), set up to monitor oil production after the 1970s oil embargo, predicted in 2007 that there will be no peak in oil production before 2030.[5]

Others believe that the world is rapidly approaching peak oil and that the adjustments that will have to be made by the industrial and industrializing countries, perhaps in the quite near future, are of epic proportions. As one prominent writer expresses it, we are likely to confront 'the kind of dramatic, earth-shattering crisis that periodically threatens the very survival of civilization. More specifically, it is an energy crisis brought about by the conflict between the rising global demand for energy and our growing inability to increase energy production.'[6] These words come from the investment analyst Stephen Leeb, who in the early 2000s predicted that world oil prices would reach $100 a barrel, a claim regarded by many at the time as ridiculous. Before 2008, Leeb was one of very few individuals talking of the possibility of oil prices reaching $200 a barrel or more. By the middle of that year – prior to the financial crisis – talk of such a possibility became commonplace;

BTU = British Thermal Unit. BTU is a measure of energy use. It is defined as the amount of heat needed to raise the temperature of one pound of water by one degree from 60 to 61 °F.

Figure 2.1 World Primary Energy Consumption

Source: Energy Information Administration.

at the same time, it was publicly endorsed by the investment bank Goldman Sachs. Oil prices had risen to $147 a barrel by July 2008, but by December, as recession started to bite, they fell back to $40 a barrel.

Leeb is one among a clutch of writers who hold that orthodox claims that world oil supplies will not peak for another 40 or 50 years are fundamentally mistaken.[7] The disagreements between those who write about oil production centre upon two main issues – how much recoverable oil there is in existing fields, and what the chances are of large new oil deposits being found. As in the climate change discussion, it will make a great difference to humanity's future who is right, or more nearly right.

The amount of new oil discovered each year has been declining for some while. According to David Strahan, discovery was at its highest point as long ago as 1965: 'These days, for every barrel we discover, we now consume at least three.'[8] Most of the world's biggest oilfields were identified long before that date. Of the 50 highest-producing oil countries, 18 have now passed their peak, even according to conservative estimates. If one includes the smaller producers, more than 60 oil-producing countries have done so too. Their production losses have so far been offset by growth in other areas and by improvements in extraction and processing technology.

Such authors reject the idea that big new oil and gas fields will be opened up under the Arctic or anywhere else, pointing to the extraction difficulties that will be involved. They argue that production in areas of the world outside the OPEC nations and Russia has remained static for years, in spite of successful finds in a range of countries. Russia's output growth of oil, although currently on the increase, looks likely to founder. The world will probably continue to have to look to OPEC and to the Middle East with all its tensions and problems.

In 2008, at the time at which oil prices reached their high point, the IEA produced a new report on global oil output.[9] The survey asserted once again that peak oil production is not imminent, but it did find that output from some of the world's largest oilfields is declining faster than earlier estimates had suggested. A significant increase in investment will be needed just to maintain the current level of production. The IEA calculates that the oil-producing countries and the oil companies will have to invest a total of about $360 billion a year until 2030 in order to replace falling oil production and to be able to meet the likely demands of the developing countries. Investment decisions by OPEC will be critical. The IEA expects oil produced from non-conventional sources, such as Canada's oil sands, to play a decisive role in keeping up levels of output. Yet the methods of extraction used in such cases are heavily polluting in terms of greenhouse gas emissions.

Supposing the theorists of peak oil are right, can natural gas step into the place of oil to some degree? After all, gas produces lower emissions than either oil or coal, and can be used for at least some of the purposes to which oil is put – for instance, cars can be converted to run on compressed natural gas without too much difficulty. It is often said that world supplies of gas far outstrip those of oil; some say there is enough to last the world for some 70–80 years from now, even given growing demand. David Victor and colleagues have suggested that there will be a worldwide move towards this energy resource.[10] By 2050, they argue, gas could supplant oil to become the most important energy source in the world. According to them, there is enough gas available to last for a century at today's rates of consumption. Yet, as in almost every aspect of energy security, controversy exists here too. There is a large distance indeed between the most optimistic estimate of recoverable gas reserves (20,000 trillion cubic feet) and the lowest (8,000 trillion cubic feet).

According to Julian Darley, the most difficult energy problem facing the United States – and by extension other major industrial countries too – in the near future, will in fact not be to do with oil but with gas.[11] In the early 2000s, as happened earlier with oil, for the first time more natural gas was consumed than was discovered – 'it is the dread hand of depletion writing on the wall'.[12] Natural gas has a vital role in the production of fertilizers – it has been called the single most important ingredient in the diets of human beings. At the moment there is no known replacement for it in this role. There are more than six billion people in the world, and that number will probably rise to nine billion later this century. In spite of the damage they can do to the soil, one cannot see how, without fertilizers, the world could possibly feed such numbers.

It is normally assumed that, in contrast to oil and gas, one thing we can be sure of is that the world has vast supplies of coal at its disposal. However, some are now saying that world coal supplies might be more limited than has hitherto been supposed.[13] There may have been large-scale over-reporting of coal reserves. Energy Watch, a German energy consultancy, has looked at the reserves listed by coal-producing countries and found that they have stayed the same even though those countries continued to mine extensively. For example, although China has mined 20 per cent of its coal since 1992, its listed reserves remain unchanged. Countries that have revised their figures have done so in a sharply downward direction, suggesting that improved techniques of assessment have produced more sober estimates than those made previously. Energy Watch has calculated that coal supplies may peak far earlier than is conventionally thought, perhaps as soon as 2025. Majority opinion, to repeat, is against such a conclusion. Indeed, one of the main worries about the world possibly running out of oil is that there could be an upswing in the use of coal.

Sweating the assets

Electricity generation is a major source of energy consumption and of the generation of greenhouse gases. To see what has happened in this area, we have to look first of all at the institutions and practices set up at the time when energy was cheap, because the thinking behind them now looks remarkably shallow. In the period following the Second World War, energy was the *locus classicus* of the state planning that was everywhere in vogue. Coal-mining was widely nationalized, while miners in numerous countries enjoyed an almost mythic status, partly because of the dangers of their jobs, but also because of the centrality of their work to the economy.

Partly as a hangover from the war years, security of energy supply was a core concern, to which government control was the response. The widespread turn to nuclear power in the 1950s and 1960s was also guided everywhere by the state. Many believed that this source would eventually provide energy in abundance; instead, it proved obstinately expensive and, in the public mind at least, hazardous. Apart from in one or two countries – as mentioned earlier, particularly France – the nuclear option was largely suspended. In many countries, nuclear power stations built decades ago are still in use, although they are now approaching the end of their lives.

The state took a back seat during the subsequent period of market deregulation from the 1980s onwards. From the late 1970s there was a more or less universal turn towards open competition in energy provision. Announcing the UK government's position in 1982, Secretary of State for Energy Nigel Lawson declared:

> I do *not* see the government's task as being to try to plan the future shape of energy production and consumption. It is not even primarily to try to balance UK demand and supply for

energy. Our task is rather to set a framework which will ensure
that the market operates in the energy sector with a minimum
of distortion.[14]

Most other industrial countries followed suit, to a greater or
lesser degree, as did the energy policy of the European Union.
Privatization and the liberalization of energy markets became
the orthodoxy, even if resisted in some quarters. In effect, there
was no energy policy as such, apart from opening up sectors to
competition so that markets could do their work in encouraging efficiency and finding appropriate prices for energy goods.
Security of supply barely appeared on the radar as prices
dropped, while electricity and oil remained plentiful.

However, these measures were to become self-undermining.
Since there was excess capacity, and hence no worries about
supply, energy companies became focused on paring back
operating costs, with pre-existing investment effectively written
off. Little new investment was made in the upgrading of plant,
save in certain sectors of the oil industry. The situation –
especially in countries where privatization had advanced
furthest – as Dieter Helm puts it, in a Marxisant way, 'contained
the seeds of its own destruction'.[15] In a whole swathe of countries in recent times there have been large-scale interruptions to
power supply, exposing vulnerabilities that derive in part from
under-investment and in part from market failures.

Since the early 2000s, what Helm calls a new energy paradigm
has emerged. It is (or was) marked by rises in the price of oil and
gas well beyond what seasoned observers had thought possible.
But it also involves a return to the protection of national energy
supplies, modernization of plant, investment for the future, a
consciousness of the finitude of oil and gas resources, recognition of the key importance of foreign policy to energy security
– and an awareness of the need to integrate energy policy with
the struggle to limit climate change. Political considerations
have come once more to intrude deeply into energy markets
because of their concentration in the hands of states which use
them as instruments of domestic and foreign policy.

The US is heavily dependent upon Middle Eastern oil producers, as are Europe and Japan, although all are now scrambling
to diversify their sources of supply. Russia's attempt to return

as a great power is based upon its fossil fuel resources and the high prices they currently command. China's very rapid rate of economic growth has led the country to take far more of an international role than it had done previously, as it makes its presence felt in the Middle East, Africa and Latin America in pursuit of oil, gas and minerals.

The EU countries import almost half their gas from Russia and a substantial proportion of their oil too. The implications on both sides for climate change policy are considerable. Russia is maximizing its income from oil and gas without the modernization that could have come about had the country permitted the introduction of outside investment and encouraged effective management. Gazprom, Russia's largest state-owned company, is notoriously inefficient and poorly managed. Domestic and industrial consumers in Russia get their energy at heavily subsidized prices, a policy that is changing only slowly, but which does nothing to promote energy conservation.

The Russian leadership has developed a confrontational approach to the EU, with consequences that also spill over into the area of climate change. It has firmly rejected EU approaches to find a meeting point: 'We intend to retain state control over the gas transport system and over Gazprom. We will not split Gazprom up. And the European Commission should not have any illusions. In the gas sector, they will have to deal with the state.'[16]

Russia has found it quite easy to do individual deals with EU member-states and thereby undercut European unity. A notable example is the Nord Stream pipeline project, which brings together Gazprom and two of Germany's biggest energy companies. Although practical and diplomatic problems mean that it may never be built, the very idea of the project runs contrary to the spirit of European solidarity. Since energy security and responding to climate change are so closely linked, an EU that cannot speak with one voice on the first could find its capabilities to make progress with the second compromised – a serious matter, since, in terms of concerns to combat global warming, it aspires to be the world leader.

A report produced for the meeting of the European Council in March 2008 pointed to some of the security questions that could be posed by the melting of the Arctic ice.[17] The mineral wealth believed to lie beneath the Arctic might become a flashpoint for new tensions. In 2007 a group of Russian scientists planted a flag on the Arctic seabed, implying that much of it is Russian territory, a case that Russia is now vigorously pursuing in international courts. Few prescriptions of international law apply to the Arctic. Most of the seabed is uncharted. The US, Norway and Denmark are all lodging ownership claims. The US is the only significant country not to have ratified the UN Convention on the Law of the Sea, which provides at least one forum for discussion for competing claims to the Arctic. However, it has largely abided by its conventions, and pressures for the country formally to ratify grew after the Russian action. In 2008 President George W. Bush recommended ratification to the US Senate.

The struggle for resources

Only the US is ahead of China in terms of oil and gas consumption. In 2007 China accounted for about 40 per cent of the worldwide growth in demand for oil. Its level of demand will rise by about 6 per cent a year over the next decade if its rates of growth are sustained and its energy policies remain the same. In casting around for oil, China is pursuing an aggressive foreign policy – following, it could be said, in the footsteps of Britain and the US. China does not work through oil corporations as Western countries tend to do, but its objectives are much the same. It essentially buys oilfields in different countries for its own use, setting the terms of sale locally. Countries where China has done such deals range from Venezuela to Indonesia, Oman, Yemen – and Sudan.

It has also made substantial inroads into the Middle East, to the chagrin of the US. Saudi Arabia has become the largest oil supplier to China, and the Chinese have been allowed to explore for gas within the country. China has forged a close relationship with Iran and is importing increasing amounts of gas and oil from that state. American oil companies are prohibited from doing business with Iran as a result of an Act of Congress, so cannot get a look in. In the meantime, along with Russia, China blocks the imposition of sanctions on Iran, which most other nations in the international community support in their attempt to stop the country from acquiring nuclear weapons and the rocket systems able to deliver them. 'Both sides behave as if an oil shortage is looming, and that it's "us or them".'[18]

India has not yet adopted such a high foreign policy profile as China in respect of oil, but it will need much more fuel as its economy advances and as consumer tastes change. In China, there has been a steep rise in car use over the past decade, with no heed at all being paid to environmental considerations. Much the same is set to happen in India. The Tata Nano car was unveiled in that country in January 2008. Costing 100,000 rupees (£1,300), it is by far the cheapest new car in the world; millions of Indians, even those on a relatively modest income, will, for the first time, be able to buy a car. The Tata Nano has a 33bhp petrol engine, which, because of being so small, is reasonably fuel-efficient. Yet the sheer numbers likely to appear on the roads will certainly result in large-scale environmental consequences.

Outside India, there are also plans to market the car in Latin America, South-East Asia and Africa. The chief scientist of the IPCC, Rajendra Pachauri, himself an Indian, says he is 'having nightmares about it'. The response from the industrialist Ratan Tata sums up perfectly some of the dilemmas surrounding both energy security and climate change: 'We need to think of our masses. Should they be denied the right to an individual form of transport?'[19]

Commentators on energy security have started to speak of 'Chindia' to refer to the combined impact of Chinese and Indian economic growth on world oil and energy markets. For most of the time since the Second World War the rise in demand for oil has been only about half that of overall economic growth. Since 2000, however, that proportion has increased to 65 per cent.[20] At the moment, measured on a per capita basis, Chindia consumes one-seventh of the total for the industrial countries. If Chindia joins the high-income group of countries within the next 20 years, as seems likely, growth in worldwide energy demand will dramatically accelerate.

In the areas of both climate change and energy security, the main divergence between the more sanguine and the apocalyptic writers is time – how much time remains before large changes will have to be made to the ways in which we live. Even if the effects of climate change are progressive rather than abrupt, and will mainly affect subsequent generations rather than ourselves, the lesson should still be to prepare early, and to start now. Exactly the same is true of energy security, even if those who say that oil and gas have several decades to run turn out to be right.

In the following chapter I return to climate change, beginning by looking at the impact of the green movement on environmental thinking. Issues to do with energy, however, intrude at most points throughout the remainder of the book, since there is no chance of mitigating climate change without radically reducing our fossil fuel dependency.

3

THE GREENS AND AFTER

Now that climate change discussions have moved into the mainstream, it isn't surprising that they reflect a variety of different perspectives. Those in the green movement tend to argue thus: 'This is our topic, since we were speaking about pollution of the environment well before anyone else.' And indeed, the green movement – or certain currents of thinking within it – has been the main source of philosophical reflection relevant to climate change objectives. Green concepts and imagery permeate the writings of even the most sober scientific writers on climate change.

However, others are pressing their claims. Environmental economists dismiss most green thinking as so much mumbo jumbo. For them, a proper approach must be hard-edged and phrased in terms of the costs and benefits of different strategies, with markets having the upper hand. They also tend to look towards carbon markets as likely to contribute most to enabling us to cope with global warming.

For writers on the left, climate change offers the opportunity to renew the case against markets that has for so long been associated with left-of-centre traditions. After all, Nicholas Stern, the author of the Stern Review on climate change, has remarked that global warming 'is the greatest market failure the world has seen'.[1] Although Stern himself doesn't draw any such conclusion, the quote is food and drink to those who would like to see the role of markets shrink and that of the state expand. As a political issue, responding to global warming also appeals to those on the left in a different way – it offers the chance to recover the radicalism that disappeared with the dissolution of revolutionary socialism. It might be seen as a means of renewing the critique of capitalism, regarded by them as the source of the troubles we face. The red–green coalitions that have been proposed by different authors, and that have existed in some real-life political contexts, have their origins in this type of reasoning.

Bandwagon effect in respect of global warming is noticeable on a strategic as well as on a more abstract plane. Thus, those who want to revive the European Union and give it more legitimacy and sense of direction find in climate change a way of doing so. Europhiles see the issue as a way of demonstrating to their own sceptics what a crucial role the EU can play in influencing global issues.

I hope I have managed to avoid bandwagon effect. Plainly it is important to be careful about using global warming as a way of surreptitiously legitimating other concerns. There is nevertheless a left/right tinge to current climate change debates: those who want to respond to climate change through widespread social reform mostly tend towards the political left; most of the authors who doubt that climate change is caused by human agency, on the other hand, are on the right. Yet it is vital that climate change policy as far as possible transcends such divisions and survives changes of government within democratic systems. I shall discuss this issue in more detail in chapter 5.

The greens

Strictly speaking, of course, there is no green movement – rather, there is a diverse range of positions, perspectives and recipes for action. I do not pretend to cover all of these, but instead will concentrate upon a number of key themes.

Like socialism, green thinking is a creation of the industrial revolution. Factories and rapidly growing cities transformed and, in many areas, came to dominate the landscape, while the 'green and pleasant land' retreated into the background. New-found wealth was brought to many, but in the eyes of critics the price paid was far too high. The 'hatred of modern civilisation' which William Morris spoke of as 'the leading passion of my life' found widespread echo in the arts and in the thinking of the early conservationists. Is it all, he wondered in a remarkable anticipation of today's social critics, 'to end in a counting house on top of a cinder heap?'[2]

Ralph Waldo Emerson's *Nature* appeared in 1836. Emerson protested volubly (although to no immediate effect) against the logging which was devastating the forests. In modern industry, he argued, nature appears as an object pressed into the service of the production of commodities. We should seek to recover the unmediated relationship to nature that our ancestors enjoyed, and which is the source of aesthetic experience and morality.[3] The theme was taken up by Henry Thoreau who, in celebrated fashion, put it into practice by living alone in the woods for two years, depending wholly on his own labour to do so. 'That man is the richest whose pleasures are the cheapest', he wrote, adding prophetically; 'what is the use of a house if you haven't got a tolerable planet to put it on?'[4] Walden Pond in Massachusetts, where Thoreau spent his two years in isolation, is considered by many to be the birthplace of the conservation movement.

The Sierra Club, founded in the US in 1892, and influenced by the ideas of Emerson and Thoreau, is widely recognized to be the world's first significant environmental organization, devoted in the first instance to protecting wilderness areas. It has a history of activism, dating back to protests against the damming of rivers in the early years of the twentieth century. Today, fighting global warming has become its main activity; it seeks to combat the 'reckless energy policy' of the US.

Most histories of the green movement tend to hop over the fact that its next significant flowering was under fascism, especially in Germany. 'Ecologism' in Germany has its origins in a similar sort of natural mysticism to that which inspired Emerson and Thoreau. The Nazi 'ecologists' promoted conservation and organic farming, and practised vegetarianism.[5] The Reich Nature Protection Law, passed in 1935, together with other legislation, had the aim of preventing damage to the environment in undeveloped areas, protecting forests and animals and reducing air pollution.

The claim that the Nazis were 'green', or had a 'green wing', which was in fact only introduced by historians in the 1980s, predictably caused a furore. The modern green movement had its origins in Germany in the 1970s, and the link to the Nazis could be seen as a way of trying to discredit it. The term 'eco-fascism' has in fact been applied by critics against greens who have favoured extra-legal direct action to pursue their goals. I see no point in denying that the fascists drew upon ideas, such as a mystic reverence for nature, that have also influenced some sectors of the greens. Different movements can make use of similar ideas, but turn them to quite opposing ends.

The term 'green' in its political sense was coined in Germany, where the Green Party was also the first to achieve a measure of electoral success. The greens have since developed into a global movement: their first worldwide gathering was held just before the UN conference in Rio in 1992. The Global Green Network has party representatives from some 80 different countries. Amid the diversity of views represented by green parties, there are some common threads that hold them all together. The Network lists a charter of principles 'defining what it means to be Green in the new millennium'. It involves the four principles first set out by the German greens two decades ago – 'ecological wisdom' (ecological harmony or equilibrium), social justice, participatory democracy and non-violence, with two others added: sustainability and respect for diversity.

Influenced by earlier social protests in the 1960s and early 1970s (for example, against the Vietnam War), the greens emerged as a movement that in some part set itself against parliamentary politics, and feared too great an involvement with the state. This is why it tends to emphasize grass-roots democracy and localism. Greens oppose established institutions of power, whether in the shape of big government or big business. They also contest 'productivism' in economics – a stress upon economic growth as a prime economic value. Growth that lowers the quality of life, or, in particular, which damages the biosphere, is 'uneconomic' growth. Orthodox economics is 'grey' – human life and nature both figure as 'factors of production' alongside other commodities. Most greens have tended to mistrust capitalism and markets, and view the large corporations with considerable hostility.

Greens often describe themselves not as anti-science, but as anti-'scientism' – against untrammelled faith in science and, especially, technology. A key aspect of green thinking in relation to technology is the precautionary principle – one of the main concepts, in fact, that the greens have contributed to the wider political discourse. It connects readily with the early thinking of Morris, Emerson and Thoreau. The precautionary principle is not easy to state – indeed, I shall argue below that it is actually incoherent. However, it has quite often been taken to mean that technologies should be rejected unless it can be proven that they will not cause harm either to human beings or to the biosphere. The precautionary principle lies behind the objections that almost all greens have had to nuclear power. The greens had a strong influence on the decision of Germany and Sweden to phase out nuclear power stations, for example.

A somewhat bewildering variety of philosophical standpoints has been associated with the greens. The Australian philosopher Robert Goodin has sought to impose some order upon this diversity. He argues that green political thinking depends upon two basic strands – a green theory of value and a green theory of agency. The first tells us what greens value and why; the second, how they do (or should) go about pursuing them.

In economics, value is assessed in terms either of prices or of welfare, the second of these defined narrowly as material benefit. In the green theory of value, by contrast, what makes something valuable is that it has been created by natural processes rather than by human beings. We can understand this position by answering a question posed by another philosopher, Martin Krieger: 'What's wrong with plastic trees?'[6] In the late 1960s, the city authorities in Los Angeles, finding that real trees planted by the freeways died because of air pollution, planted plastic ones instead. They were surprised when these were pulled down by irate citizens. Goodin suggests that even if artificial trees could be made in such a way as to be indistinguishable from the real thing, we would still (rightly) tend to reject them – much as we would a forgery of a picture. We value nature, because it is larger than ourselves and because it sets our own lives in a much more encompassing context.

Unlike the 'deep ecologists', who try to derive values from nature itself, Goodin accepts that objects in nature can only have value through us – when we speak of values there is inescapably a human element involved, since there must be someone to hold these values. Such values are at the same time relational: they presuppose and depend on a world larger than ourselves. A landscape doesn't have to be wholly untouched by a human hand for us to value it in this manner. Thus the English fields and hedgerows are human modifications of nature – they house (or used to) a way of life in which people broadly live in harmony with nature. This situation is different from circumstances where we seek to impose our own order on nature in a tyrannical fashion. Goodin gives the example of Los Angeles, in fact, where, he argues, nature has been obliterated.[7] Sustainability, a basic green concern, can be inferred from such an emphasis; so can concern with the interests of future generations. Many greens have argued against further economic growth on the grounds that it is too damaging – they would like to see a 'no-growth society'.

Values do not realize themselves. They have to be connected to a 'how' that explains the means whereby they can be realized. Greens, as mentioned, have a distrust of power and the state – the desire for participatory democracy is found in the manifestos of virtually all green parties. Goodin searches for a logical connection between green values and the typical green political framework – advocacy of participatory democracy, distrust of large-scale power, and non-violence – and finds none. This is an important conclusion, for reasons I shall mention later. He also argues – I think correctly – that a green theory of value should have priority, in cases of clash, over the green theory of agency. As he points out, such an emphasis runs counter to the intuitions of most greens, who believe that direct personal action should have priority over orthodox politics, and see this belief at the core of what it means to be green.

Although Goodin does not discuss the issue in an extensive way, one should point out that the relationship between the greens and the question of global warming is problematic. Global warming is not simply an extension of more traditional forms of industrial pollution; it is qualitatively different. Scientists, and scientists alone, have directed our attention to it, since it is not visible in the way London smogs were, or smoke-stack pollution is. We are also wholly dependent on the research and monitoring work of scientists to track the progress of warming and map its consequences.

Some concepts which play a major role in current environmental thinking, such as the aforementioned precautionary principle, come from the green movement broadly defined. Other notions sound as though they have green origins, but in fact do not, such as 'ecological footprint', a phrase first introduced by William Rees in the early 1990s.[8] One might think it refers to a footprint in the sand, but it actually has high-tech origins – it came from the comment of a computer technician, who spoke admiringly of the small space his new computer took up on his desk.

A lot more order needs to be brought into this jumble of ideas and concepts. I see no problem in accepting that there are green values which are relevant for significant aspects of political life. However, such values are not necessarily the same as those connected to controlling climate change, and may indeed run counter to them. For example, a key green value is that of 'staying close to nature' – or, more briefly put, conservation. It is a value that has a certain aesthetic quality to it. It is very possibly important to the good life, but it has no direct relevance to climate change. Clashes can easily occur between conservationist values and policies relevant to global warming – for example, conservationists might resist the building of a nuclear power station, or a wind farm, in a given area of the countryside.

The desire to protect animal species from extinction might also be a worthy one, but its only connection to climate change is if extinction threatens the ecosystems that help reduce emissions. For these reasons, although being 'green' has become synonymous with acting against global warming, I don't use the term. Of course, green values or policies could be and are relevant to political convergence. In other words, actions that are politically attractive because they serve widely held green values could also serve the goal of limiting climate change. It is quite right to say that economic growth shouldn't be valued in and of itself, especially as a society becomes more affluent.

The green movement will lose (or has already lost) its identity as environmental politics become part of the mainstream. Although green groups and parties holding these ideas will of course remain, the absorption of the greens into the mainstream means discarding those aspects of green theories of agency that have nothing intrinsically to do with green values. These include the theses that participatory democracy is the only kind of democracy that counts; that the best kind of society we can aim for is a radically decentralized one (decentralization may quite often be a valuable political goal, and even relevant to green objectives, but only alongside other forms of political organization); and the commitment to non-violence (plainly an important goal in most contexts, but arguably not a universal one, and in any case one that has no intrinsic connection with climate change objectives as such).

We must also disavow any remaining forms of mystical reverence for nature, including the more limited versions which shift the centre of values away from human beings to the earth itself[9] – tackling global warming has nothing to do with saving the earth, which will survive whatever we do. Living in harmony with the earth, respecting the earth, respecting nature – these ideas fall into the same category.

The green movement leaves behind it some central dilemmas. In what sense, if any, does coping with climate change and energy security mean that economic growth, in its usual sense, is inevitably compromised? Can and should political life in the industrial countries, and perhaps elsewhere too, be reshaped so that well-being replaces affluence as a core aspiration of development? We also have to ask how useful the concepts are that have come, at least in some part, from the green movement. They include especially the precautionary principle, sustainability and the principle that 'the polluter pays'. One of the consequences of the greens' distaste for orthodox politics is that we lack a set of concepts relevant to analysing how climate change policy can effectively be integrated into orthodox political practice.

Managing risk: the precautionary principle

The precautionary principle (PP) has been used well beyond the green movement to handle risk in the context of climate change and other environmental areas. The notion has been incorporated into numerous official documents concerned with global warming: it was built into the 1992 Rio Declaration and has been applied widely since, including in the programmes of the European Commission. Its core meaning can be summarized as the aphorism 'better safe than sorry', although it is invariably clothed in more technical garb. Like other aspects of everyday wisdom, 'better safe than sorry' is a theorem that dissolves into ambiguity when subject to scrutiny. Moreover, there is no reason why 'better safe than sorry' should be prioritized over its opposite: 'he who hesitates is lost'. All popular maxims, in fact, have their opposite, which explains their lack of explanatory or predictive capacity. We tend to apply them retrospectively depending on what the outcomes of a course of action prove to be.

The PP concentrates only on one side of risk, the possibility of harm. The reason why it has become so prominent is bound up with its origins in the green movement and the attitude of that movement towards nature. Conservationism easily slides over into the view that we should beware of interfering with natural processes as a matter of principle. Risk, however, has two sides. The opposite of precaution is boldness and innovation – taking the plunge. Taking risks adds edge to our lives, but much more importantly is intrinsic to a whole diversity of fruitful and constructive tasks.[10] Risk-taking is essential to new thinking in all spheres, to scientific progress and to wealth-creation. We have no hope of responding to climate change unless we are prepared to take bold decisions. It is the biggest example ever of he who hesitates is lost.

The American legal scholar Cass Sunstein has produced a devastating critique of the precautionary principle. He notes how divergent are the situations it has been taken to cover. The definition of the PP most often offered is 'that regulators should take steps to protect against potential harms, even if causal chains are unclear and even if we do not know that those harms will come to fruition'.[11] Yet thus formulated, the PP can be invoked in quite contradictory ways. It could be used to endorse interventionist action to prevent a given state of affairs from arising, as in the case of taking action against global warming – or, as Sunstein points out, the invasion of Iraq. More often, however, the PP is invoked to justify exactly the opposite – inaction, on the grounds of being better safe than sorry. Such is the case, for example, when groups oppose the introduction of GM crops, in the belief that it is better to maintain the status quo than to make risky interventions into nature.

Since it can be used to justify completely opposed courses of action, it isn't surprising that there is little consistency in definitions offered of the PP. Sunstein traces some 20 different such definitions, in fact, remarking that 'they are not compatible with one another'.[12] They range from 'weak' to 'strong'. A weak definition is one such as the following: that 'a lack of decisive of harm should not be grounds for refusing to regulate, in relation to a specific hazard'. Strong definitions are those such as 'action should be taken to correct a problem as soon as there is evidence that harm may occur'. Sunstein shows that both types of definition are worthless as guides to action. Weak versions of the PP do no more than state a truism. Governments could not possibly demand certainty in risk situations before taking regulatory action.

However, stronger versions, if they were applied strictly, would paralyse all action. Take the example of GM crops. The risks to human health and local ecologies are not known with any precision. A strong version of the PP requires that they be banned completely, on the basis that this way we avoid any risks they are likely to pose. However, prohibiting their use creates significant risks too, including the possibility, for example, of rising levels of starvation and malnutrition. The strong definition of the PP would entail that we avoid these risks too. Hence the strong definition is logically incoherent; it goes against both the cultivation and the non-cultivation of

GM crops. The PP in its strong form, Sunstein shows, tends to lead to extreme conclusions, as a means of concealing its incoherence. It tends to focus only on worst-case possibilities, producing either a paralysing focus on the status quo, or endorsements of extreme reactions.

Precautions against some risks almost always create others. This observation is important to my arguments about climate change, since there is always a balance of risks (and, crucially, opportunities) whenever a given course of action is considered. We cannot therefore justify a 'bias for nature' – leaving nature intact – as an argument relevant to dealing with global warming. We will need to push the boundaries of the end of nature further rather than (as green thinkers want) pull back from them.

How can it be that the PP is self-contradictory, yet is so widely accepted as a framework for policy? The reasons, Sunstein says, lie in the social perception of risk. We tend to focus on some risks to the exclusion of others, and use rules of thumb that are quite often very misleading in judging risks. Sunstein lists a number of such rules of thumb or 'heuristics', including:

1 The 'availability heuristic'. We may pick on certain risks simply because they are in the news, ignoring other relevant threats. For instance, Sunstein says, at the moment there is a distinct tendency to overplay the risks posed by terrorism.
2 'Probability neglect'. We tend to focus on worst-case scenarios, even if they are very improbable. This tendency is noticeable among some of the writers on climate change, as noted earlier.
3 'Loss aversion'. People tend to have a bias in favour of the status quo because they are more concerned about losses than about future gains, a well-established finding in behavioural economics. This tendency is related to future discounting, as discussed in the Introduction.
4 A belief in the 'benevolence of nature' that makes risks created by humans particularly suspect.
5 'System neglect'. This tendency prevents people from seeing the risks created by their own attempts at risk avoidance.

If one adds to these points the exploitation of risks by special interest groups, it is easy to see how biased risk assessments arise. Since people usually concentrate only on some risks, filtering out others, and since they tend to concentrate on worst-case scenarios, strong versions of the PP result. They offer no proper policy guidelines however, because of their self-contradictory starting-point.

I draw several conclusions from Sunstein's analysis. The first is that we have to operate in terms not of the precautionary principle, but of another PP – the 'percentage principle'. In assessing risks, no matter how catastrophic, some form of cost-benefit analysis of possible forms of action is nearly always involved. That is, we have to assess risks and opportunities in terms of costs incurred in relation to benefits obtained. Risks which shade over significantly into uncertainties, like those involved in global warming, however, inevitably mean that there will be an element of guesswork, perhaps a large element, in whatever we do (or do not do).

Second, cost-benefit analysis in democratic settings presumes public debate, since choice among risks is involved. For instance, nuclear power can help reduce emissions, but it creates other risks, such as those involved in the disposal of radioactive waste. Debate, however, will not necessarily lead to agreement, and policy-makers will in the end have to make the leap one way or the other.

Third, all risk assessment is contextual. It depends upon values, which inevitably shape the threats considered most salient at any point, given that no course of action is ever risk-free. Consider the introduction of a new medical drug. From a regulatory point of view, it is certainly sensible to test it thoroughly before it is used on a wide scale. However, those suffering from a condition that the drug could help may well decide to take it before full testing has taken place. In such a case, 'he who hesitates is lost' trumps 'better safe than sorry', because sufferers have little to lose by not taking the drug.

The issues just discussed are relevant to all areas of risk and public policy. They are important to the arguments of this book, since how people assess and respond to risk in general is a key part of the politics of global warming. However, they are also relevant in an immediate way to strategies for mitigating climate change and also to problems of adaptation.

'Sustainable development'

The year 1972 was important in the history of environmental thinking, since it was the date at which a landmark study appeared: the Club of Rome's *Limits to Growth*. The work argued that our civilization is exhausting the resources upon which its continued existence depends.[13] It sold in its millions and, although it was subjected to numerous criticisms, its overall emphasis is now widely accepted. In the same year, a major UN conference on the 'Human Environment' highlighted the importance of reconciling economic development with the more efficient use of resources. The term 'sustainable development' was introduced in the 1987 report of the World Commission on Environment and Development – now usually referred to as the Brundtland Report, since it was chaired by the Norwegian ex-Prime Minister, Gro Harlem Brundtland.[14] Like *Limits to Growth*, it focused on the possibility that modern industry is using up its source materials at an alarming rate, which cannot be maintained for much longer without major change.

The Brundtland Report recognized that economic growth is necessary in order to bring greater prosperity to the developing world. However, development overall has to become sustainable. The Commission defined sustainable development as 'development that meets the needs of the present without compromising the ability of future generations to meet their own needs'.[15] The 1992 UN Rio Earth Summit endorsed a declaration setting out 27 principles of sustainable development and recommended that every country produce a national strategy to achieve these ends. A few years later the Treaty of Amsterdam embraced sustainable development as integral to the aims of the EU, and a comprehensive Sustainable Development Strategy was established in 2001.

The introduction of the notion has had a valuable effect. At least to some degree it has helped bring together two previously discrepant communities – on the one hand, greens and others who were 'anti-growth' and, on the other, pro-market authors. As Richard North has observed, it 'has exposed green extremists as being indifferent to human realities [the plight of the poorer countries] and hard-nosed industrialists as obsessing about the short-term. And it has provided some solid middle ground from which former hotheads, dreamers and radicals can hone workable policy.'[16] The meeting-point came through world poverty. Greens and conservationists could argue that a no-growth policy made sense in the industrial states. However, they also support global social justice, whose realization means that poorer countries must be given the opportunity to become richer – that is, to develop economically.

The term gained such popularity that it is now deployed almost everywhere and has figured in thousands of books, articles and speeches. Yet it has had its detractors from the beginning and their voices have become ever more strident. What accounts for its popularity, they argue, is precisely its anodyne quality – an intrinsic vagueness, coupled with a have-your-cake-and-eat-it quality. The two prime terms 'sustainability' and 'development' – as many have observed – have somewhat contradictory meanings.[17] 'Sustainability' implies continuity and balance, while 'development' implies dynamism and change. Thus environmentalists are drawn to the 'sustainability' angle, while governments and businesses (in practice, anyway) place the focus on 'development', usually meaning by this term GDP (Gross Domestic Product) growth.

One response to the elusive nature of the concept has simply been to avoid defining it and instead to substitute a cluster of goals in its place. In *Implementing Sustainable Development*, for example, William Lafferty and James Meadowcroft argue: 'Sustainable development indicates an interdependent concern with: promoting human welfare; satisfying basic needs; protecting the environment; considering the fate of future generations; achieving equity between rich and poor; and participating on a broad basis in decision-making.'[18] Such an all-encompassing list, however, surely empties the notion of any core meaning. It is an example of 'the way that sustainable development has become an all-embracing concept to the extent that it has no clear analytical bite at all'.[19]

'Sustainable development' is more of a slogan than an analytical concept, and I shall avoid using it in this book. Rather, I will consider its two components separately. 'Sustainability' is a useful notion, although itself a little slippery to define, since it concerns an indefinite future. We don't know what technological innovations will occur down the line, and hence assessments of the limits of the earth's resources usually operate under a question-mark. Sustainability in its simplest meaning implies that, in tackling environmental problems, we are looking for lasting solutions, not short-term fixes. We have to think over the medium and the long term and develop strategies that stretch over those time scales. There is an obligation to consider how present-day policies are likely to affect the lives of those as yet unborn.

It can be given substance in various ways. For example, the World Economic Forum has elaborated an Environmental Sustainability Index, which has been applied to more than 100 countries.[20] Environmental sustainability is defined in terms of five elements:

1 The condition of ecological systems such as air, soil and water.
2 The stresses to which those systems are subject, including their levels of pollution.
3 The impact of such stresses upon human society, as measured in terms of factors such as the availability of food and exposure to disease.
4 The social and institutional capacity of a society to cope with environmental hazards.
5 The capacity to create stewardship of global public goods, especially the atmosphere.

We should also look again at the idea of 'development'. 'Development', on its own, has two somewhat different meanings. It can simply mean economic growth, as measured by GDP, in which case it applies in principle to all countries. However, it can also refer more narrowly to the economic processes that take people out of poverty. This is the sense in which we contrast the 'developing' countries with the 'developed' ones. In the first sense of the term, of course, 'development' never stops.

In both senses, 'development' means the accumulation of wealth, normally measured in terms of GDP, such that a society becomes progressively richer. It implies that this wealth is generated in some large part by the economic trans-formation of the society in question, as a self-perpetuating process. We wouldn't say that a society is developing eco-nomically if, for example, it were simply getting income from selling off its mineral resources. We speak of 'developed' as opposed to 'developing' countries for a reason – namely, that growth is much less important to the former than to the latter. 'Developed' countries may continue to expand their econo-mies, but the need for growth is much less pressing – they have reached some sort of equilibrium, albeit a dynamic one.

For the poorer countries there is a *development imperative*. It is not only that they have the right to become richer, but that such a process has direct implications for sustainability. Poverty is closely associated with population expansion, one of the root causes of the pressure that is now threatening resources. There will continue to be two separate trajectories of 'development' in the world, at least until the poorer countries reach a certain standard of wealth. Just what this 'certain level of wealth' should be is a massively important question, which has to be negotiated politically. Wherever possible, such as through technology transfer, reductions in emissions – at least relative to past practices in the developed countries – should be sought. The state of play in terms of the dangers involved in climate change, together with a peak in the production of oil and gas, will determine in large part how far 'development' today can mimic the trajectories followed by the existing industrial coun-tries. We have already reached a point where the outcome of those trajectories are under immense pressure. Nevertheless, a certain 'licence to pollute' has to be acknowledged.

'Contraction and convergence' – whereby developed coun-tries reduce their emissions first, and radically, with poorer countries following suit as they become richer – is a necessary point of connection between the two types of development. There are different versions of this idea around, but the underlying principle is simple.[21] The developed countries must aim to make large cuts in their greenhouse gas emissions, starting now. Developing nations can increase their emissions for a period in order to permit growth, after which they must begin to reduce them. The two groups of countries will then progressively converge.

Over-development

We can legitimately talk of *over-development* as a possibility in the affluent societies. The continued expansion of the economy may well bring benefits, but at the same time the problems of affluence tend to pile up.[22] The implication is not that economic growth has to stop, but that it should not be pursued irrespective of its wider consequences. For these countries it is essential to create more effective measures of welfare than GDP. GDP is normally defined as the total market value of all final goods and services produced in an economy a given year. The formula includes personal consumption expenditures, gross private domestic investment, government purchases and net exports. It was not invented as an indicator of welfare, but has almost everywhere come to be used that way.

Using GDP as a measure of growth has distinct advantages, not least those of simplicity and ease of calculation. However, its inadequacies as an index of economic welfare are well known. It is essentially an indicator of the size of an economy and a measure of market transactions. Activities that are environmentally damaging can appear to be wealth-generating in GDP measures, as can many other harmful ones. GDP makes no distinction between industrial growth which acts to increase emissions and that which does not. Nor does it factor in economic inequality – GDP can continue to rise even though only a small minority of the population is making any gains.

The critique of GDP as a measure of welfare now dates back many years. Broader measures of welfare have to be introduced to get a true measure of how societies are faring as a result of economic growth. One such measure is the Genuine Progress Indicator (GPI), which was initiated in 1995. It starts with similar personal consumption measures to GDP, but adjusts for factors such as income distribution, the value of household and volunteer work, crime and pollution. As John Talberth and Clifford Cobb, who were responsible for producing the GPI, observe, in the developed societies 'GPI started declining around 1975, while GDP keeps increasing'. In their most recent report, they comment scathingly on the reactions of economic analysts to hurricanes Katrina and Rita in the US. Whereas most analysts wrote about how well the economy reacted to the disasters, with growth rates unaffected, Talberth and Cobb wrote:

> In one fell swoop, these headlines dismissed the inequitable and catastrophic toll associated with 1,836 preventable deaths, over 850,000 housing units damaged, destroyed, or left uninhabitable, disruption of 600,000 jobs, permanent inundation of 118 square miles of marshland, destruction of 1.3 million acres of forest, and contamination caused by millions of gallons of floodwaters tainted by sewage, oil, heavy metals, pesticides, and other toxins as irrelevant to the US economy.[23]

Another measure is the Index of Sustainable Economic Welfare (ISEW). It uses both national and local data to identify trends. A study looking at the period between 1975 and 1990 showed that although GDP continued to rise, the ISEW went down by a quarter in the US. Over the same period, the ISEW in the UK declined by a full 50 per cent.[24] In common with other industrial countries, both societies showed record ISEW growth over the post-war period until the 1970s – the threshold point, it appears, for over-development.

A third index, the Sustainable Society Index (SSI), was set up in 2006.[25] This makes use of a wider range of environmental measures than the others, including resource depletion affecting wetlands, forests, farmland and non-renewable raw materials, together with the level of carbon emissions and other potential causes of environmental damage, such as the ozone-depleting materials. Also incorporated are indices such as income distribution, level of volunteering and dependence on foreign assets. The results show similar conclusions to those of the ISEW: as measured by the SSI, growth in most industrial countries has been stagnant since the 1970s.

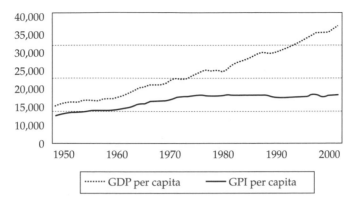

Figure 3.1 Real GDP and GPI per capita in the United States

Source: The Genuine Progress Indicator, 2006, p. 19, fig. 3.

Why are most countries so reluctant to use such measures in a prominent way? There is an obvious answer – they show economic development in a far harsher light than GDP does. A government that seems to have a good record of economic success is suddenly shown to have presided over a decline in welfare. Yet we have to bite the bullet. Every country, but especially the developed ones, should introduce alternative measures of, and frameworks for, welfare alongside narrow economic measures, and they should be made public.

Polluter pays

As a concept 'the polluter pays' is more easily dealt with than the others. It means that those who cause pollution – with carbon emissions at the top of the list – should be charged in ratio to the harm they cause. This is the logic behind climate change taxes and carbon markets; and it is also the origin of the principle that countries which have contributed most to greenhouse gases in the past should make the largest cuts today.

In practice, the notion can be difficult to pin down. Where does responsibility for pollution start and stop? The idea of 'extended polluter responsibility' has been coined in order to try to clarify this question. Those who cause emissions through manufacturing, for example, should bear the responsibility for the goods they produce throughout their life cycle, including their eventual disposal. Making such calculations is rarely easy in practice, however, simply because of the complexities involved. We cannot know, for example, which polluters are most culpable in the case of floods that have been influenced by global warming. Hence the costs of such damage have to be covered either by insurance companies or by the public authorities, or by a combination of the two.

Moreover, harmful consequences may take some time to unfold, or, in the case of new technologies, be difficult to assess. As in most areas of climate change policy, inventive solutions will be required. One way of dealing with these situations, for example, is through assurance bonds, which are a way of getting the polluter to bear insurance costs that might arise later. Funds are put up by the company or industry to insure against possible adverse environmental impact. The bond is recoverable, with interest, after it is demonstrated with reasonable confidence that the process in question is benign. If damage occurs the bond is used for environmental ends. The idea is that an incentive is provided for the potential polluter to reduce CO_2 emissions as far as possible.

Although 'the polluter pays' principle has its practical limits, it is nevertheless a guiding thread in bringing climate change into the sphere of orthodox politics. It is a principle of justice which not only stands behind that of the differential responsibility of developed and developing countries for responding to climate change, but offers the means of building such responsibility into law. The fact that it provides incentives to modify behaviour is also highly important.

The politics of climate change: concepts

To summarize the above discussion: we should discard the precautionary principle and the concept of sustainable development. The first should be replaced by more sophisticated modes of risk analysis, as discussed at many points in the book. The second is something of an oxymoron, and it seems most sensible to disentangle the two component terms again. In the case of 'development', we should focus on the contrast between the developed and developing societies. In so far as the rich countries are concerned, the problems created by affluence have to be put alongside the benefits of economic growth. I shall argue that dealing with these problems proves to be of direct relevance to the politics of climate change.

Below, I propose a list of concepts that I shall deploy in the remaining chapters. They mostly concern how to analyse and promote climate change policy in the context of political institutions. From the preceding discussion, I take the notions of 'sustainability' and 'the polluter pays'. The other concepts are:

1 The *ensuring state*. I talk about the state a lot in this book, both in the sense of the institutions of government and in the sense of the nation-state, but I don't want readers to get the wrong idea. I don't mean to go back to the old idea of the state as a top-down agency. The state today has to be an 'enabling state': its prime role is to help energize a diversity of groups to reach solutions to collective problems, many such groups operating in a bottom-up fashion. However, the concept of the enabling state isn't strong enough to capture the state's role, which also has to be to deliver outcomes. Nowhere is this principle clearer than in the case of responding to climate change. The ensuring state is a stronger notion. It means that the state is responsible for monitoring public goals and for trying to make sure they are realized in a visible and acceptable fashion.

2 *Political convergence*. This idea refers to the degree to which policies relevant to mitigating climate change overlap positively with other areas of public policy, such that each can be used to gain traction over the other. Political convergence is likely to be crucial to how far we can effectively respond to global warming; being abstract, and concerning mostly future dangers, global warming tends all too easily to give way to more everyday concerns in people's minds. Some of the most important areas of political convergence are energy security and energy planning, technological innovation, lifestyle politics and the downside of affluence, as just discussed. The largest and most promising

convergence is between climate change policy and an orientation to welfare going well beyond GDP. For instance, the car is supposed to confer freedom and mobility, but can lead to the opposite – being stuck in traffic jams. Reducing congestion by upgrading public transport and other measures responds to this issue, and is also a positive gain for reducing CO_2 emissions.

3 *Economic convergence.* This notion refers to the overlap between low-carbon technologies, forms of business practice and lifestyles with economic competitiveness. Again, it will have a fundamental impact upon our efforts to contain global warming. Economic convergence has some similarities to what has been called 'ecological modernization' – the idea that environmentally progressive policies often coincide with what is good for the economy and for wider political goals. Ecological modernization has been defined as 'a partnership in which governments, businesses, moderate environmentalists, and scientists co-operate in the restructuring of the capitalist political economy along more environmentally defensible lines'.[26] At the time when it was first mooted, in the mid-1980s, the concept of ecological modernization marked an important step forward in the environmental literature, and a major deviation from green orthodoxy. The authors who introduced it distanced themselves from the pessimism of the 'limits to development' literature, and also from those in the green movement who set themselves against modernity and, to some extent, against science and technology more generally.[27] The basic thesis was that environmental issues (not just climate change) could best be dealt with by being normalized – by drawing them into the existing framework of social economic institutions, rather than contesting those institutions as many greens chose to do. A strong emphasis was placed on the role of science and technology in generating solutions to environmental difficulties, including in coping with the problem of diminishing world resources. However, 'modernization' also included reforming governmental institutions and markets with environmental goals in mind; and it attributed an important role to civil society groups in keeping both the state and business

on the right track. I have no quarrel with any of these emphases and am therefore in general a supporter of the ecological modernization approach. Valid criticisms have been made of it, however, at least in its original formulations. It seemed as though we could have the best of all worlds. Yet while I am strongly in favour of a win–win approach to climate change policy, we must at the same time recognize the compromises that have to be made and the difficult decisions that have to be negotiated. It is also a mistake, as I have said, to assume that growth is an unalloyed benefit, especially in the more developed countries.

4 *Foregrounding*. Given its potentially cataclysmic implications, we need global warming to be a front-of-the-mind issue; however, both in the political sphere and in the minds of citizens, it all too readily becomes a back-of-the-mind one. Foregrounding refers to the use of the various political devices that can be deployed to keep global warming at the core of the political agenda.

5 *Climate change positives*. It won't be possible to mobilize effectively against global warming simply on the basis of the avoidance of future dangers – that is, in a wholly negative way. We will need some more positive goals to aim for. I believe these can come mainly from areas of political and economic convergence. Climate change policy involves thinking in the long term, and it involves an emphasis on the 'durable' rather than the ephemeral. I shall try to show that these concerns overlap significantly with well-being, rather than with sheer economic growth.

6 *Political transcendence*. Responding to climate change must not be seen as a left–right issue. Climate change has to be a question that largely transcends party politics, and about which there is an overall framework of agreement that will endure across changes of government. I have never agreed with the idea that the political centre – where the parties converge – is the antithesis of radicalism. Sometimes overall political agreement is the condition of radical policy-making, and coping with climate change certainly falls into that category.

7 *The percentage principle*. This concept marks the recognition that no course of action (or inaction) is without risks; and

that, consequently, there is always a balance of risks and opportunities to be considered in any policy context.

8 *The development imperative*. Poorer countries must have the right to develop economically, even if this process involves a significant growth in greenhouse gas emissions.

9 *Over-development*. In the rich countries, affluence itself produces a range of quite profound social problems. Economic growth correlates with measures of welfare only up to a certain level; after that point, the connection becomes more problematic. Addressing problems of over-development forms a major area of political convergence with policies relevant to controlling climate change.

10 *Proactive adaptation*. Given that climate change will happen whatever we do from now onwards, a politics of adaptation will have to be worked out alongside that of climate change mitigation. We must as far as possible prepare beforehand in a pre-emptive fashion, basing what we do upon risk assessment, with policies evolving as scientific information shifts and matures.

In the next chapter, I shall consider where the developed countries have got to in their attempts to begin a switch to a low-carbon economy. I shall look to some extent across the board, but take the UK as a key example, since its experience is in some ways typical of the problems that all will have to face.

4

THE TRACK RECORD SO FAR

Some environmentalists argue that liberal democratic societies are not equipped to cope with ecological problems, especially climate change, given the far-reaching character of the social and economic reforms that will be needed. Is it really possible to formulate policies for the long term in such societies, given the concentration of most citizens on the immediate issues of their lives?[1] In *The Climate Change Challenge and the Failure of Democracy*, David Shearman and Joseph Wayne Smith argue that the answer is 'no'. Democratic states, they say, are too dominated by sectional interests and by a hapless materialism to be able to create policies substantial enough to meet the scale of the challenge we face. We should accept that confronting our environmental dilemmas will require a more authoritarian approach from government: 'For us, freedom is not the most fundamental value and is merely one value among others. Survival strikes us as a much more basic value.'[2]

The difficulties facing liberal democratic states as they confront climate change are indeed many. Yet one should not use them to reach a counsel of despair. After all, it is these countries that have helped create the conditions under which environmental issues have come to the fore.[3] Totalitarian states have generally had poor or disastrous environmental records. So also have most of those that have undergone processes of 'authoritarian modernization', such as China, Russia or South Korea.

Several factors explain the difference. Democratic countries not only permit but positively encourage the open development of science, the very basis of our awareness of the problems of global warming and also of most other forms of environmental threat. They provide for the possibility of the mobilization of social movements, environmental pressure groups and NGOs. By contrast, non-democratic states usually maintain a high degree of control over civil society organizations, involving registration of members and supervision of their activities, with the right to close them down if they are deemed a challenge to the world-view of the authorities. Non-democratic societies have proved themselves able to stimulate technological advances in the military sphere, by concentrating their resources there; but they have lagged far behind the democratic countries in most other areas of technological development.

Taking a wide set of indices of environmental criteria, the best performers are all democratic countries. As ranked by the Environmental Performance Index developed by Yale and Columbia Universities, the top five countries in the world are Sweden, Norway, Finland, Switzerland and, interestingly, a developing society, Costa Rica.[4] Costa Rica is a middle-income country, but one that has long-standing democratic traditions – a notable exception in this respect among Central American states.

However, there is no nation that gets even close to what might be regarded as an effective performance in terms of reduction of greenhouse gas emissions. A comparison of trends in the 56 most polluting nations in terms of emissions shows that, in the words of its authors, 'If climate change protection was an Olympic discipline, no country in the world would deserve to climb the winner's victory podium.'[5] Among the industrial countries, those that have done most to improve their performance since 1990 are Sweden as number one, followed by Germany, Iceland and the UK. Some of the EU 15 countries come out poorly. For instance, Spain is 29th on the list, the Netherlands 30th, Finland 36th and Austria 37th. The US ranks 55th out of the 56 countries, ahead only of Saudi Arabia.

Leaders of the pack

It is worth having a look at the policy records of the countries which have been most successful in controlling their carbon emissions. I shall concentrate on them rather than on the laggards, of whom there are all too many, in order to form some idea of best practice. To do so, we have to begin well before the Kyoto baseline year of 1990. I shall start with Sweden, which, according to most criteria, is the outright leader in environmental performance, and will move on from there to consider some of the other states mentioned above.

Sweden took major steps to improve its level of energy efficiency following the OPEC oil embargo of 1973. Shortly afterwards, because of worries about oil dependency, several major regions in the country announced programmes for reducing domestic and commercial energy use through improvements in insulation and generation of local block heating – programmes that have been refined and improved over the years.[6] The country also turned to nuclear and hydroelectric power. Since the early 1980s the use of oil has fallen by nearly 50 per cent. In 1970 fossil fuel imports corresponded to 80 per cent of the total energy supply of the country; today the figure is only 35 per cent.

Sweden has an ambitious programme to become the world's first oil-free economy by 2020 and has been in the forefront of states pressing for international regulation of emissions. It plans to cut its own emissions from transport by the extensive use of biofuels, derived from its vast forest areas. Biofuels have been used in transport in the country for some while (for the story of how this happened, see below, pp. 125–6) and biomass, mainly from wood pulp, has been used increasingly since the mid-1970s. The green movement has been influential in Sweden and a referendum was held in 1980 which led to a decision to phase out nuclear power. In spite of protests from green groups, the government allowed the development of six new reactors before the resolution actually came into force, and for the two decades after that date nuclear power more than doubled its share of energy production.[7]

Sweden is one of six EU member-states to have a carbon

tax, which – together with nuclear power – helped cut emissions from industry and energy production by about a third between 1970 and 1990. When the tax was introduced, in order to neutralize the overall fiscal effect, income taxes were cut by half. Sweden's greenhouse gas emissions were 9 per cent lower in 2005 than they were in 1990. Over that period the economy grew by 44 per cent.

Sweden has adopted 16 environmental quality objectives, representing goals to be achieved by 2020. There are 72 interim targets to be met. Progress towards the objectives is monitored by the Environmental Objectives Council. Reducing carbon emissions brooks large among these, but they also cover other aspects, such as air quality, the soil, the forests and the Baltic Sea, which is a site of very heavy pollution.

Germany was the original home of the greens and has proved to be an environmental leader, especially among the bigger countries. Since the mid-1980s there has been substantial agreement among Germany's political parties about the need to lower greenhouse gas emissions. A report published by a parliamentary commission in 1984, *Protection of the Earth's Atmosphere*, set the tone for subsequent discussion, arguing for substantial reductions.[8]

The country has a large motor industry and coal-mining is still important; however, the early opposition of these industries to regulatory measures has become more muted across the years. The proportion of electricity generated from renewable sources grew from 6.3 per cent in 2000 to more than 14 per cent today, and Germany is now the world's biggest user of wind power, boasting some 20,000 wind turbines – wind generates about 6 per cent of the country's total energy use. The country is also the world's largest producer of photovoltaic solar power and has the fastest growing market in terms of domestic installations. The Waldpolenz Solar Park will be the most extensive solar power installation in the world when it is completed in 2009; almost 80 per cent of all European solar energy production capacity is in Germany. The country's production companies in these areas currently dominate world markets.

These achievements have been strongly influenced by the introduction of feed-in tariffs for renewable energy in the 1990s pioneered by industrialist Hermann Scheer. Anyone who attaches a renewable energy source to his or her property can have it connected to the grid at a subsidised rate fixed for 20 years. More than 300,000 private home-owners and small businesses have been incorporated into the scheme.

Yet Germany faces significant problems in further building upon its environmental successes. At the moment, the country is heavily reliant upon coal for energy production. Coal-fired power plants supply about half of Germany's electricity, with nuclear energy making up 27 per cent. As of early 2007, more than two dozen new coal plants were either in the planning stage or in the course of construction, and, like Sweden, the country has been committed to phasing out its nuclear power stations. In 2000 the then-Chancellor Gerhard Schröder announced that the country's 19 plants would be shut down after a life-span of 32 years. According to such a schedule, Germany's last nuclear plant would close in 2020. The legislation was enacted as the Nuclear Exit Law, and two plants have been turned off – one in 2003 and one in 2005. However, in 2008 Schröder's successor, Angela Merkel, from the centre-right, shifted the government position to oppose the phase-out of the nuclear industry, and its future is therefore now unclear.

In August 2007, a climate plan – the 'Meseberg programme' – was published by the government. It was promoted by the Social Democratic Party within the governing coalition, and called for a reduction in Germany's greenhouse gas emissions by 40 per cent over 1990 levels by 2020.[9] Energy efficiency, a further extension of renewable energy sources and the cleaning up of coal and gas power stations are the basis of the plan. Nuclear energy did not figure, but without it, critics argue, the figures do not stack up.

Iceland is an idiosyncratic country, partly because of its small size and partly because of its location. However, in terms of climate change it is interesting for various reasons. Because it is so far north, it is on the front line of global warming, as its glaciers melt and its weather patterns start to change. Iceland has very large resources of hydro and geothermal energy. At present, only about 15 per cent of its hydro-power potential and 1 per cent of its geothermal potential are being tapped. Nonetheless, 66 per cent of its energy supply already comes from these sources, while 99 per cent of electricity and nearly all heating for buildings derive from hydro and geothermal energy. It took 25 years for the country to convert from oil to the other energy sources, a process achieved by the creation of an energy fund, used to connect even remote areas to the grid, and by subsidies for the use of renewable energy. No other country uses such a high proportion of renewable energy sources.

Iceland is one of four small countries which have signed a pact to become carbon-neutral within some two decades. The others are New Zealand, Norway and Costa Rica. How realistic such proposals are is difficult to judge. In order to diversify the economy away from fishing, the Icelandic government has supported the building of several new aluminium smelting plants in the country. A large dam to generate hydroelectricity is being constructed in what was an environmentally protected area to help power the industry. Aluminium smelting is a heavily polluting process in terms of greenhouse gases, in spite of recent technological advances in the industry. It is hard to anticipate what will happen in the country, especially after the heavy losses it suffered as a result of the troubles in financial markets in 2008.

New Zealand's aspiration is to generate 90 per cent of its energy from renewable sources by the year 2025, and to halve its transport emissions by 2040. The agenda is an ambitious one given that the country at the moment looks unlikely even to meet its Kyoto commitment. The idea is that the government would lead the way by making its own institutions carbon-neutral within a relatively short period of time. A plan for an emissions trading scheme is meeting obstacles, partly because it excludes agriculture, the largest contributor to emissions.

Norway's ambitions are even higher: the country is aiming for carbon neutrality by 2030, in spite of being one of the largest exporters of oil and gas in the world. It already gets 95 per cent of its electricity from hydroelectric power. However, the country's carbon emissions in fact rose by 80 per cent over the period from 1990 to 2005, mainly as a result of transport, even though it has high taxes on cars and fuel. In the short term, Norway can reduce its emissions count by financing environmental projects in poorer countries, as the Kyoto Protocol allows. It is not clear, however, how the country will be able to reduce its own emissions in a substantial way, although an emissions trading scheme will be set up to cover 35–40 per cent of greenhouse gases emanating from Norwegian sources.

Costa Rica proposes to move faster than any of the other three, with the aim of reaching carbon neutrality by 2021, the date of the 200th anniversary of its independence. A major part of the strategy is the planting of trees to soak up emissions. In 2007, five million new trees were planted, easily the highest per capita planting in the world. Tax incentives are available for landowners who manage their resources in such a way as to encourage carbon sequestration and the promotion of bio-diversity. There is an initiative to make the banana industry carbon neutral within a few years. Costa Rica is the only developing country to have adopted a tax on fuel for environmental purposes. However, motor traffic has increased fivefold in the country over the past 20 years, and air traffic went up by 700 per cent over the period from 2001 to 2007.

Denmark is also an interesting case, because of its forceful programme for expanding renewable sources of energy and because of the ambiguous results that have followed.[10] At the time of the OPEC oil embargo in the late 1970s the country was heavily dependent upon oil, all of which had to be imported. The government of the time determined that this level of dependency should be reduced and its successors continued similar policies. Taxes on natural gas and petrol were introduced to stimulate energy efficiency. Oil fields in the North Sea belonging to Denmark also started production at this time. In the early 1990s the country introduced a system of subsidies to facilitate the expansion of wind power. At that point renewables accounted for some 5 per cent of its electricity.

The fluctuating nature of wind energy was compensated for by importing hydroelectricity from Sweden and Norway, and by the use of small-scale power stations which run on biomass of various kinds and which can be switched on and off quickly. By 2005 the proportion of electricity generated by wind power had jumped to well over 20 per cent and contributed 17 per cent of total energy use. Over the period from 1997 to 2003, under the aegis of a social democratic government (which fell in 2001) an average of 325 megawatts of wind power capacity was installed each year. Under the successor right-of-centre government, that figure dropped to only 3 megawatts a year. Three projected new wind farms were cancelled and in 2007 more wind-power capacity was dismantled than was put up. The country has the notable achievement of having kept energy consumption stable during a lengthy period of economic growth. However, over the past three years CO_2 emissions have risen once again.

These are at most thumbnail sketches. Rather than looking at such initiatives from around the world in depth, I shall take the United Kingdom as a type case. Each country will tread a somewhat different path, but some core problems are generic.

The case of the UK

The fact that Britain is on track to meet its Kyoto commitments comes in some part from Prime Minister Margaret Thatcher's decision to privatize the large state energy monopolies. She was determined to face down the power of the unions, especially in coal-mining. The switch from coal-fired to gas-fired power stations was driven by these aims, but also by the fact that gas was seen as the cheapest available source of energy. The closure of the coal mines coincided with the availability of natural gas supplies from the North Sea. Coal production declined from 84 million tons in 1988 to 35 million tons in 1995, and has since fallen by a further half.

According to current government estimates, about 20 per cent of the UK's performance in terms of controlling emissions of CO_2 can be put down to the 'dash for gas', although its contribution to reducing other greenhouse gases is considerably higher. Improvements in energy efficiency (in some part driven by privatization) contributed about 40 per cent. A much smaller proportion can be attributed to environmental policy, such as the Climate Change Levy set up in April 2001, and voluntary energy agreements (in which companies pay a reduced rate of the levy in exchange for meeting more rigorous energy efficiency targets over a 10-year period).

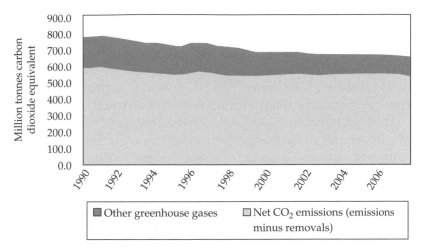

Figure 4.1 UK Greenhouse Gas Emissions, 1990–2007

Source: © Crown Copyright. Department of the Environment, Food and Rural Affairs (DEFRA), *The House Magazine*.

A Climate Change Bill was introduced in the UK in 2008. It marked a new level of ambition for the Labour government, which previously had only a modest record on environmental issues in general, and on combating global warming in particular. The bill introduced statutory targets for emissions reductions. According to its original version, greenhouse gas emissions were to be reduced by at least 60 per cent by 2050 over a 1990 baseline. This proportion has since been raised to 80 per cent. A report on progress will be published every five years and reviewed by Parliament, as well as the ongoing results of an adaptation programme. A carbon budget will be established to cover each five-year period. Late in 2008 the bill was endorsed by Parliament and became the Climate Change Act.

A Committee on Climate Change has been set up to advise the government of the day on the level of the carbon budgets and, therefore, on the optimal path towards emission reduction targets. The Committee will also consider and advise on issues such as how international aviation and shipping should be included in the targets (initially they were excluded) and the balance of reductions to be achieved domestically as compared to the use of international trading schemes. The Act requires that emissions from international passenger travel and imports or exports of goods must be included in the targets within five years from the time at which it became law. The Committee will also consider whether other greenhouse gases, estimated to account for 15 per cent of the UK's overall impact on climate change, should be incorporated within the targets.

The legislation includes provision for 'banking' and 'borrowing' between carbon budget periods. Banking is the capacity to carry over unused quotas from one budget period to a future one; borrowing allows the government to count future anticipated reductions against the current five-year period, such borrowing to be limited to 1 per cent of the following carbon budget. Banking is supposed to provide an incentive to 'overperform' during a given period, or at least remove disincentives that might kick in if a given budget were achieved early. It is accepted that there are costs involved in reducing carbon output and that energy prices will increase (and, therefore, so will other prices). The European Trading Scheme (ETS) is already having this effect in the UK, because power generators are able to pass extra costs on to consumers. However, it is suggested that the cost will not be large for individual households, and it might even act as an incentive to reduce energy use.

Recognizing how closely climate change and energy change policy are intertwined, the government introduced an Energy Bill at about the same time as the Climate Change Bill. It was passed as the Energy Act in November 2008. At that time the government also created a new ministry, the Department for Energy and Climate Change. North Sea oil and gas have supplied most of the UK's energy needs for the past 20 years, but stocks are declining. Most of Britain's nuclear and some of its coal-fired power stations will reach the end of their lives by around 2020 – fully one-third of the country's electricity generation system will need to have been replaced by this point.

The UK has a huge task if it is to meet the target set by the EU, which is that 15 per cent of its energy (including electricity, transport fuels and heating) must come from renewable sources by 2020.[11] To do so, about 40 per cent of its electricity will have to come from renewable sources – an increase of 800 per cent over present-day levels. The government has accepted that nuclear power has to be part of the mix, and included in the Act are plans to build a new generation of nuclear plants. At least eight are scheduled to be constructed, with locations to be finalized under new fast-track planning procedures; some, but not all, will be built on existing nuclear sites.

The remainder of the mix is to come mainly from a strengthening of the Renewables Obligation. Introduced in 2006, this piece of legislation requires suppliers of electricity to generate a specific and annually increasing percentage of energy from renewable sources. The Energy Act also includes provisions to stimulate the development of carbon capture and storage.

What are we to make of these efforts? The introduction of the two pieces of legislation shows a determination to confront the twin problems of climate change and energy security; the bills received a high degree of cross-party support in their passage through Parliament. Although some climate change sceptics used the opportunity to air their views during the debates, it turned out that the main clauses in both Acts were strengthened rather than weakened. However, a number of weaknesses and problems remain, outlined below:

1   The policies are more about the 'what to do' in response to climate change then the 'how to do'. The Climate Change Act sets out a number of ambitious targets, but provides little insight into how they will be met. Indeed, the 'how' seems to be left largely to the Climate Change Committee to set out. The Energy Act fills in some of the gaps, but is open to considerable criticism, as we shall see. The Climate Change Act leaves aside the issue of the 'export of pollution' – the fact that the large developing countries, especially China, are carrying out much of the industrial production of the manufactured goods consumed in the developed societies. Yet will the developed countries simply be able to ignore the question? In some sense it is likely to form part of whatever bargain is to be worked out between the developed and developing world.

2   Both Acts are organized mainly in terms of negatives – scenarios we have to avoid. In so far as solutions are suggested at all about how targets for emissions are to be reached, they are posed in terms of 'out there' solutions, such as the expansion of carbon markets and encouragement

for the development of certain technologies. A positive vision is lacking.

3   The Climate Change Act seeks to provide legal backing for medium- and long-term decisions made about controlling emissions. It recognizes one of the core problems that democratic countries face – how to construct plans that survive successive changes of government. Much will depend upon the Climate Change Committee. Yet how strong will this group be? It has to hold the government to account; but its role is explicitly set as only an advisory one.

4   The government has not hesitated to politicize the two Acts, in spite of the fact that an enduring cross-party consensus will have to be sustained if they are to have long-term effects. It is reported in an official Labour document that the current Conservative leader, David Cameron, 'is more concerned with his image and PR than the long-term decisions needed to meet the challenge of tackling climate change'. Indeed, he has been held up to ridicule. He travelled to the Arctic, the document continues, 'to be photographed with huskies'; he attached a wind turbine to his house, only having to take it down later because he didn't have planning permission; and he cycled to work while being followed by a (large) car carrying his shoes and his briefcase.[12]

5   Nuclear power forms an important part of the government's package, and with good reason, since a diversification of energy sources seems crucial to reducing emissions. However, even setting aside the objections of those who see no place for nuclear power at all, there are formidable difficulties in the way. The government argues that a new generation of nuclear power stations can be built without any form of state subsidy. Yet there are serious doubts about whether such a strategy is realistic. The government underwrote all the debts of British Energy when it was on the verge of bankruptcy in 2001, at very substantial cost. In the meantime, the expense of cleaning up Britain's existing nuclear legacy has been calculated at £73 billion – which does not augur well for the future.[13]

6   Taxes on fuel are described by the government as environmental taxes, as indeed they are. In the shape of the

'Fuel Price Escalator', they were introduced in 1993 by the Conservative government and remained in place when Labour came to power. The escalator was initially set at 3 per cent above the annual rate of inflation and was later increased to 5 per cent. The incoming Labour government raised it further, but, following widespread protests, abandoned it in favour of ad hoc budget decisions. The result of this somewhat eccentric history is that fuel tax has lost almost all its environmental connotations; it is seen as 'just another tax' with which the government has chosen to burden the public. In a recent poll, 70 per cent of respondents said they believed fuel levies to be simply a smokescreen for raising taxes.[14]

7 It is not clear how the stated objectives of the Climate Change Act can be reconciled with other aspects of government policy. For example, the government has endorsed proposals to build a third runway at Heathrow Airport in London. An earlier commitment that flights to and from the airport would be capped at 480,000 a year has been discarded. With the building of a new runway, the number of flights will rise very substantially, and the government anticipates that the number of passengers passing through airports in Britain will go up from 230 million in 2006 to 465 million by 2030. It is argued that such expansion is of key importance to the economy; and that if it is not catered for in Britain, it will simply move elsewhere. A report published by the Sustainable Development Commission (SDC), set up a few years earlier by the government, stated that the data used to justify expansion were inadequate and argued that the proposed strategy should be put on hold while a full-scale enquiry was carried out. The report was rejected by the government itself; a statement was issued saying that it 'fundamentally disagreed' with the SDC's findings. Further deferral of a decision, it was stated, was not an option. But if the considered findings of a government-supported agency are to be dismissed so lightly, how much influence will the Committee on Climate Change actually have? Hugh Raven, SDC Commissioner, commented upon the decision about the third runway: 'Pressing ahead with the expansion of Heathrow is highly irresponsible.'[15]

8 Little attempt has been made to expand the national railway network or to encourage electrification. In the UK, 33 per cent of the network runs off electricity, one of the smallest proportions in the EU. Trains powered in such a way emit substantially lower levels of CO_2 than do diesel locomotives. A report published by the government in July 2007 argued that the long-term benefits of systematic electrification are 'currently uncertain and . . . do not reflect today's priorities'.[16] A five-year plan for the future of the railways published by the government in July 2008 has been justifiably attacked as being too modest. Early in 2009, the government announced that proposals for some new high-speed lines were being looked at.

9 Only marginal attention seems to have been given to how the proposals in the two Acts will impact upon issues of social justice. Rising carbon and fuel prices will affect the poor more than the affluent. Average fuel bills in 2008 in the UK increased by some 40 per cent over the previous year. The consequences were particularly severe for over-65-year-olds living below the poverty line – some two million people in Britain. Specific redistributive measures are needed to counter these effects, but those introduced so far are relatively minor.

10 It could be argued that the clauses in the Energy Act fall well short of providing the stimulus that will be needed for the UK to reach its climate change targets. The Renewables Obligation does not look strong enough to increase sufficiently the percentage of energy delivered by non-fossil fuel sources. In 2007, the power companies were 'obligated' to make 6.7 per cent of their electricity production renewable; they only succeeded in delivering 4.7 per cent. A new and more far-reaching blueprint for increased energy supply from renewable sources was introduced in mid-2008. It envisages a big expansion in the development of wind power, biomass from wood and sewerage, biofuels, micro-generation from homes, plus a rise in house insulation. The level of the Renewables Obligation would be raised, and changes introduced to speed up planning applications for energy-related projects. There would be a contribution to the economy from the new technology

industries, plus the creation of new jobs. Tax breaks, tax credits, grants and one-off subsidies are among the ways in which it is proposed to stimulate the needed changes. The government says that there will be significant net cost to the country, put at £6 billion a year by 2020, and that the policies will add further to energy prices in the short term. In November 2008, as the Energy Bill was being debated in Parliament, the government suddenly shifted its position on feed-in tariffs. Ed Miliband, Secretary of State for Energy and Climate Change, announced that a feed-in tariff would be introduced to complement the Renewables Obligation.

11 The government is considering whether to sanction the building of a coal-fired power station at Kingsnorth in Kent. The proposal is to replace the existing plant with a new one. It could be the first of a number of new coal-fired plants. Critics point out that the Kingsnorth station would produce more CO_2 per year than a country the size of Ghana. The commercial development of carbon capture and sequestration, which would make coal far more environment-friendly, is, in practice, years away from being realized.

12 The Climate Change Act and the Energy Act do not cover adaptation and the problems of insurance that go with it. In 2007 unprecedented floods affected East and South Yorkshire, Gloucestershire and the Thames Valley. A year later, 11,000 people were still living in temporary accommodation. Many of those whose homes have been repaired say they live in fear whenever rain threatens to turn heavy. In a report that came out in 2008, it was stated that preparations for further possible floods are quite inadequate. More than 90 recommendations were put forward, to be implemented as soon as possible, ranging from better preparation from the water companies, new building regulations and the creation of a national electronic map of the country's drainage ditches and streams, with clear allocation of authority for keeping them clear.[17] (For further discussion, see chapter 7.)

Britain's level of emissions of greenhouse gases fell by 2.2 per cent in 2007, compared with the previous year, due mainly to the continuing switch to gas for electricity generation.[18]

However, over the decade from 1997 to 2007, the number of cars owned by households rose by a net total of 5 million. The mileage covered on average by cars rose by some 2 per cent each year. Air passenger numbers increased by 54 million over the five years from 2002 to 2007. Perhaps it isn't surprising that many critics argue that the UK will struggle to reach the goals it has set itself.

In December 2008, the Climate Change Committee published its first report on how the country should go about reaching those goals. The report includes recommendations covering the first three budgets defining the path to emissions reductions to be followed up to 2022. Wind, solar, tidal and nuclear power, together with carbon capture and storage of 'clean coal', are the principal technologies listed as needing expansion. Home and office insulation together with increased vehicle efficiency also brook large. At the time of writing, the government has not made a formal response to the document.[19]

Most of the issues noted above will be faced in one form or another by every country that sets itself demanding climate change targets, although a few may be in a better position than the UK in terms of their starting-point. The majority, however, start from much further back. It is a sobering thought, and gives an indication of the scale of the task that awaits. Looking at where the countries discussed above stand drives home how far there is to go in order to make significant progress towards major emissions reductions. The nations discussed are among the best performers in the world and even their progress is relatively limited. Some points of general interest emerge:

1 With the partial exception of Germany and Denmark, countries that are at the top of the league are there because of a preoccupation with energy security rather than climate change. In this sense, they have arrived where they are largely by accident. There are potential lessons here for the future. The impact of Giddens's paradox might be reduced by focusing on energy efficiency as much as on climate change as such.

2 The left–right dimension can significantly affect the continuity of energy and climate change policies. Thus far, effective policies have mostly been driven by left-of-centre regimes.

The Scandinavian countries, for example, are in prime position largely because they have had long periods of left-of-centre government. Germany provides a better model for the future, since there has been something of a consensus among the parties about environmental measures.

3 Carbon taxes do work – although, as I shall discuss at a later point, they are rarely straightforward to implement. Putting a price on carbon is an essential component of climate change policy. Carbon taxes have the great advantage over other strategies in that they are universal and binding, although ways have to be found to reconcile them with issues of social justice, since the poor are very often the hardest hit.

4 It is essential for the state to subsidize renewable technologies if they are to make an impact. One reason is the need to preserve a stable basis for investment, even as oil and other fossil fuel prices fluctuate. Subsidies can also be used to provide positive motivation for the take-up of possibilities on offer. The feed-in tariffs made available in Germany provide a model which can and should be copied elsewhere.

5 Despite objections, nuclear power is likely to have to form part of the energy mix, at least in some, perhaps many, states. The worries that many people have about the use of nuclear energy are real and significant. Yet we have to bear in mind the percentage principle. The risks involved when a country has little chance of reaching its emissions reduction targets without nuclear energy as part of the mix must be taken seriously too.

6 In only a few countries – such as Sweden or Germany – could it be said that climate change policies have truly moved to the centre of the political field, and even there they are still to some degree contentious and under attack.

7 The more detailed consideration of the British case shows how difficult it will be for governments to maintain coherence in their policies in different areas. Of course, such a difficulty is to some extent intrinsic to democratic politics, given the push and pull between political leaders, interest groups and the public – coupled to the need to win elections. However, a key aim in all countries must be to push

for consistency in climate change and energy policy across the board.

8 We should bear in mind that the past 20 years have been a period during which manufacture continued to decline in Western countries. They have become dependent upon manufactured goods produced in China and the other developing countries. The levels of emissions produced by the developed countries would be higher than they currently are without this 'transfer of emissions' eastwards.

5

A RETURN TO PLANNING?

Key arguments of this book are that the industrial nations must take the lead in addressing climate change and that the chances of success will depend a great deal upon *government* and *the state*. Whatever can be done through the state will in turn depend upon generating widespread political support from citizens, within the context of democratic rights and freedoms. I don't want to deny that reaching international agreements is essential, or that many other agencies, including NGOs and businesses, will play a fundamental role. However, for better or worse, the state retains many of the powers that have to be invoked if a serious impact on global warming is to be made.

What should the role of the state, as ensuring state, be? Its main function must be to act as a catalyst, as a facilitator, but certainly, as far as climate change and energy security are concerned, it has also to strive for guarantees. These are areas where solutions simply have to be found, and where there are timetables involved. If your living room is a mess, you can wait until you have time to clear it up. We can't do the same with emissions, as they pile up in the atmosphere and as oil and gas start to run out.

These are some of the tasks in which the state has to be prime actor. The state must:

- *help us to think ahead*: it is the responsibility of political leaders to introduce policies for the long term. For this shift in orientation to come about, there has to be return to planning, in some guise or another. In case it isn't self-evident, thinking long term is not the same as setting targets for some distant date in the future and then sitting back and relaxing. 'Rigorous' targets set two or three or more decades down the line might make government ministers feel good, but really there has to be an all-out concentration upon *means*. In the Soviet Union, five-, ten- and twenty-year targets were announced with a great deal of huffing and puffing. The results normally fell well short of expectations and new plans would then be instituted. Empty promises for the future won't do in the case of climate change, since the emissions in the atmosphere continue to mount. Planning, of course, isn't the sole prerogative of the state. Governments should encourage a shift towards long-term thinking among companies, third-sector groups and individual citizens.

- *manage climate change and energy risks in the context of other risks faced by contemporary societies*: risk and opportunity are the two poles around which a great deal of social and economic policy now revolves. We face a future in which the past history of industrialism, as it were, is rapidly catching up with us, and major adjustments have to be made. However, the risks associated with climate change intersect with a variety of others, locally, nationally and internationally.
- *promote political and economic convergence*, as the main driving forces of climate change and energy policy. Both can and should be targets for the short and the longer term, and should form the foundation of forward planning. In the long term, a whole diversity of areas has to be considered, including preparing for the large-scale social and economic restructuring that a low-carbon economy inevitably will involve.
- *make interventions into markets to institutionalize 'the polluter pays' principle*, thereby ensuring that markets work in favour of climate change policy, rather than against it. In almost all developed countries at the moment environmental costs remain largely externalized. I am dubious about how effective carbon markets as such will be, but there is a great deal that can be done to introduce full cost pricing, and therefore to allow market forces to become centred upon promoting environmental benefits. Government should act to reduce

'negative externalities' – situations in which environmental costs are not brought into the marketplace – in order that markets can work to environmental ends.

- *act to counter business interests which seek to block climate change initiatives*: large-scale change is needed here, and at first blush this seems a tall order indeed. For business, especially big business, has a dominant role in contemporary societies. It is able to influence governments, even sometimes hold them to ransom and also influence consumers through advertising and other means. When governments threaten regulation, businesses can simply announce that they will up sticks and move elsewhere – the so-called problem of 'leakage'. Yet couldn't all this be turned around and the power of business become deployed to climate change objectives? I believe it is possible, even in the short term, as long as governments act together with enlightened corporate leaders. Here again we see the key importance of economic convergence. Joint action can emerge from a confluence of interests; it doesn't have to come from a sudden burst of altruism on the part of business firms.

- *keep climate change at the top of the political agenda*: for most people, most of the time, global warming is not a worry that intrudes deeply into the routines of daily life. It can drift off the agenda as other concerns come to the fore, or as elections approach. There should be an agreement among competing political parties that climate change and energy policy will be sustained in spite of other differences and conflicts that exist. In addition, climate change should feature in the curriculum of all schools.

- *develop an appropriate economic and fiscal framework for moving towards a low-carbon economy*: subsidies are needed if new technologies are to thrive, since, in the beginning, they will be unable to compete with fossil fuels. I shall argue below that a holistic approach is needed to carbon taxation – it will not do just to think in terms of a handful of specific tax measures. The overall tax system needs continuous auditing in terms of its generic impact upon economic behaviour and lifestyles.

- *prepare to adapt to the consequences of climate change*, which will now be felt in any case. Thinking ahead in this area is crucial – as in the case of mitigation, we can't just wait around to see what develops. We must try to anticipate exactly how and where the effects of global warming will be felt and act pre-emptively to counter or minimize them.

- *integrate local, regional, national and international aspects of climate change policy*: without robust national programmes, international agreements will not work. Conversely, however, international collaboration of one sort or another is a necessary condition for coping with climate change.

Is this all asking too much, given the fact that governments often find themselves hemmed in by the pressure of events of the day? The political theorist John Dryzek argues that the combination of capitalist markets, vested interests and state bureaucracy means that government will be 'thoroughly inept when it comes to ecology'. He adds that 'any redeeming features are to be found only in the possibilities they open up for their own transformation'.[1] The first comment is too dismissive, but I agree with the thrust of the second. Responding to climate change will prompt and require innovation in government itself and in the relation between the state, markets and civil society.

The above points provide the basis for this and the following two chapters. In the current one, I shall discuss what a return to planning might imply, what surveys show about public attitudes towards climate change and how we might keep the issue at the forefront of the political agenda. I will then move on to consider how consistent policy might be maintained between otherwise antagonistic political parties. In the following chapter I discuss technological innovation and what help government might play in furthering it, plus how taxation can play a role. In chapter 7 I move onto the ticklish but necessary topic of the politics of adaptation.

Planning, then and now

Planning was in vogue for some two or three decades in Western countries after the Second World War and was, of course, the very basis of the economy in Soviet-type societies. Between 1928 and 1991, as many as 13 successive national plans were instituted in the USSR. Planning was not only in fashion, but was *de rigueur* in Western countries too for a lengthy period after the Second World War, before falling into disrepute. In 1949 the economist Evan Durbin wrote: 'We are all planners now. . . . The collapse of the popular faith in *laisser faire* has proceeded with spectacular rapidity . . . all over the world since the War.'[2]

In the post-war period, 'planning' normally meant strong central direction by the state in the interests of overall economic prosperity and social justice. In the mixed economies of the West, it signalled the nationalization of industry, especially those industries seen as strategically important, such as the energy industries, communications and iron and steel. It also referred to the creation of 'planned communities', such as 'new towns' and garden cities.

The reasons why the world retreated from planning, especially in its more centralized versions, were various. In Soviet-style society it was associated with an authoritarian, oppressive state. Even in the West many came to resent the heavy-handed outlook of government planners – faceless bureaucrats who could intervene in communities without much thought for local concerns or sensitivities. Moreover, centralized planning of the economy, supposed to overcome the irrationalities of capitalism, proved quite unable to cope with the complexities of a developed economic system. Bets were placed by governments on industries which promptly then went on to fail. Critics such as Friedrich von Hayek were proved correct when they argued that only markets can cope with the enormous numbers of on-the-ground decisions about prices and products that have to be made every moment of the day in modern economies.[3]

When the counter-revolution set in, from the 1980s onwards, involving widespread privatization, coupled with minimal macroeconomic steering, the very word 'planning' came under a shadow and has, until recently, remained there. Yet whenever we think about the future in a systematic way, in the sense of attempting to shape or guide it, planning of some sort is inevitable. The post-war period was one of reconstruction, in which large-scale investments had to be made in order to recover from a situation of immense material damage.

Many forms of planning were in fact carried on 'below the radar' by states, even after the time at which the idea fell into disrepute. Governments have had to monitor demographic shifts, for instance, in order to plan ahead for future needs in education, health and pensions. They have had to do the same with roads and railways in terms of future projections of use. Contingency plans have to exist in case of possible disasters. Even as 'planned communities' fell out of fashion, so urban planning of one sort or another continued.

There has now to be a return to greater state interventionism, a conclusion that is reinforced by the failure of deregulation. That failure can be summed up as too much 'short-termism' and a corrosion of public institutions, coupled to a lack of controls for system risk. In terms of the economy, ways will have to be found to introduce regulation without crippling that sense of adventure and entrepreneurialism upon which a successful response to climate change will also depend. In a nutshell, overall macroeconomic steering, the main economic role of government for the past three or four decades, is no longer enough. There needs to be a greater emphasis on industrial policy. This point is obvious in the case of the fostering of low-carbon technologies, but surely must apply more broadly – although the issues involved stretch well beyond my specific concerns here. Supply-side mechanisms will continue to be vital areas for state investment, as in the case of education or the provision of infrastructure.

A return to planning will in no sense be a straightforward process. Planning has to be reconciled with democratic freedoms, some of which should be actively extended, rather than reduced, in relation to the demands of climate change. There will be a push and pull between the political centre, regions and localities, which will have to be resolved through democratic mechanisms. It will not be easy to decide where the balance should lie. National planning will demand that local concerns sometimes be overridden – but how and to what degree?

This issue arises, for example, with the creation of new towns. Planned communities are back in fashion – this time as eco-towns, now being built or envisaged in many countries. In Britain, for example, 10 eco-towns are to be constructed, starting in 2012–13. They will be designed for between 5,000 and 20,000 people. The towns will be largely pedestrianized, with only a few roads, where the speed limit will be 15 miles per hour. There will be no garages or parking places for the houses, and all the main facilities will be within walking distance of every dwelling. The buildings will be heavily insulated; underground vacuum recycling will be installed; and solar panels, wind turbines and biomass from local sources will supply much of the energy. Will these new venues meet the fate of the pre-existing 'new towns'? Already they have their critics. Some claim the carbon emissions needed to build them will outstrip the benefits; others fear that the inhabitants will be marooned on car-free sites in the middle of nowhere.

The Planning Bill recently introduced in the British Parliament brings these dilemmas into relief. The aim is to facilitate infrastructural planning, for example, in relation to the building of power stations, railways and roads. The current planning system, the government believes, is too cumbersome and slow-moving to permit effective long-term decision-making. Currently, more than 100 major projects are stuck in the pipeline, including proposals for the building of barrages, waste recycling plants and wind farms. Alongside these are others of more dubious environmental value, such as widening motorways or expanding air traffic. The government puts forward climate change and energy concerns as its main motivating reason for the legislation.

The bill empowers the government periodically to issue national policy statements, some of which would identify major developments on specific sites, where it considers them to be in the public interest – such as the building of a new nuclear power station. There will be local consultation, but a newly created agency, the Infrastructure Planning Commission, will take a final decision about whether a project should be permitted to go ahead. The bill is set to pass through Parliament, but the objections have been many. From an environmental point of view, the central problem is that it is not confined to schemes relevant to climate change objectives. It could be used as what opposition groups describe as a 'developers' charter', not just to encroach on the countryside, but to push through projects that are actively damaging to the environmentalist cause.

However, one can understand the government's point of view. Planning has to be generic. It can't be limited only to environmental projects as such, because climate change and energy conservation are not the only considerations that government must face up to and take decisions about. There isn't a problem-free solution. It will be up to interested parties to monitor what the new agency does and raise objections where necessary, but they won't have the power to block decisions that it makes.

It is clear also that planning must stretch across the boundaries of nations. National plans can't be hatched without due consideration of what neighbouring countries are doing. Compared to other countries, EU states should have a distinct advantage in this respect, since coordinated planning should, in principle, be much easier.

In thinking about planning, it won't do to consider only the form it will take; we also have to decide about its content. Lessons can be learned from those who make a speciality of studying that nebulous entity, the future.[4] How do we plan for a future which is inherently uncertain and in order to limit risks which, since we have no prior experience of them, cannot be assessed with complete precision? How can the mistakes made by the previous generation of planners be avoided? Planning in the old days was based on forecasting, but the limitations of this method are by now well known. It works best for short-term planning and also in cases where present-day trends are to some degree set in stone. In the case of energy forecasting in Britain, for instance, we know that the existing generation of power stations will need replacing within a certain timescale.

We often want to predict the future in order to change it – and where our attempts to change it become part of that future. This situation holds in the case of climate change. One way of dealing with it is by *backcasting*: asking what changes have to be made in the present in order to arrive at alternative future states. A successful outcome is imagined in the future, and different scenarios are calculated as to how it might be reached. We are talking therefore of alternative and plural futures, where adjustments, even radical revisions, are made as time unfolds and then built into other scenarios. This approach is essentially that used by the IPCC. The distinct advantage over traditional forecasting is that it allows much greater space to unforeseen contingencies that might dramatically alter predictions made at any specific date.

The point of backcasting is not to reveal what the future will be, but to weigh up future options and policy goals. Backcasting is especially relevant for environmental and energy planning issues, since they fit the circumstances to which the approach is most relevant. These are that the context is complex, a major reorientation of current trends is demanded and a timescale of several decades or more is involved. There are many examples from around the world. A project was instituted in the Netherlands in the late 1990s, for example, to look for alternatives to meat production and consumption. Its key assumption was that by 2040 new protein foods should replace 40 per cent of current meat consumption. The foods would have to be at least as tasty as the most popular forms of meat, while, among other qualities, having superior health value. The project considered how tastes might change to promote acceptance of such foods. It concluded that new protein foods could be produced 10–30 times more efficiently than meat, as measured in terms of reducing emissions, while at the same time producing a health bonus.[5]

Backcasting sounds technocratic. In fact, it almost always involves a visionary element, since, by definition, it projects a future that is different from that seen from the present. Of course, forecasting will not disappear and will continue to be part of government planning. It is obvious that backcasting and forecasting are often complementary. Take, as an example, planning for the future of the water industry in Australia, a country suffering from droughts that are probably influenced by global warming and where water is becoming an ever more scarce resource.[6]

Cynthia Mitchell and Stuart White argue that forecasting can identify policies that will produce results in the short term – it can help pluck the low-lying fruit. Backcasting is needed to think more radically about future possibilities. Forecasts about security of water supply in urban areas in Australia indicate major problems in guaranteeing adequate supply within a few years. Several policies that could quickly make a difference within the existing water system were identified, such as installing water-efficient shower heads and tap regulators, dual flush toilets, waterless urinals, taps operated by sensors and local water collection and recycling. In Queensland, where there have been prolonged periods of drought, reductions in customer demand of up to 30 per cent have been attained using such means.

Backcasting, however, has helped suggest more far-reaching innovations. Thus at the moment it is commonly assumed that water, sewage and storm-water systems should be considered and planned for separately. Thinking 'backwards' from a hypothetical situation of a total water cycle has produced quite a different perspective. What can be achieved has been demonstrated in a residential development in Melbourne, which generated a 70 per cent reduction in water demand. Another possibility is, instead of simply providing a water stream, to think of providing a service of a more general nature. Thus, in central Queensland about 80 per cent of raw water demand comes from industry, and some 80 per cent of it is for cooling. A high proportion of that demand could in fact be transferred to air cooling, reducing the need to use water.

In thinking about planning, especially over the longer term, we find ourselves back with risk and uncertainty. 'Planning' sounds like a straightforward process, but this is far from the case – it is highly complex and contingent. One of the main reasons for this is the fact that predictions, forecasts and plans that are made become themselves part of the universe of events which they are about. In an important sense they have to do so, since the point is to shape the future; yet, at the same time, an inherent element of unpredictability is introduced and has to be coped with. Trying to alter public attitudes towards risk is a key part of planning policy, and it is to this topic that I now turn.

Changing lives

Looking at public attitudes in a number of industrial countries 10 years ago, a group of researchers concluded 'Our interpretation of existing data is that, all things being equal, a majority of citizens in most countries will support national and international initiatives designed to cope with global warming as long as these initiatives do not demand a significant alteration of lifestyle.'[7] Perhaps surprisingly, in spite of the greater prominence that global warming has in the media today, broadly speaking that statement still holds good.

In a national survey carried out in the UK in 2008, 30 per cent of respondents said they were 'very concerned' about climate change, with a further 47 per cent saying they were 'fairly concerned'.[8] However, many expressed doubts about the status of the scientific findings on the issue: 60 per cent either 'strongly agreed' or 'agreed' with the statement that 'many scientific experts still question if humans are contributing to climate change', demonstrating the influence of the sceptics, which is out of all proportion to their numbers in the scientific community. Only 7 per cent 'strongly disagreed' with the statement, and 42 per cent either 'strongly agreed' or 'agreed' that 'I sometimes think climate change might not be as bad as people say'. Almost 60 per cent thought the government is using the climate change agenda to raise taxes. A large majority (77 per cent) endorsed the statement that 'most people are not prepared to make big sacrifices' to help stop climate change.

In terms of ranking the problems facing the country, 33 per cent chose the economy as their main worry – even before the 2008 financial crisis. Only 7 per cent put global warming at the top of the list. Climate change tends to be seen as a risk the responsibility for which lies with 'the authorities'.[9]

In such surveys, a high proportion of people agree that 'We are too small to make a difference', and that 'We shouldn't take action until bigger countries do'. The responses echo a problem in climate change policy which crops up in many different contexts – that of *free-riding*. Free-riding can arise in any area of social or economic life in which collective outcomes hinge on decisions taken by individual actors. For example, suppose that the residents in a street vulnerable to crime get together to set up a neighbourhood watch scheme – each has to pay £100 to make the scheme work. Some might refuse to contribute, yet the system is set up anyway. These people are free-riding, since they benefit from the scheme for nothing.

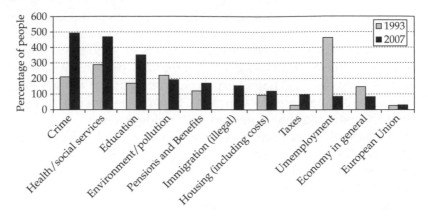

Figure 5.1 Issues regarded as most important by the public, 1993 and 2007

Source: © Crown Copyright. Department for Environment, Food and Rural Affairs (DEFRA), 2007 Survey of Public Attitudes and Behaviours Towards the Environment.

Problems of free-riding exist everywhere in the area of climate change policy, from the level of ordinary citizens right up to the international arena. People who continue to drive SUVs are free-riding off those who have switched to smaller cars. Countries that have done little or nothing to reduce their greenhouse gas emissions are free-riding off those that have been more active. Feelings about free-riders in the area of climate change are very strong. The result is the 'I won't unless you do' syndrome, which is widespread.

Polls show that most people only a have a vague idea about the causes of climate change. Many believe, for example, that healing the ozone layer will help stop global warming. A survey taken in 2002 in the Seattle area – one of the most advanced in terms of environmental consciousness – showed that 45 per cent of respondents thought that stopping the use of aerosol sprays would be very helpful in reducing global warming.[10] Many did not appreciate that greenhouses gases are not just another form of pollution; a significant proportion believed that they can be removed from the air as easily as the pollutants which cause acid rain. Most people had a clearer understanding of problems surrounding energy, and in focus groups their opinions were often framed more in terms of energy requirements rather than of climate change.

A national survey carried out in the US in 2006 showed that 44 per cent of respondents rated global warming as 'very important'. However, it was only 18th in a list of other concerns about which they were worried.[11] Fewer than one in five said they were concerned 'a great deal' about the issue. An international survey taken in the same year revealed that, among 29 other countries, the US had the highest proportion of citizens who believed that global warming is not a serious problem.[12]

Surveys taken on a global level show that people in the developing countries are the most concerned about climate change. A cross-cultural study of nine developed and developing countries indicated that about 60 per cent of people interviewed about climate change in China, India, Mexico and Brazil felt a 'high level of concern', in contrast to figures of only 22 per cent in the UK and Germany.[13] Furthermore, in the poorer countries, around 47 per cent of respondents expressed high levels of personal commitment to responding to climate change, compared to just 19 per cent in the UK. Although the proportion was even lower in the US, respondents there were by far the most optimistic of any that the problem could be solved. This finding is in line with a further study, which showed that 71 per cent of Americans agreed that steps taken to reduce emissions will help the US economy 'become more competitive . . . in the long run'.[14]

Research produced in Britain by DEFRA divides up the public into seven clusters in terms of their appreciation of the threat of climate change and their willingness to respond on the level of their day-to-day lives.[15] One group, the 'positive greens', accept that they should do as much as they can to limit their impact on the environment. They made up 18 per cent of the sample of the population studied. Those comprising this group came mostly from affluent backgrounds – social classes A and B in Census terminology.

A second group, the 'waste-watchers', follow a 'waste not want not' philosophy, relevant to environmental goals, but not especially inspired by them. Thrift is part of their lives, presumably most often simply because of lack of resources. They represented 12 per cent of the sample, and were concentrated mainly among older age groups. The third cluster, the 'concerned consumers', making up 14 per cent, say they 'already do more than a lot of people' and are not willing at the moment to do much more.

A fourth cluster, the 'sideline supporters', accept that climate change is a major problem. Yet they are not contemplating any particular changes to their lifestyles. They say, for example, 'I don't think much about how much water or electricity I use, and I forget to turn things off', yet do seem to feel minor pangs of guilt about their attitudes. They comprised 14 per cent of the sample. A fifth group, the 'cautious participants', do little to help the environment, but would do more if others did – they form another 14 per cent.

The sixth cluster, labelled the 'stalled starters', say they don't know much about climate change, and, in any case, lack the means to take any steps to help with the issue – they are mostly from non-affluent backgrounds. Most can't afford a car, but would like to buy one if they could. Finally, the 'honestly disengaged' are either sceptical about, or indifferent towards, climate change. As one interviewee remarked: 'Maybe there'll be an environmental disaster, maybe not. Makes no difference to me, I'm just living life the way I want to.'

It follows, the DEFRA report argues, that policy concerned with securing more environmentally responsible behaviour should vary. The 'positive greens' have a high potential to do more, and are willing to do so – and, at least to some degree, so are the 'concerned consumers' and the 'sideline supporters'. In these instances, policy should be to 'enable and engage' – it should be aimed at providing the means for individuals to build on the attitudes they already hold. Examples include providing information about how to lower carbon consumption, encouraging community action, improving infrastructure and so on.

For the 'cautious participants' and the 'stalled starters', the report says, the emphasis should be not only on enabling and engaging, but, in addition and in particular, on 'exemplifying'. In the terms I used earlier, people in these groups are worried about free-riding. Community leadership and neighbourhood groups can play a part in reducing the impact of feelings of unfairness about free-riding. As for the 'sceptics', their attitudes will be harder to sustain if others move the centre of gravity of public opinion onwards. The problem, as far as public policy is concerned, is one of 'engagement' – how to get such groups to take climate change seriously at all.

DEFRA hosted a 'citizens' summit' to see how far a deliberative process might shift public attitudes towards global warming and foster lifestyle changes. It formed part of a wider public consultation process as part of the lead-up to the introduction of the Climate Change Bill. A representative group of citizens from different regions in the country took part in a series of workshops. Information packs were provided, and the participants were requested to try out taking steps to reduce their carbon consumption before the final meeting, the 'summit', took place.

As in wider surveys, the desire for the government to take the lead came through clearly. People feel strongly about the gap they see between what they can do as individuals and the global scope of the problem. At the end of the deliberative process, the proportion of participants who agreed with the phase 'I am well informed about climate change' more than doubled – 66 per cent at that point claimed to be well-informed. The percentage agreeing that 'action needs to be taken urgently' rose from 65 per cent at the beginning to 82 per cent by the close. Before the workshops started, just over half of the participants agreed that the responsibility for countering climate change 'belongs to all of us'. That proportion increased to 83 per cent.

About 40 per cent of emissions in the UK come from domestic sources if one includes household travel. There are many areas of day-to-day conduct where changes in behaviour would help lower this total. DEFRA separates them into 'one-off purchasing decisions', 'habitual everyday lifestyle activities', 'occasional purchasing decisions' and 'habitual purchasing decisions'. Those in the first category include, for example, installing home insulation or buying a more energy-efficient car. The second consists of such factors as energy consumption in the home and the level of car usage. Occasional purchasing decisions include buying energy-efficient products such as low-energy light bulbs. The fourth category is made up of activities such as the purchase of food and household goods.

The list of day-to-day activities outlined by DEFRA as relevant to reducing emissions is long. Should we be concentrating upon a blanket strategy, focusing on all of them? Many would say so. A proliferation of how-to-do-it books exist on how to reduce one's carbon footprint, and, if the majority of the population were to follow them, the impact upon carbon consumption would be significant.

I am quite hostile to such endeavours, however, no matter how well intentioned they may be. They are based upon a quite unrealistic assumption – that everyone is willing and able to live like the small minority of 'positive greens' in DEFRA's sample. It is possible that they may even be counterproductive, by actively putting off the majority of citizens from other steps they may take. Giddens's paradox holds. For most of the time and for the majority of citizens, climate change is a back-of-the-mind issue, even if is a source of worry. It will stay that way unless its consequences become visible and immediate. In the meantime, no strategy is likely to work which concentrates solely upon provoking fear and anxiety, or which is based not only on instructing people to cut down on this or that, but also on expecting them to monitor that process on a continuous basis.

A different approach is needed from that prevalent at the moment. It must place an emphasis on positives as much as on negatives, and on opportunities rather than on self-induced deprivations. I would set out its main principles as follows.

Incentives must take precedence over all other interventions, including those which are tax-based. 'No punishment for punishment's sake': in other words punitive measures should either supply revenue spent directly for environmental purposes, or be linked in a visible way with behaviour change – and preferably both. The drivers of gas-guzzling vehicles, for example, should face heavy tax duties for the privilege, as heavy as is politically feasible, under 'the polluter pays' principle. Clear and self-evident options for behaviour change are available – switch to smaller cars or drive less.

The positives must dominate. This isn't as difficult as it might sound. Take the issue of making homes more energy-efficient. There are several countries in the world that have managed to make major progress in this respect. How have they done so? Not by trying to scare people, but by emphasizing the advantages of having homes that are snug, protected against the elements and which also save money. An example is what has been achieved in Sweden, which was done by placing a strong emphasis on what was called 'community, style and comfort'.

Low-carbon practices or inventions that initially have only limited appeal can be fundamentally important if they set trends, or if they are seen as in some way iconic.[16] Most initiatives, whether social, economic or technological, are, in the early stages, open only to a small elite. In California, for example, there are long waiting lists for the hydrogen-powered Lifecar, due on the market shortly, although the first models will be extremely expensive. However, investment in such a car will provide the opportunity to see whether the vehicle could have a wider market, and also gives it an avant-garde cachet. This is what happened with the Toyota Prius hybrid car, nearly a million of which have been sold worldwide. It was a vanguard model in the sense that it stimulated other manufacturers to start producing low-emission vehicles, whether hybrid or not.

Most initiatives that have successfully reduced emissions so far have been driven by the motivation to increase energy efficiency, rather than the desire to limit climate change. This observation applies to whole countries as well as to regions, cities and the actions of individuals. It should still be the lead principle today, since greater energy efficiency *ipso facto* reduces emissions. People are able to grasp and respond to this perspective more easily than they have done to climate change, with all its surrounding debates and complexities; it is not difficult to present energy efficiency in a positive light. What is at issue is energy efficiency in the economy as a whole, since efficiency gains in one context are of little or no value if savings made are spent on energy-consuming activities elsewhere. The fundamental problem at the moment is to make clean energy sources competitive with fossil fuel energy sources, whether through public provision of subsidies or through technological advance. Utility companies in the US have been offering electricity generated from wind or solar sources to consumers for at least the last ten years. Initially, take-up was very small, however, since the prices were not competitive. In early 2006 Xcel Energy in Colorado and Austin Energy in Texas offered tariffs below those of the regular energy sources. Austin Energy encouraged its customers to sign up for 10-year energy contracts, and were able to prosper even when the price of electricity dropped.

The role of technology in promoting low-carbon lifestyles is bound to be considerable. Technological innovation rarely determines what people do, since we often react to it in ways in which its initiators did not suspect. Thus the telephone was invented in 1876 as a signalling device; no one imagined that it would become so intrinsic to our lives as a medium of talk and conversation.[17] Yet, at the same time, our lives can change dramatically through such interaction with technology. It is said that we are 'creatures of habit'. And it is often true, especially if habits become addictive. Yet such is far from always the case – we can change our behaviour quite rapidly and dramatically, as has happened, and on a global level, with the arrival of the internet.

Government should be actively encouraging the creative economy and the creative society, even when these don't seem to have an immediate bearing upon climate change, since creativity has to be the order of the day. Richard Florida, who has written extensively on the subject, argues persuasively that the creative sectors of the economy – where innovation, lateral thinking and enterprise can flourish – are increasingly becoming the driving force of the economy as a whole. Florida rejects the idea that creativity – the capacity to innovate, to question conventional wisdom – is limited to the few. Creativity is a 'limitless resource. . . . It's a trait that can't be handed down, and it can't be owned in the traditional sense.'[18] R&D investment is important, but in pioneering responses to climate change, we need to be bringing science, the universities and social entrepreneurs closer together.

Step changes or 'tipping points' aren't confined to the field of climate change science. They apply to social and economic life too – that was the context, in fact, in which the author who popularized the term, Malcolm Gladwell, originally discussed it.[19] We should be looking to create tipping points when it comes to the transition to low-carbon lifestyles. From small beginnings, much larger changes can occur when a certain threshold is reached. It is easy, for example, to envisage such a thing happening with SUVs. If public opinion were to turn against them, they could become almost unmarketable over-night – perhaps they already are, with the recession playing a part.

Governments have an important role in 'editing choice', and, in pursuing that aim, they shouldn't be afraid to take on big business when it is necessary to do so. Corporations influence our choices in many direct and indirect ways – the state shouldn't be reluctant to take a leaf out of their book. For instance, supermarkets usually place sweets and chocolates close to the exit, where customers line up to pay for their purchases. The reason is that at that point they are open to impulse buying, having relaxed after making their main purchases. Given the advance of obesity, I see no reason why such a practice shouldn't be either prohibited or actively discouraged (although thus far it has not). How far we should go with choices that affect carbon consumption is a moot point. Some examples of choice editing appear to be completely unobjectionable. Thus, for example, we could propose that heating and air-conditioning should be organ-ized such that everyone knows immediately how much he or she is spending at any given time. The effect would be even more powerful if we knew how our expenditure rated com-pared to that of our neighbours. A study showed that heavy users made bigger cuts in consumption if a smiling face was inscribed on bills below the average, with a frowning face on the bills of those having higher than average expenditure. Other examples are more complicated. I see no civil liberties issue in cases where our behaviour is already being signifi-cantly influenced, or manipulated, by companies, and where the object of government policy is to counter that influence.[20] An example would be when a firm heavily advertises a product or service known to have adverse environmental effects. Should governments go further? The Australian government, for example, has instituted a total ban on all light bulbs that aren't of the low-energy type. Is it justified in doing so? In my view it is, given that the energy gains are substantial, while the difference in other ways between the conventional and low-energy bulbs is negligible. In any case, it is up to governments to explore these boundaries in conjunction with the electorate.

Foregrounding

Combating climate change demands long-term policies: how are these to be kept at the forefront of political concern? What can be done to keep global warming firmly on the political agenda? Agenda-setting theory in political science helps supply some of the answers.[21] It concerns how and why different policy questions figure prominently in the programmes of governments while others tend to recede into the background or even disappear altogether. How far a given set of problems receives public and policy attention does not just depend upon its objective importance, but upon a range of other factors too. In democratic countries, numerous areas of concern at any one time jostle for attention in the public sphere. Very often, transient issues outweigh more permanent and profound ones in terms of the attention they receive in the political arena.

Three aspects of the political agenda can be identified. First, there is the 'public agenda', which refers to issues felt to be most important by voters at any specific point in time. Second, the 'governmental agenda' is about the questions that are under debate in parliament and surrounding agencies. Finally, the 'decision agenda' refers to a more limited set of policies that are actually being enacted. Each of these dimensions is limited in terms of the numbers of issues that can be considered at any particular moment. Hence, there is competition between items that press for attention.

According to John Kingdon, the leading author in the field, who coined these terms, the political agenda at a given time is the result of the interaction of different 'streams' of concerns, which he labels problems, policies and politics. They sometimes converge, but also often flow on largely independently of one another, with their own rules and conventions, personnel and dynamics. What actually gets done depends upon the points at which they connect, which canny political players manage to exploit. There is much more chance that an issue will command the interest of policy-makers at such a point – a window of opportunity opens. His now classic work, *Agendas, Alternatives and Public Policies*, starts with a resounding quote from Victor Hugo, 'Greater than the tread of mighty armies is an idea whose time has come.' [22] But how can we know when the time for an idea has come? Why do those in and around government, at any particular point, attend to some issues and not others?

The problem stream comes to the attention of policy-makers, Kingdon says, through indicators, focusing events and feedback. Indicators are measuring devices that reveal the scale of the problem in question. They allow a process to be monitored. Thus a continuing issue may actually become a 'problem' when a change is witnessed, as when unemployment or crime rates go up. Shifts in indicators may be enough to push an item onto the agenda, but issues are more likely to attract attention when propelled into the limelight as a result of dramatic events that bring them into focus. A focusing event may be anything that catches the headlines, such as a particularly violent crime.

Feedback concerns the responses of different groups, or the public at large, to particular policy programmes. It is almost always negative feedback that highlights a given problem – policies or practices that are working well don't get reported. Nor do they tend to spark the interest of the public, which is most often stimulated when things go wrong or are seen to be going wrong. How events and reactions to them become framed – for example, how far a given problem is seen as open to government intervention or not – is of great importance in determining actual outcomes.

Work in the policy stream tends to be continuous. It goes on without much day-to-day reference to what moods may grip the public, and is pursued by specialists and experts within policy communities. Such work generates many possible policy proposals, but only a few ever make it onto the concrete political agenda. They are quite often 'solutions' waiting for problems – that is to say, they provide avenues for political intervention when the need for it arises as driven by a specific focusing event or set of events. The availability of 'solutions' is very important. Problems which do not come with potential courses of remedial action attached are not likely to get onto the agenda. Rather, they are accepted as situations that have to be lived with, and normally do not rate highly among the worries expressed by the public.

Organized interest groups of one kind or another play a role in shaping public opinion and limiting or opening out space for governmental action. However, what Kingdon calls the 'national mood' has a major impact upon when, where and how the problem, policy and political streams converge. For instance, when the mood is 'anti-government', voters may simply tune out from whatever strategies the government of the day might propose.

Some windows of opportunity are predictable – annual budgets, for example, usually provide an opportunity for a new departure. Most, however, are not, and policy entrepreneurs must therefore be prepared to grasp the opportunity when it presents itself, or to mobilize to block it. Public enthusiasm for a given policy agenda rarely lasts long, even when an issue is of continuing and manifest importance. In fact, studies show, it most often turns to disillusionment or indifference when the problem is not one that admits of a simple solution. Cynicism, unwillingness to make sacrifices, the perception that the costs are too great, or simply boredom can supplant the initial burst of public concern and support. With a constant search for novelty, and a distaste for 'yesterday's news', the media undoubtedly play a substantial role in public shifts in attention.

The implications for climate change policy are clear and significant. Public support for such policy is not likely to be constant and can only form a general backdrop to effective policy action. I have argued that anxiety about future risk can't be used as the sole motivator of public opinion, and that conclusion is backed up by studies of other risks and how people respond to them. For instance, concern about terrorism tends to move up and down the list of major public concerns depending exactly upon the factors identified by Kingdon – for instance, whether or not there has been a focusing incident of some kind. Worries not linked in the public mind with clear modes of response quickly slip down peoples' ratings of what disturbs them most. Talk of impending catastrophe –whatever the risk in question – has little impact and indeed may induce an attitude of fatalism that blunts action. Fatalism in response to risk is a common reaction, visible in many who choose to pay no heed to health warnings about their lifestyle habits.

A cross-party concordat, as discussed below, would give a firm anchor for climate change as a continuing preoccupation of the 'policy stream'. A diversity of groups in civil society – also discussed below – will certainly continue to press to keep necessary reforms and innovations going. Yet public support will be needed and it cannot be only latent. Based on Kingdon's work, Sarah Pralle suggests a number of ways in which public interest and concern can be charged and recharged. Indicators, if they are straightforward and easy to grasp, could have an important role; and with the continued advance of climate science, they are certainly abundant. A few key indicators, especially where they can be linked to focusing events, should be highlighted. However, they shouldn't be of the doom and gloom variety, but linked to potentially positive outcomes – to efforts that groups and communities are making to lessen the threats.

Problems that relate to peoples' immediate experience are most likely to be taken seriously. Rightly or wrongly, hurricane Katrina and the 2003 European heat waves made the impact they did upon the consciousness of citizens in the developed countries because they were 'close to home'. Only a small proportion of people in the industrial countries currently agree with the statement, 'My life is directly affected by global warming and climate change.'[23] They are also far more likely, on average, to be taking concrete measures to reduce their own carbon consumption. Most important of all, policy entrepreneurs should always connect problems with potential remedies or solutions. However, those solutions themselves must have 'salience' – they have to supply the motivation to act. One hundred books on one hundred ways to reduce your carbon footprint will have less effect than just one that is geared to what people are positively motivated to do.

A political concordat

Many have bemoaned the convergence of parties towards the centre ground in contemporary politics, but in the environmental field at least this could be a major advantage. Equating being in the political centre with an absence of radicalism only applies in the case of traditional left–right issues. As I have argued earlier, if one doesn't think in this way, it is entirely possible to have a 'radicalism of the centre' – indeed, in terms of climate change and energy policy it is an essential concept.

What does a 'radicalism of the centre' mean? It means, first of all, gaining widespread public support for radical actions – that is, for the conjunction of innovation and long-term thinking which is the condition necessary for responding to climate change. It implies the reform of the state. Climate change and energy security are such serious issues, and they affect so many other aspects of the political field, that a concern with them has to be introduced across all branches of government. Most of the industrial states are coming to recognize this, although progress on the ground tends to be slow. Climate change is generally allocated to the environment ministry, which, in turn, is rarely one of the most powerful in influencing government. Such ministries are quite often separate from those dealing with transport and energy, health or overseas development. Power lies mostly where the money is: in the Treasury or finance ministry. Yet from now on, where the money is will be influenced enormously by climate change and energy questions, so it is in everyone's interest that these issues achieve the primacy of place they deserve.

Climate change should be lifted out of a right–left context, where it has no place. It is normal and acceptable for political parties to claim that they, rather than their opponents, are the ones to turn to for firm action on global warming. Yet beyond a certain area, and beyond the rhetoric of immediate party politics, there has to be agreement that the issue is so important and all-encompassing that the usual party conflicts should be suspended or muted.

How a cross-party consensus might be achieved was explored in a British context in a comprehensive report on the issue produced by an all-party group in Parliament. The group tried to reach a consensus about consensus and, to a significant degree, it succeeded in so doing. The objective was to investigate 'the potential of a cross-party consensus on climate change to try to look beyond the tendency of politics to dwell in the terrain of competition for short-term advantage'.[24] Is a consensus desirable and, if so, what form should it take?

A wide range of opinions was solicited for the inquiry. Some argued that a consensus would in fact be undesirable, since it would be likely to stifle debate and the critical examination to which all political proposals and policies should be subject. Moreover, they pointed out, a consensus could potentially lead to a loss of public attention and awareness for the issue. In addition, reaching shared agreement might mean opting for the lowest common denominator (much as has happened in the Kyoto and post-Kyoto negotiations).

However, while recognizing the force of these points, the large majority of contributors accepted that a consensus across the parties was not only possible but necessary. There was more agreement about the need for a consensus on targets for emissions reductions than upon how they should best be reached. Yet many emphasized the importance of overall agreement about means as well as ends. Policies initiated by one government in areas such as fiscal measures or investment in R&D and technology, would have to have a core of stability across changes of government.

Cross-party agreement has to be robust, since there will be a clear temptation for parties to sacrifice longer-term goals in pursuit of immediate political advantage, especially when unpopular decisions have to be taken. A consensus that focuses only on goals, even if it involves a general agreement on targets, is likely to be too weak to be effective. The chairman of the committee, Colin Challen, MP, expressed the point forcefully:

> Until a binding consensus is reached, there will always be the danger that any party proposing the really tough measures necessary to tackle the problem will face. . .the strong likelihood that another party will present the electorate with a 'get out of jail free card' for their own electoral advantage. . .There seems little point in drawing together a consensus that is merely promoting motherhood and apple pie. It is clear that the purpose of the consensus is to overcome the severe tension between short-term electoral politics and long-term climate change goals, a tension which has to date resulted in the triumph of short-termism.[25]

The committee concluded that a consensus doesn't have to be 'all or nothing' in order to work. It should concentrate upon targets and upon a long-term policy framework that would offer a reasonable chance of meeting the targets. Examples already exist where a cross-party consensus has been formed and clear results have been produced – such as that which helped lead to a settlement in Northern Ireland.

A main recommendation was that an independent body be set up to monitor progress towards targets; and that the prime minister of the day should be held directly responsible for the cross-party consensus process. Such an agency was in fact later set up, in the shape of the Climate Change Committee, coupled with the introduction of legal obligations on the part of successive governments to make specific progress towards the targets (see pp. 81–8 above). Several other countries, such as the Netherlands, Demark and Japan, have set up similar programmes to try to create and preserve cross-party agreements.

Although it is important that there should be consensus, it cannot be too minimalist. We should perhaps speak of a *concordat* rather than a consensus, because there should be a clear statement of principles that are publicly endorsed. In accordance with the overall themes of this book, I would emphasize that it must cover means as well as ends, and it has to home in on the short term as well as the long term in order to be effective. Agreement on targets set for decades down the line will be of little help, however demanding those targets appear. Should such a consensus imply a 'suspension of hostilities' between the parties, as far as parliamentary debate about climate change is concerned? Yes, it should. Left-of-centre parties or coalitions have a particular responsibility to tone down their rhetoric, especially of the red–green variety, since it stakes a claim to the privileged position of leftist thinking – a claim which is false. Such restraint is all the more important given the fact that it is the right-of-centre parties which tend to be most reluctant to support climate change policy.

A stronger monitoring body should be established than the Climate Change Committee set up in Britain. It should not be merely advisory, but have the capacity to intervene in legislation by, for example, having clearly specified rights to take the government to the courts if it has gone back on its obligations. Its composition is likely to be crucial, and appointment to it should not simply be the prerogative of the government of the day. Its brief has to extend beyond climate change and there has to be clear coordination with whatever major agency is responsible for energy and energy planning.

It will be essential to stop such a body from becoming too bureaucratic and fixed in its practices. Hence there must be a method of ensuring a regular turnover in its composition, whether by having relatively short terms of service or by other means. It must be subject to regular parliamentary as well as wider public scrutiny.

Moreover, government must not only be an agent of change as far as combating global warming is concerned; it must be an exemplar too. Government and its officialdom shouldn't find themselves in the position of the doctor who carries on smoking while advising his patients not to do so. 'Do as I say, not as I do' is not good enough. For example, governments shouldn't only be in the business of setting targets; they should also be in the vanguard of showing concretely how to reach them.

State and society: business and the NGOs

An ensuring state must work with diverse groups and, of course, with the public, in order to deliver upon climate change goals. The classical liberal view of the rights and responsibilities of individuals, simply put, is that every individual should be free to pursue whatever lifestyle he or she chooses, so long as those choices do not harm others. However, the liberal state has not been accustomed to extending that principle to environmental goods, or to the avoidance of harm to future generations; both now have to become absolutely central.

The rights of future generations should be incorporated within standard democratic procedures. Environmentalists often bolster their arguments about climate change by asking rhetorically, 'What would we say to our children's children

in 50 years' time when they ask how we could have allowed
such damage to occur, knowing that it was almost certain
to happen?' That question should not be an isolated one,
however, but part of what we ask ourselves on a regular basis,
as a normal feature of the democratic process. It has many
implications. For instance, the debate about oil and gas is
about when available supplies will be half gone, and therefore
at what date they will be largely exhausted. Yet it could, and
should, be asked how far we (the current generation) have the
right more or less to destroy such a natural resource forever,
whatever other sources of energy are developed in the future.
The same question could, and should, also be asked about
other mineral resources.

Environmental rights and responsibilities, incorporating
due attention to the rights of subsequent generations, should
be introduced directly to the existing framework of liberal
democracy. In other words, they should be added to and integrated with such rights and responsibilities as the right to vote,
to enjoy equality before the law, freedom of speech and assem-
bly. Robyn Eckersley[26] suggests that environmental rights and
responsibilities should include the following:

- as just mentioned, a responsibility on the part of government to include future generations and non-human species
  as moral referents;
- right-to-know legislation in relation to pollutants and toxic
  substances, which the state is mandated to provide, both
  on a regular basis and when asked by citizens' groups or
  communities;
- the provision of public forums where the environmental
  impact of new technology or development proposals can be
  assessed;
- third-party litigation rights to allow NGOs and concerned
  citizens to ensure that environmental standards are being
  upheld;
- thoroughgoing acceptance of 'the polluter pays' principle,
  with penalties for those who cause environmental harm;
- the obligation of citizens, businesses and groups in civil
  society to act as positive agents of environmental change,
  rather than simply preventing destructive acts.

Such a framework would help integrate the diversity of groups whose activities are relevant to climate change policy. NGOs and businesses are the most prominent types of such groups and have long defined themselves partly in relation to one another. In each case they are quite often global in scope and their leading organizations are household names. Industry is, by any reckoning, a major force in the environmental area; it accounts for more than a third of the energy consumed across the world, and of course is involved in its production too. The NGOs like to portray themselves as minnows pitting themselves against the industrial giants, but, in truth, their influence has become very large. The best-known NGOs enjoy far higher levels of public trust than do their business counterparts.[27]

NGOs have long regarded large corporations as the prime agents of the irresponsible squandering of resources. In some large degree they have had good reason for such a view. Particularly important, in terms of climate change, have been the fossil fuel lobbies, representing heavy industry, transportation, coal, oil and chemicals. Until recently, the lobbies and the large majority of their individual members have argued that action to reduce greenhouse gases would be a mistake. They have mostly taken a sceptical position, as is shown in surveys of their literature and that of the think tanks they help fund. The American Petroleum Institute, an industry research organization, claimed as its main goal to make sure that 'climate change becomes a non-issue'.[28]

Industrial lobbies are especially well organized and powerful in the US, and undoubtedly played a major role in influencing the hostile attitudes of the Bush administration towards efforts to take action against global warming. During the first term of George W. Bush's presidency, John H. Sununu, a prominent climate change sceptic, was the White House Chief of Staff. The lobbies had easy access to him, and to Vice-President Dick Cheney; they managed to block or dismember legislation regarded as a threat to fossil fuel interests. When Sununu stepped down, a newspaper headline announced: 'Sununu resigns . . . coal lobby in mourning.'[29] Industry groups have been a major influence in Europe too. They lobbied fiercely and effectively against the original commission proposals for a universal carbon tax, arguing, as their counterparts in the US did, that it would undermine competitiveness.

However, one should guard against the easy demonizing of the industry lobbies, and of big business more generally, that pervades much of the environmental literature. Business leaders are not all cut from the same cloth, while the lobbies themselves (as is true too of environmental lobbies) are quite frequently divided. For instance, in the run-up to the Kyoto Summit, the major oil interests were hostile to the proposals put forward, but the gas and electricity companies were in favour. John Browne, the head of BP, in a speech at Stanford University in California in 1997, was the first to break ranks with the other major oil companies. He acknowledged the dangers of global warming and accepted that BP should contribute to solutions. It was not a sudden, but more of a gradual, conversion by the company. When BP discovered a large oil field in Alaska some 30 years earlier, its proposals to exploit the resource brought determined resistance from environmentalists. After that point, no exploration was carried out by the company without an assessment of its likely environmental impact.

NGOs tend to cloak themselves in moral garb and are no doubt sincere in their desire to better the world. Yet they too are lobbying groups, like the new associations springing up that represent the renewable technology industries. As has often been pointed out by critics, NGOs are neither elected bodies nor subject to the market discipline that industrial bodies have to face. It is difficult to assess the level of their influence, since their activities tend to be less formalized than those of the industry lobbies.

The Climate Change Network is an organization of 365 NGOs from diverse countries and regions, and includes the well-known ones, such as Greenpeace, Friends of the Earth and the World Wildlife Fund. The network boasts a world membership of 20 million people, which is the basis of its claim to speak for large constituencies of concerned citizens. It follows a 'three-track' approach. One involves putting pressure on nations to set themselves rigorous targets, as agreed at the 2007 Bali Summit, to set up a new round of international agreements to limit climate change. The second, the 'greening track', is about helping developing countries to adopt renewable technologies. The third, the 'adaptation track' is concerned with helping the most vulnerable countries anticipate and prepare for unavoidable consequences of climate change.

NGOs are not only pressure groups, but also play a significant role in coordinating scientific information and bringing it to the notice of decision-makers and the public. The two workshops set up in the late 1980s which led to the emergence of the IPCC were organized by NGOs. NGOs have also been closely involved in the setting of climate change policy in many countries, where they have tried to prompt governments to act, and have then pushed for their actions to be far-reaching.

A new generation of business leaders – who quite often work directly with NGOs – is arising which not only acknowledges the perils of climate change, but is active in the vanguard of reaction to it. Businesses such as Wal-Mart, which for years were seen by environmentalists as public enemies, have swung behind the climate change agenda, and in much more than just a face-saving way. Wal-Mart has planned substantial reductions in its own emissions, in the short as well as the long term, and it has demanded that its suppliers measure and report their emissions too. Tesco has pledged to put 'carbon labels' on all its 80,000 product lines, so that consumers know what volume of greenhouse gases has gone into their production. The firm has set itself the goal of halving its emissions per case of goods delivered worldwide by 2012 against a baseline of 2006. Of course, there are many who doubt the authenticity of these commitments. The NGO Corporate Watch lists no fewer than 20 kinds of 'corporate crimes' of which Tesco is accused.

As far as the environmentalist claims of businesses are concerned, it is important to separate the wheat from the chaff. The making of disingenuous or false claims to environmental credentials – 'greenwash' – has become a real problem. In front of me as I write, I have two large ads from a daily newspaper. One is for one of the most thirsty SUVs on the road, which, in this case, is seen in a field rather than the city streets where most of its counterparts roam. The makers announce how proud they feel to be doing their bit for 'the environment' because they have made some improvements in the energy efficiency of their production processes. The second ad, even more absurdly, makes similar claims for a sports car that, when driven in town, travels fewer than 10 miles per gallon of fuel consumed.

In most countries, regulatory authorities do not have sufficient authority, or resources, to intervene in an official and effective way. The same standards, backed by law, should be imposed that apply in other areas, such as those governing racism. Attacking 'greenwash' is not, I believe, a trivial or marginal pursuit. One reason, of course, is that it is necessary to ensure that companies take seriously their obligations to reduce their emissions. Perhaps even more important, though, is the fact that 'greenwash' is a way of wilfully misleading the public.

The standards that companies should meet can be fairly easily described. Their claims should apply across the whole of their carbon output, not just one selected part of it where some sort of improvement has been made. Assertions made should be backed up with concrete and measurable actions, set against a given baseline, or they should not be made at all. Corporations could call in third parties to audit their performance, and their results should be published, just as are those of their financial operations.

We must wait and see with Wal-Mart and other supermarket chains, but some corporations have in fact already delivered on their promises. Nike, for example, has reduced its carbon footprint by 75 per cent over a period of 10 years. The company has stated that it aims to achieve zero waste, zero toxicity and complete recyclability across its product range by 2020. It might not happen, but there seems no more reason to doubt the firm's seriousness of intent than the declarations made by countries about what they will achieve by that date. Of course, as in the case of the state, NGOs exist in order to put pressure on organizations whose activities don't match up to their proclaimed intent.

There are many corporations today, such as those mentioned above, that are transforming their attitudes just as radically as are states. They are doing so partly for business reasons and in order to respond to the coming of carbon markets and carbon taxes – but they are doing so also because the message of the need for change has struck home.

The chairman of Coca-Cola announced in 2007 that the guiding principle of the firm's activities in the future has to be that, 'We should not cause more water to be removed from a watershed than we can replenish.'[30] The company has entered into a partnership with the World Wildlife Fund to pursue the cause of water conservation. The partnership has come about because both Coca-Cola and the WWF have recognized that a change of tack is required. WWF's chief operating officer, Marcia Marsh, observed: 'The simple fact is that we are failing relative to our wider goals. Despite our successes in raising public awareness and funding, species are disappearing at historic rates. Habitat continues to be destroyed. Working alone, NGOs are simply unable to reverse the tide of global change.'[31]

Coca-Cola carried out an extensive project on world fresh-water supplies in 2002, at a point when most governments had not yet appreciated the scale of the problem of looming world water shortages. However, the company was a long way from having analysed the impact of its entire supply-chain, and the firm later agreed that the WWF will be able to report publicly its findings about the environmental consequences of the company's worldwide activities. The two organizations will work together to develop binding targets for improved water efficiency.

In *Green Inc*, Christine MacDonald takes the NGOs to task for the closeness of the ties they have forged with business, on the grounds that they are being corrupted.[32] And, indeed, NGOs, businesses and governments to some degree have differences of interest that neither could nor should be eradicated. All are to some extent interest groups, with agendas that do not by any means always conform to the public interest; yet it is hard to see that much progress will be made unless they can form active and effective partnerships. NGOs not only have moral credibility, but have accumulated a fund of environmental knowledge and expertise that companies normally lack. The role of businesses, small and large, is going to be absolutely crucial in responding to climate change, not least because they will have to supply a good deal of the funding and also pioneer new technologies.

Coca-Cola and the WWF are not alone; many similar partner-ships are developing around the world.[33] Unilever is working with the Rainforest Alliance on the environmental effects of its Lipton tea business; IKEA is collaborating with Brazilian NGOs to work towards regulating logging in the Amazon rainforest. Alcoa, the aluminium-producing company, a target for attack by many NGOs in the past, is doing the same as part of a new-found commitment to reducing its environmental impact. A great deal of water is used in the production of aluminium. The production process is also a major source of greenhouse gas emissions, while also generating waste that has to go to land-fill. Since aluminium ore (bauxite) is found near to the land surface, it is often extracted by open-cast mining. In the smelting process, CO_2 and perfluorocarbons (PFCs) are produced. PFCs are among the most harmful of greenhouse gases, more so even than methane. Alcoa has set itself targets of a 70 per cent reduction in water discharge from its plants by 2010 and zero discharge by 2020. It has introduced similarly radical programmes for recycling and emissions – its goals are to achieve 25 per cent recycled aluminium content by 2010 and 50 per cent by 2020.[34] Recycling not only saves emissions directly but will help in another way too. Aluminium cans may use bauxite mined in Australia, be smelted in China, and pressed into cans and filled in the US or Europe. When cans are recycled, the whole process can be completed domestically, reducing emissions by as much as 75 per cent.

It is not only manufacturing companies that are undergoing such a change of attitudes, but those in other sectors too. In February 2007, Citigroup Bank issued a 'Position Statement on Climate Change' accepting that serious risks are posed by global warming.[35] The key questions now, it says, concern the rapidity and severity of the changes and the practical implications that flow from them. During the Bush years, the company argued that the US government must shift its position quite dramatically and assume a world leadership role in countering climate change. Citigroup committed itself to a 10 per cent reduction in its own greenhouse gas emissions by 2011 and pledges investment in alternative energy technology.

In the same year the corporation announced that it will direct $50 billion over the next 10 years towards climate change projects, through investment to support the activities of its clients and through its own operations. To date, it has invested $10 billion. Citibank already has a substantial portfolio of equity investments in solar, wind and hydroelectric power, as well as in low-carbon building projects. According to its originators, the firm's comprehensive programme 'is not a wish-list, but a realistic, achievable plan'.[36] How far that plan will survive the serious economic difficulties the bank got into late in 2008 remains to be seen.

The influence of policy entrepreneurs

States, businesses and NGOs are not the only agents involved in active policy to counter global warming. We must also recognize the importance of local and city-based initiatives. As emphasized earlier, 'the state' does not only refer to the national level, but to regional, city and local government too. In the global age, many influences come in below the level of the nation-state, impinging directly upon localities, which in turn can have an impact much greater than their size would suggest. Moreover, at all levels inspirational individuals can break the mould of conventional wisdom.

Sweden is the country furthest along the line towards overcoming its dependence on fossil fuels, and one man, Per Carstedt, can take a certain amount of the credit.[37] Carstedt is a Ford car dealer who spent a number of years in Brazil, the first country to develop ethanol on a large scale as a motor fuel. He went to the Rio Summit in 1992, and came away clear in his mind that humanity couldn't carry on for long on its current path. When he returned to Sweden, he started looking into how ethanol might be introduced into the country. Initially he made no headway at all. There was no technical know-how, no filling stations were interested in supplying ethanol and, it was said, the fuel wouldn't work in Sweden's cold climate anyway. Eventually, he located a small flexi-fuel programme at Ford in Detroit, and through this contact managed to import three ethanol cars into Sweden, showing that they could run perfectly well there. Later he imported some more, but neither Ford nor any other manufacturer he approached showed any interest, arguing that there was no market for them. Carstedt then spent several years travelling the country, building up support in a consortium of local governments, companies and individuals who would buy the vehicles.

There was still no ethanol in filling stations, but Carstedt finally managed to persuade one close to his home and another in Stockholm to put in an ethanol pump. He and his colleagues then toured other stations, trying to persuade them one by one to do the same, offering finance if necessary. By 2002 there 40 stations were offering ethanol, and from then on they rapidly multiplied. About 1,000 such stations had come into existence by mid-2007, constituting 25 per cent of the overall number in the country. Some 15 per cent of vehicles in Sweden today run on biofuels.

Carstedt anticipated early on the backlash that has occurred against biofuels. What is needed, he argues, is investment to develop fuels that do not compete with food production. The research group with which he is currently involved is producing biofuels from cellulose, coming from wood chips or industrial waste, which will meet that requirement. A new bio-energy refinery using this technology has been built, and a far larger one is planned. The refinery produces a total energy efficiency of over 70 per cent, which is much higher than the level produced by orthodox forms of ethanol.

The US federal government prior to 2009 was a notable laggard in climate change policy. The same cannot be said of the individual states, cities and local communities. Cities from across the world have linked together in networks to take common action, and US cities have been prominent in such endeavours. As early as 1995, 30 cities from different countries adopted a target to reduce their emissions by 20 per cent within 10 years, as compared to a 1998 baseline. In the event, by 2005 only a handful of cities had in fact met their targets.

In the same year, 1995, the mayor of Seattle, Greg Nickels, challenged other US cities to meet or surpass these targets, a proposal that was accepted by many.[38] By 2006, 358 mayors, coming from 49 different states, had signed the Climate Change Agreement which the Seattle mayor had drafted. Almost as many cities belong to the Cities for Climate Protection (CCP), which is linked to an international association of local governments. The CCP agreement commits cities and communities to programmes of action which demonstrate how detailed targets will be achieved and which involve gathering data that will document the results.

Seattle has been a particular centre of activism. The city began investing in waste recycling in the late 1970s, and has long emphasized water conservation over the exploitation of new sources of supply. Unlike most US cities, it has invested extensively in public transport, including trams, light rail, an effective bus system and cycle lanes. A task force which reported in 2006 set out a plan for meeting radical emissions targets.

California has produced the most comprehensive climate change plan of any US state so far. It includes mandatory emissions reporting from all major industries, coupled to a carbon trading scheme. Education about climate change will become part of the curriculum in public schools; it will be coupled to a larger educational campaign aimed at all citizens. Publicly owned utilities provide some 30 per cent of the electricity used in California, and they will be required to take the lead in achieving steep efficiency targets. The targets the state has set itself overall are to reduce emissions to 1990 levels by 2020 and by 80 per cent relative to a 1990 baseline by 2050.

Like California, Oregon has a long history of involvement with environmental issues. Oregon and California are among a number of states in the US seeking to organize regional groupings of states committed to carbon markets and to shared emissions goals. Similar associations are being planned in the north-east and in other regions. Some US states have also signed climate change agreements directly with other countries, with a view to developing mutual carbon trading schemes, exchanging information about other programmes and sharing technological advances. California has signed an agreement with the UK, for example, as has Florida.

Cities and regions in many other parts of the world have also been well in advance of the nations of which they form a part in seeking to take action against climate change – and often they have done so in collaboration with one another. The reason is partly the need to deal with directly toxic forms of air pollution faced in city environments, which can cause or worsen a range of major diseases, especially those affecting the lungs or throat. It is relatively easy to promote clean air and water campaigns when their harmful effects are visible for all to see. However, such campaigns have created a consciousness of longer-term forms of pollution and hence a concern to develop policies against those too. Moreover, in principle, and often in practice, local areas and communities, including large cities, can often mobilize themselves more rapidly and effectively than national government can.

Especially when they act together, local, regional and city leaders can have a major influence on central government policy. Thus it is city governments that have pioneered congestion charging as a means both of preventing traffic gridlock and bringing about emissions reductions. Much the same applies to the insulation of homes and workplaces, investing in public transport, furthering the recycling of waste and in many other areas of environmental policy, including those concerned with adaptation.

Why not go the whole hog and argue, as some environmentalists do, that climate change issues should be dealt with piecemeal and primarily from the bottom-up? The reason why not, in fact, is easy to see. Unregulated markets have no long-term perspective, and, in so far as they create externalities, may actively undermine such a perspective. Much the same is true of the thousands of local initiatives that exist, even if many of them on their own are worthy or necessary.

TECHNOLOGIES AND TAXES

Ambitious attempts have been made to anticipate how the spread of renewable technologies will transform modern economies. Some speak of the coming of a new industrial revolution, which will be initiated by such technologies. The American political thinker Jeremy Rifkin argues that the great changes in world history have taken place when new sources of energy have emerged in tandem with developments in communications. Thus the convergence of coal-based power and the printing press gave rise to the first industrial revolution. Previous forms of communication would not have been able to handle the social and economic complexities introduced by the new forms of technology. The 'second industrial revolution' started in the late nineteenth century. It was marked by the invention of electric communication, beginning with the telegraph and branching out into the telephone, radio and television. These developments converged with the emergence of oil as a major form of power generation and as the dominant source of energy for transport.

We now stand on the verge of a 'third industrial revolution', Rifkin says, which will have as its backdrop the development of networked communication, represented by personal computers and the internet. The potential of these technologies lies in their convergence with renewable energy. We can envisage a global energy economy where millions of people produce renewable energy and share it with others through national and international power grids – as happens today with information. Just as personal computers have vastly more power than the early machines, which took up several rooms, so intelligent energy networks will become more powerful and ubiquitous than anything we know at the moment.

Rifkin has his favourite renewable energy source to help point the way ahead: hydrogen.[1] Hydrogen, he says, is the 'forever fuel', since it is the most ubiquitous element in the universe – and it produces no greenhouse gas emissions. Fuel cells using hydrogen are already being introduced into the market for home and industrial use. The top-down energy regime that exists today with big oil and gas will be replaced by decentralized energy production and use. It will be 'the first truly democratic energy regime in history'.[2]

Such ideas aren't particularly compelling. In the first place, they reflect a view in which history is driven in large part by technology, a partial notion at best. The dating and nature of the supposed second industrial revolution are vague – as can be seen by the fact that other authors who propose similar ideas come up with quite different versions of when it happened and what its content was. Some, for example, date it 40 or 50 years later than Rifkin does. No one knows as yet what role a specific energy source such as hydrogen might play. Moreover, technologies never operate on their own – they are always embedded in wider political, economic and social frameworks, which are likely to govern both how they develop and what their consequences are.

In addition, the 'next industrial revolution' hasn't as yet actually happened. The original industrial revolution did not occur in a conscious way. The next one, however, has to be created as a deliberate project to protect us against future dangers – a very different situation. We don't know how things will turn out. It could be, as Rifkin hopes, that energy and politics will march in line – decentralized network systems, rooted in local communities, will replace current forms of political and economic power. It is the vision that many in the green movement would like to see realized. I'm not sure such an outcome is either likely or desirable. Certainly, it is very possible that most households will help create energy, rather than just consume it – as is already the case, for example, with feed-in tariffs. However, we will also need coordinated energy management on a national as well as an international level.

Technological innovation has to be a core part of any successful climate change strategy and the same is true of energy policy. The state and government must have a significant role in making such innovation possible, since a regulatory framework, including incentives and other tax mechanisms, will be involved. What role should this be exactly? The issue overlaps with that of planning. For a while, it became conventional wisdom that markets cannot be second-guessed; nor can we predict with any precision where innovation will happen. Today the pendulum is swinging back again. Various technologies or non fossil-fuel energy sources are touted as the answer to our need to reduce emissions; large amounts of investment are flowing into them. People are again placing bets on the future.

Technologies: where we stand

Hydrogen is only one of many fuel sources and technologies that figure on most people's lists as relevant to mitigating climate change. At the moment it is impossible to say which are likely to be most important. Nuclear and hydroelectric power are the most tried and tested technologies. The first has vociferous critics, and is not (currently) a renewable resource, while the second has intrinsic limitations depending upon the flow of water within a given country or region. The following technologies or proposed energy sources are also in play: purified coal (carbon capture and sequestration, or CCS); wind power; tidal or wave power; biofuels; solar power; geothermal energy; smart electricity grids; geo-engineering technologies, such as heat shields that would turn back a proportion of the sun's rays; and 'scrubbers' – devices that would suck CO_2 and other greenhouse gases out of the atmosphere.

Each of these, at least in principle, could overlap with the others in specific contexts; and most could contain or link up with sub-technologies, or with gadgets (such as plug-in cars running off electricity supplied from one or other clean energy source).

The literature on climate change technologies is a minefield of claims and counter-claims. All the technologies on offer have their enthusiasts, who like to assert that their chosen one is more advanced than most think. Each has its detractors and, to use a familiar term, its sceptics. Take hydrogen as a starting-point. Rifkin sees it as the ubiquitous energy source of the future. Others take quite an opposite view. Hydrogen, they point out, cannot be drawn upon from natural resources; it has to be made, either from other fuels, or from water by means of electricity. It is far more complicated to deal with as a source of energy supply than other gaseous fuels because it has to be stored at very high pressures. Even small leaks can be dangerous.[3] Of course, as in every other area, these and other problems presented by hydrogen could at some point be solved. At this point, we don't know.

Nuclear power remains mired in controversy, but as mentioned in chapter 4, it is difficult to see how it will not figure in a prominent way – not for all industrial countries, but certainly for some of them. In Britain, nuclear power generated 19 per cent of the country's electricity in 2006, compared to 36 per cent from gas and 38 per cent from coal. In 2007 this proportion dropped to 15 per cent and it will decline more as the ageing plants lose capacity. The differential was partly made up in 2007 by the import of 3 per cent of electricity demand from nuclear plants in France. Since the proportion of electricity generated from renewable sources is so small, it is difficult to see how the UK could possibly meet its EU 2020 target of 16 per cent from renewables if nuclear were allowed to lapse.

Risks and problems there are plenty. Yet, as I have stressed throughout the book, it is the balance of risks we have to consider and there are no risk-free options. A nuclear reactor emits virtually no CO_2, although emissions are involved in the building of nuclear power stations. The IPCC calculates that the total life-cycle level of emissions per unit of energy is some 40g CO_2 equivalent per kilowatt-hour, the same as that for renewable energy sources.[4] Supplies of uranium are plentiful and not concentrated in unstable countries. The biggest difficulties concern the connection between nuclear power and the building of nuclear weapons; the possibility of nuclear terror-ism; and the difficulty of disposing of the nuclear waste. No one could possibly be sanguine about how serious these ques-tions are. The first is arguably more dangerous than the second or the third. Many countries that have nuclear power do not possess nuclear weapons. Yet some states, at the moment most notably Iran, almost certainly want to develop nuclear power in order to build a nuclear arsenal.

I do not want in any sense to downplay such risks; like many others, I am a reluctant convert to nuclear power, at least in so far as some of the industrial and developing countries are concerned. But there simply is no substitute on the horizon at the moment and the risks of taking nuclear out of the mix are too great. It is possible to design nuclear power stations that are almost impervious to terrorist attack, at least in terms of such an episode causing a release of radiation. The reactors currently being built in Finland incorporate such safeguards. It is at least possible that the waste-disposal issue could be resolved at some point in the future. Some have argued that fourth-generation nuclear technology could burn almost all the energy available in the uranium ore, and also run on the depleted uranium left behind by conventional reactors. Pie in the sky? It may be, but almost all renewable sources of energy need comparable technological breakthroughs if they are to serve to replace oil, gas and coal.

Wind, wave, tidal and geothermal energy, together with biofuels, are all reasonably well developed. They are likely to play a part – albeit in most countries only a relatively small part – in the total energy mix. None is problem-free. Thus, wind power delivers energy in an erratic way, although it can be topped up from other sources to produce a more stable output. There is some concern that wind farms could interfere with the radar used in air-traffic control. In Britain, a number of proposed wind-power installations have been deferred because of such worries. Widespread enthusiasm for the use of biofuels has diminished as it has become clear that growing them can seriously affect world food production. They could have an important role to play in the future, but further tech-nological advance is needed if they are to be employed on the large scale.

Geothermal energy looks promising. At present, apart from some areas in Iceland, Japan and New Zealand where volcanically active rocks are near the surface, it is too far below the earth's crust to be accessible. However, technology has quite recently been introduced which could overcome the difficulty. It involves fracturing hot rocks and injecting water which heats up as it circulates through them.[5] A commercial plant has been set up in Landau, Germany, which already produces 22 gigawatt-hours of electricity annually. As with most other technologies, substantial government subsidies are needed to get the industry off the ground.

The technologies whose development will probably be most consequential, as far as we can see at the moment, are nuclear power, CCS and solar energy. CCS potentially is enormously important, because even if world reserves have been exaggerated, coal exists in some abundance; and also because of the fact that coal-fired power stations are very widespread and a major source of global warming. If most of these cannot be retro-fitted with carbon capture technology, then the battle to contain emissions will be seriously handicapped, or even simply lost.

Some environmentalists more or less write off 'clean coal' – CCS – altogether. For them, it's not a clean technology at all, because of the number of mine-related deaths and the fact that even de-carbonated coal contributes to illnesses such as asthma and heart disease.[6] Moreover, they worry that the promise of CCS is being used as a justification for building more coal-fired power stations, in spite of the fact that no one can be sure how effective or affordable the technology will turn out to be. Yet CCS has to stay very high up the agenda for the reasons given above. There are difficult problems to be faced. The CO_2 extracted from the coal has to be interred deep underground, with enough pressure such that it turns into a liquid. No one knows how far it will in fact stay buried. If the technology comes into widespread use, it may be difficult to find enough sites.

The other major problem is expense, which is partly caused by the need for storage, but mainly results from the costs of the process of carbon extraction. CCS is nowhere close to being competitive with orthodox coal production. Four major projects exist at the moment, in North Dakota in the US, in Algeria, in Germany and off the coast of Norway. They are all experimental and none is connected to an electricity grid. Each will require the storing of a million tonnes of CO_2 a year. The electricity system in the US alone produces 1.5 billion tonnes of CO_2 annually, which would mean finding 1,500 appropriate sites.[7] Crucial though it undoubtedly is, no one knows at the moment how far, and within what timescale, the problems of CCS can be overcome. In the meantime, untreated coal, which a few years ago seemed a fuel from yesteryear, is on its way back. Some 180 new large coal-fired power stations were built in the world in 2007, 100 of them in China. For these alone, 600 million tonnes of new coal needs to be dug. World consumption of coal rose by nearly 10 per cent in 2007, compared to 1.5 per cent for oil and 3 per cent for gas; across the world, 40 per cent of electricity and 25 per cent of total energy comes from coal.

And so – on to solar energy, for many the best hope of all. The energy that comes in the form of sunlight every day is far greater than we would ever need to fuel our needs. Such energy can be generated effectively even in temperate climates, but at present it only works well when there are long sunny periods. Solar energy has a range of practical advantages. It can be deployed on the small or the large scale and, once installed, has high reliability and low maintenance costs, with a life of 30 years or more. So far it only supplies about 1 per cent of the world's electricity. Solar power has been around for some 30 years, which could mean that the technology has got stuck; or it might mean that the long lead-up time will set the stage for major expansion.

Silicon semiconductors, which so radically altered the nature of computers, may be set to do the same for solar technology. The search is also on for non-silicon materials that are cheaper to produce. Solar technology takes various different forms, but the most advanced is photovoltaic, which turns sunlight into electric current; it can be directly connected to the grid. One of the main difficulties, which also arises with other intermittent energy sources, is how to store the electricity so as to have stocks in reserve. Various modes of storage exist at the moment, but none is of the capacity needed to use solar power on a large scale. For instance, the heat energy can be stored in containers in which stones are placed, which can conserve the energy temporarily; the same can be done with water. A pilot study, funded by the EU, is under way to study how solar energy might be converted into chemical fuels that can be stored for long periods of time and transported over long distances.

Some place faith in the possibility of constructing a technology that will extract CO_2 from the air and allow it to be stored.[8] Small-scale models of such 'scrubbers' exist. Just as in clean coal technology, the CO_2 would have to be stored – which, given the quantities involved, is a problem. It will be a big task to develop the technology on the scale needed to make a meaningful impact. Yet its potential is large, since it is the only technology known at the moment that could actually reverse the causes of global warming. As such, of course, it is subject to Giddens's paradox: many are wary of discussing the technology at all, on the grounds that, if the prospect is taken seriously, it would inhibit other necessary measures that have to be initiated.

Finally in this lengthy list there is geo-engineering, although none of the projects of this sort being mooted at the moment is more than a gleam in the eye of their potential inventors. One idea is to sow the oceans with iron particles to boost the growth of surface plankton that would then suck up CO_2 from the atmosphere. Another is to seed reflective particles in space which would reflect back a certain portion of sunlight. In its Fourth Assessment Report, the IPCC concluded that at present geo-engineering projects are 'largely speculative and with the risk of unknown side effects'. Most would agree, but in Britain the Royal Society has nonetheless commissioned a report on them, on the grounds that we have to explore all possibilities in the struggle to limit climate change. They would be used only as a last resort, since their scale means that if they went wrong they could provoke greater disasters than those they help prevent. A major difference between technologies designed to extract CO_2 from the atmosphere and those listed previously is that they do nothing to promote greater energy security.

Since there are no guaranteed technological solutions, radically increasing energy efficiency has to be high on the agenda.

The constructing of eco-homes and other environment-friendly buildings is likely to be very important for the future. The German *Passivhaus* has such high levels of insulation that it can be heated by the warmth of the human body alone, even in sub-zero temperatures. Dramatically heightened energy efficiency is the essence of Amory Lovins's notion of 'natural capitalism', which he defines as capitalism that includes a full economic valuation of the earth's eco-systems.[9] It involves ensuring that natural resources – not just energy, but also minerals, water and forests – stretch many times further than they do today. His ultimate aim is not just to reduce waste but to eliminate it altogether. In closed production systems, every output would either be returned to the eco-system as a nutrient or become an input for another manufacturing product. A further objective would be to move away from the usual notion of making goods for consumers to purchase; instead, they would rent them. At the end of a given period, the producing company would buy them back. Manufacturers would thereby have an interest in concentrating on the durability of their products; when they are exchanged against new ones, they would be wholly recycled.

These ideas may sound unrealistic, but in some ways and contexts they are closer to being realized than most of the hoped-for technological innovations, since they have already been put into practice. For example, a large glass-clad office tower in Chicago needed a major renovation after having been in existence for 20 years. The glazing was replaced by a new type that let in six times more daylight than the old units, while reducing the flow of heat and noise fourfold. The need for lighting, heating and air-conditioning was reduced by 75 per cent. Lovins claims that in the US there are some 100,000 office towers of a similar type that are due for renovation, where the same order of saving could be made.

In terms of the near future – the next 20 years – it seems certain that a diversity of energy sources will be required to reduce emissions and break dependence on oil, gas and coal. In a now well-known article published in *Science* magazine, two Princeton professors, Robert Socolow and Stephen Pacala, identified 15 energy 'wedges' that, combined with one another, could stabilize world emissions over the next 50 years.

They calculated that, given current patterns of economic development, emissions must be reduced by about seven gigatonnes to hold the increase in world temperatures at or below 2 percent. Each wedge could reduce emissions by one gigatonne, so, all other things being equal, seven of the wedges out of the substantial number they identify would be enough to reach that end. The wedges include factors such as the successful deployment of CCS technology, nuclear power, increased fuel economy for vehicles, and improvements in building insulation. [10]

The role of government

The issue for governments is how best to encourage technological innovation without prejudging where the most relevant and profound innovations are likely to occur. Subsidies are needed to provide a platform, since virtually all new technologies are more costly than fossil fuels. Innovation, however, is obviously not all of a piece. In a classic study, Christopher Freeman distinguishes a number of different levels of innovation, each of which might have to be dealt with in a different way as far as industrial policy is concerned.[11]

There can be incremental improvements in a given technological context, based upon improved design and efficiency, as in the case of the evolution of jet engines. This situation can be distinguished from new inventions, which alter the nature of a product – as when those engines were invented in the first place. On a more comprehensive level, changes in a technological system can occur when innovations are made which affect that system as a whole – an example would be the impact the computer has had on office work. Finally, changes can be introduced whose effects are felt in almost all fields of social and economic life, as has happened with the coming of the internet. Those in the final category are, by definition, the most significant, but they are least predictable and hence the most difficult to encourage by active policy.

Analysis of the economics of innovation helps suggest where government might be effective in its interventions.[12] For instance, new processes or inventions may not become cost-effective until significant investment is made and experience developed as to how they might effectively be applied. An industry might wait around for someone to take a leap of faith, which might not happen, with the result that the industry (and consumers) remain locked in to old technology. This point is one at which state-provided subsidies, in the form of challenge schemes, for example, could promote a breakthrough. Another major area is patenting, since companies will be reluctant to innovate unless they receive protection against their competitors simply taking over what they have pioneered. Government must look for an appropriate balance. If patents are too strong, innovation may in fact be discouraged, since other firms will find it difficult to build on the work of the originating company. Much the same applies on the international level, where safeguarding intellectual property is more difficult. Allowing poorer countries to bypass patents will be vital. Yet a similar dilemma to that operating nationally applies here too. If the international regime is too loose, it could militate against much-needed technological advances.

Of particular importance will be what happens in the power industry, especially given its history of widespread deregulation over the past three decades, as described in chapter 2. Power supplied through national grids is a public good, but in the 1970s and 1980s governments took the decision to turn much of it over to private firms – with the UK leading the way. Planners emphasized quantity first and foremost, having in mind issues of security, which were uppermost in policymakers' minds; cost was a secondary consideration. Following privatization, these emphases were in effect reversed. Once the major companies had been privatized, prices were pushed down towards marginal costs, leading, in effect, to a writing-off of the sunk costs. Much-needed investment was put off or scrapped, and the concentration on extracting the maximum from existing assets meant there was little capacity to cope with external shocks. Moreover, electricity generation became caught up in the more extreme edges of financial speculation, with consequences seen most spectacularly in the case of Enron in the US. Enron's troubles came from the corrupt activities of its leadership, but these developed when the complex system of trading in deregulated energy markets which Enron set up failed, creating a 'regulatory black hole'.[13]

One of the results of the sweating of assets in power generation is the low level of R&D in the industry generally – a major problem now the emphasis has swung so heavily in favour of innovation. In earlier days, state-owned industries invested a good deal in R&D, drawing upon an indigenous manufacturing base that was much stronger than is now the case. The proportion of turnover spent on R&D varies in a major way between different industries. In the big pharmaceutical companies in the UK, as of 2007, R&D intensity was 15 per cent. A survey of power-generating firms found the average to be only 0.2 per cent. In-depth studies have shown that the decline in R&D corresponds closely with electricity reform.[14]

As elsewhere, the response cannot simply be a return to top-down measures on the part of the state or the regulators appointed by the state. Policies that encourage consumers to become active partners in the supply chain are very likely to be important in terms of innovation; among other advantages, they create markets for smaller firms to enter. Yet, as elsewhere, wholesale decentralization would not work. A system like an electricity grid has to have organized coordination mechanisms, especially if smart grids are to be introduced.

It is up to government to move towards a thorough clean-out of anti-environmental subsidies. In the energy market, major hidden – and not so hidden – subsidies exist, even more so if we emphasize that producers must face the full environmental cost of their decisions. The subsidy for fossil fuels has been estimated at $20–30 billion in the OECD countries, without counting externalities at all.[15] Unless some of that money is directly and explicitly turned towards new technologies, innovation is likely to be blocked. Indeed, without substantial government intervention there is virtually no chance of effective transformation in electricity production. National grids are geared towards a centralized system of power plants; since cost reductions with new technologies usually take years to come about, there is a gap that capital markets cannot fill.[16] Some of these factors also apply to transport, the fastest-growing source of emissions.

Against this backdrop, consider the example of the hypercar, first proposed by Amory and Hunter Lovins.[17] The hypercar aims to reduce fuel consumption by over 80 per cent and the emissions involved in making the vehicle by as much as 90 per cent compared to the most economical vehicles of similar capacity that exist at the moment. The machine would be made out of materials that reduce its weight to a fraction of the average vehicle today, without sacrificing its ability to with-stand accidents. It would be modelled to reduce air resistance to a minimum and be powered by a hybrid-electric drive using hydrogen fuel cells. Trucks and cars made this way would be able to return from between 80–200 miles per gallon and they would be neither small nor sluggish.

The hypercar, the Lovinses argue, would transform other industries around it. It would displace one-eighth of the steel industry, saving that proportion of emissions. A wholesale move towards hypercars could save the equivalent of the total OPEC production of oil. It would also aid in introducing inex-pensive fuel cells in other industries. In addition, hypercars would generate surplus electricity that could be fed back into the national grid.

At the moment, manufacturers are managing steadily to increase the overall economy of their vehicles, but nowhere near to the degree which is already in fact practicable. The main reason is the 'technological inertia' bound up with an industry locked into existing markets and the surrounding structure of supply. Public policy is required to begin a transition to new networks and surrounding support systems. Such policy will have also to help ensure that the electricity consumed by low-emission vehicles itself comes from low-carbon sources.

How can government minimize the problem that the money spent funding best guesses for innovation might be wasted? One way is to support a range of technological possibilities, the equivalent of a portfolio approach in spreading market risk. Diversity in energy supply has additional benefits too, including provision of greater security should any one source become threatened. There is a downside, however, since there is a danger that subsidies and incentives may become spread too thinly to have their desired effects. Governments and busi-nesses have to accept that some technologies may fail or prove to be a dead end, while others, perhaps even the most influen-tial ones, may slip in from the side.

We should recognize also that it is not only large, established industries that can form lobbies which tend to act in favour of the status quo. The same can be true of smaller producers, especially where there is a clear mechanism of subsidy involved – the proponents of wind or solar power, for example, are likely to push their own cases forcefully. One responsibility of government is to make sure that state funding does not produce the equivalent of welfare dependency, where those who receive support come to treat it as a natural right and then resist change.

There are few technologies that do not have spill-over effects, so in practice government support of innovation has to be connected with broader concerns. Where spill-over effects are positive, they may need state support, or an appropriate regulatory framework, to have greatest effect. Thus, materials developed in the motor industry may have direct application to building more energy-efficient homes and workplaces if technology-transfer is actively rewarded. For these reasons, holistic thinking is going to be essential in promoting technological innovation. Any fundamental technological breakthrough is going to be felt throughout society, as happened in the case of the internet. Urban planning and land regulation must be flexible enough both to promote and to respond to transformations of this sort.

Eco-towns might help explore the advantages and difficulties of future changes that later become more generalized. It is evident that innovative forms of technology could create complex problems of urban and rural land planning. The days when power stations could be located in the centre of cities, as used to be the norm in the early twentieth century, are long gone. Even in remote areas there may be deeply felt opposition to the building of nuclear power stations, which is why countries contemplating nuclear renewal are proposing to build on existing sites. Many citizens also have aesthetic objections to wind-farms.

Wherever new initiatives are made, whether in technology itself or in areas where its impact is felt, areas of uncertainty are created. A technology that is unproven has no confirmed price and it is difficult to cost the consequences of its widespread adoption, given all the factors just discussed. Take for an example a problem of far-reaching importance – the development of new ways of storing electricity. As in the case of the hypercar, the starting-point is likely to be a shared vision of what could be achieved, involving industry, government and other agencies.[18]

Creating new ways of storing electricity is an issue that goes well beyond only solar power and other intermittent renewable energy sources. It could have an enormous impact upon the power grid, on transportation and other areas. For instance, it would help directly with one of the problems of some leading renewable technologies, that they only provide intermittent supply. Various means of electricity storage are conventionally recognized, such as batteries, fly-wheels and compressed air.[19] A range of other possibilities exists, awaiting possible commercial development. These include flow batteries, lithium battery systems, supercapacitors and power conversion systems. *Smartgrids*, published by the European Commission, offers a vision of the future of Europe's electricity networks that includes anticipating more effective storage technologies.[20] It not only traces out the implications in a holistic way, but proposes how partnerships between governments and business can overcome early investment hurdles.

As already stated, some of these technologies will turn out to be going nowhere, as is the case in all other areas where governments offer subsidies or incentives – or where private firms invest without such support. Failures can be accompanied by lessons, since they may generate significant knowledge along the way, and closing down possibilities can, in principle, lead to better focused investment. However, exit strategies should be in place from the beginning, at least as far as the state is involved, or there is the chance that good money will follow bad. Anyone who studies the history of early post-war planning will recognize that this danger is very real.

Promoting job creation: a 'Climate Change New Deal'?

Job creation through the spread of renewable technologies sounds like a prime form of economic convergence – and so, in principle, it is. 'Wind power has created thousands of new jobs', it is often said of a given country – for instance, Germany. Yet put that way the claim is too simplistic, since jobs in new technology areas may come at the expense of others in more traditional energy industries where some workers, as a consequence, become unemployed. Moreover, most new technologies reduce the need for labour power. Wind and wave power, for example, typically employ fewer workers per unit of energy produced than coal-mining. Industrial policy planned with climate change objectives in mind cannot be based upon an easy equation between economic convergence and job creation.

In the environmental literature, lifestyle change is normally identified with reducing waste and profligacy. These emphases are no doubt correct, but there is no reason why other avenues of taste and self-expression should not open up as new technologies develop. We live in a post-industrial society and that will not change whatever else happens. The transition to a low-carbon economy can be expected to create new jobs, but they are likely to come about as much through developments in lifestyle or taste as from changes in the energy industries as such. Who would have thought that, having put up with inferior coffee for years, US and British consumers were secretly longing for a better product and for numerous varieties of it? Well, presumably they weren't, but an opportunity was spotted, and initiated a trend. Much the same is likely to happen, along a variety of dimensions, as the world moves towards low-carbon technologies and lifestyles. Just where the space for such initiatives will exist, however, is essentially unpredictable.

The United Nations Environment Programme (UNEP) has published a comprehensive analysis of how environment-friendly jobs might be created.[21] In true UN style, it starts with a glossary of acronyms used in the text – no fewer than 182 of them (one of which is 'UNEP' itself). Such jobs are defined as work in agriculture, manufacturing, research and development and services 'that contribute substantially to preserving or restoring environmental quality'.

The report says that employment will be affected in four main ways by an increasing concern with environmental quality, including responding to climate change. Some additional jobs will be created without substituting for others, such as where pollution control devices are added to existing equipment. Certain jobs that are lost as new technologies advance will be directly replaced, as for instance where landfill or waste incineration are replaced by recycling. Others will disappear without being replaced – as where the production of packaging materials for manufactured goods is simply discontinued. Yet others will be transformed and redefined, either through technological change or as the tasks involved are altered – such as in the construction industry. The report has the virtue of emphasizing that some industries will have to go through difficult processes of restructuring and there will be winners and losers.

The role of public policy, the report rightly continues, will be vital. Subsidies for environmentally harmful industries will have to be phased out, alongside the introduction or improvement of those promoting energy-efficient practices. Carbon taxes should be used to transfer the tax burden away from labour and towards taxing the sources of environmental pollution. Direct regulation is needed in many areas, in the shape, for example, of building codes, energy-efficiency standards, or the control of land-use and the eco-labelling of products. Governments should commission in-depth modelling and econometric studies to assess the likely consequences of investments and controls.

The proportion of workers currently involved in renewable technology industries is currently tiny, but will inevitably expand greatly. At present, some two million workers worldwide are estimated to be directly employed in such industries. About half of these are working in biofuels, mostly in growing and collecting the plants used to produce them. Since there are major worries about the implications of first-generation biofuels for food scarcity, this proportion may actually decline, at least in the short term. As far as other renewable technologies go, almost all the employment generated thus far is concentrated in a handful of industrial countries.

The problems of planning noted earlier apply with some force to environmental job creation. Innovations in renewable technologies cannot be predicted except in a general way, while by definition the implications of possible breakthroughs are unknown. There are huge gaps in available data about the environmental consequences of existing work practices and ways of life, especially as far as the developing world is concerned. In all countries, should environment-friendly jobs dramatically increase, there are major implications for education and training, knock-on implications for the work–life balance, pensions and many other areas.

The current financial crisis has prompted excited talk of a low-carbon 'New Deal' that would promote economic recovery through state-led investment in energy conservation and renewable technologies. The model is the strategy launched under that name by President Franklin D. Roosevelt in the US following the 1929 Great Crash, plus the modifications later added by John Maynard Keynes. The Green New Deal Group in Britain, for example, has called for 'a programme of investment and a call to action as urgent and far-reaching as the US New Deal in the 1930s and the mobilization for war in 1939'.[22]

The group proposes an annual £50 billion crash programme of spending on renewable technologies in the UK. It would be aimed at making 'every building a power station', to generate energy and improve energy efficiency. The programme would concentrate on investment in off-shore wind-power stations, in solar energy and in building insulation. A 'carbon army' made up of 'hundreds of thousands of workers' would provide the labour power for this. The 'carbon army' would form part of a 'wider shift of an economy narrowly focused on financial services and shopping to one that is an engine of environmental transformation'. Britain, the group says, should emulate Germany, where 250,000 jobs have been created in renewable technology industries (that naive claim again!).

Well before the arrival of the current financial crisis, US authors Michael Shellenberger and Ted Nordhaus had proposed a 'New Apollo Project', aimed at freeing the States from its dependence on oil and at the same time creating new jobs. In a swingeing critique of America's environmental movement, which they see as having been narrow-minded and negative, they argue for a strategy that will 'create something inspiring' and will 'remind people of the American dream'. Together with others, they have put together a coalition of groups, involving business, labour unions and community agencies, to push forward their proposals, which involve large-scale expenditure on the part of government to advance low-carbon technologies and thereby create 'millions of jobs'.[23]

In *The Green Economy*, Van Jones proposes that state-led investment in low-carbon energy and energy efficiency could be a means of involving the less well-off in the concerns about climate change.[24] Many of the jobs involved in the two areas, he says, are not high-tech, but are middle skill ones. A detailed programme, centred on stimulating economic recovery, has been set out by others at the Center for American Progress. This involves public-sector spending in six main areas: improving the energy efficiency of buildings; expanding public transport and freight; setting up smart electricity grids; building wind farms and solar power installations; and developing next-generation biofuels.[25] According to its initiators, Robert Pollin and colleagues, the programme would help renew manufacture and the construction industry and also be a major source of new jobs.

Unlike others who make such claims, Pollin et al. offer an analysis of the conditions under which job expansion can proceed without significant job loss elsewhere, at least in circumstances of recovery from recession. A $100 billion government investment programme, according to their analysis, could generate 1.7 million new jobs. Like Van Jones, they stress that such investment will offer a substantial proportion of entry-level jobs as well as more skilled and technical ones.

I am in favour of such proposals, especially in an American context, since the US has so much ground to make up on most other industrial countries in terms both of emissions reduction and energy saving. However, care will have to be taken about how they are instituted and plenty of difficulties have to be resolved. If they are to work, training will have to be provided, at all levels, and on a substantial scale – this means up-front expenditure without any immediate pay-back. Investment in infrastructure will be crucial, and will have to be planned over a longer period than just at the time of economic recovery. Consistency of policy will be called for. There is not much point investing in renewables on the large scale if the effects on such investment are negated by policy decisions taken elsewhere. In the US, for example, a lot will depend upon what attitude the government takes towards the failing car industry, which is now demanding state support.

Most important of all, policy initiated to aid short-term recovery will have to be directed towards what happens later. The current financial crisis is not just a routine cyclical movement of the economy. I would see it as a '1989 of deregulation' – a transition perhaps as fraught with implications as was the collapse of Soviet communism, and as likely to be as protracted and complex in its consequences and implications. I have no quarrel with the view that there has to be a profound restructuring of financial markets themselves and of banking.

However, as with most forms of peering into the future, it isn't at all clear at the moment just what actions will be taken. Moreover, we will have to be very careful not to revert to a traditional model of the state, or to throw away the benefits that complex market instruments offer, including derivatives and the hedging of risk. For instance, as is discussed later in the book, complex insurance mechanisms, which are all about risk transfer, will be essential to cope with adaptation to climate change. The state will never be able to provide more than a bare minimum of the cover that will be needed.

Big-bang solutions are intuitively attractive, but we are also going to have to feel our way forward and cope with the mixture of implications that recession and the need for widespread restructuring will have. Plans have to be in place for the return to high oil prices, which is almost certain to follow world economic resurgence. Taxation is sure to play an important part, with the strong likelihood that taxes in the industrial countries will have to rise. What matters here is that such increases should be integrated with a broader movement towards carbon taxes.

In such a context, I shan't try to discuss the implications of the financial crisis in general. The shakeout is almost certain to be mixed as far as climate change policy is concerned. Agenda-setting is likely to be crucial and could be seen as part of what those calling for an environmental New Deal are trying to produce – to prevent climate change sliding down the agenda by making a pre-emptive bid for the attention of policy-makers and the public.

It is up to policy entrepreneurs to deploy the range of interventions against such an eventuality mentioned earlier in the chapter. Possibilities of job creation in conditions of recovery will, in my view, have to be much more broad-ranging than those mentioned in the sources discussed above; and the knock-on consequences of job-creation strategies will have to be thoroughly examined. The best way of keeping climate change policy in the forefront will be to deploy the strategy suggested throughout this book – work to keep it at the cutting edge of economic competitiveness, integrate it with wider political programmes and avoid empty moral posturing.

Carbon taxes

Taxation regimes will play a significant part in stimulating innovation and, to some extent, in controlling its direction. Taxation is one of the main levers of state policy, and will of course have a broader role too in the struggle to reduce emissions. In the debate between writers who favour carbon emissions markets and those who place most emphasis on carbon taxes, I incline towards the latter, although obviously the two can coexist.

In what follows, I shall argue that we should not focus only on carbon taxes as such, but upon the consequences of a given fiscal system as a whole for outputs that are relevant to climate change. We should recognize that existing taxes which have not been devised for environmental purposes may nevertheless in some part serve them – in that sense, they are carbon taxes. For instance, taxes invested in railways can serve to reduce emissions in spite of the fact that such a concern was not what prompted them originally.

The reverse also applies. Taxes may have adverse, although unintended, effects as far as environmental issues are concerned. Such effects might be fairly obvious, as in the case of airline fuel being exempt from taxes applied to other forms of transport. But they can be more diffuse as, for example, where the location of a supermarket is left open to market forces, with no thought given to environmental implications.

Directly motivated carbon taxes can be of two sorts: those whose revenue, part or all, is spent for environmental purposes; and those whose purpose it is to influence behaviour in ways compatible with climate change objectives. Taxes invested in developing renewable technologies, for example, fall into the first category. Those aimed at persuading people to drive more fuel-efficient cars, or reduce the mileage they drive every year, fall into the second. As with other taxes, they can serve as incentives or they can be punitive.

Carbon taxes should be transparent to citizens rather than presented in some other guise or under some other pretext, as happened with the fuel levies in the UK. They are likely to be most successful where they combine several of the qualities just noted – i.e., if they are explicitly designed as such; directed at changing behaviour, whether of agencies in society, such as business firms, or citizens as a whole; wherever possible are incentives rather than negative taxes, since incentives draw upon positive motivations; form part of an overall fiscal strategy; and where their environmental consequences are openly stated and visible.

From an economic point of view, the point of carbon taxes is to help eliminate externalities as far as the environment is concerned – to ensure that they are fully costed, including costs to future generations. As in so many other areas of climate change policy, the principle is easy to state, but quite often difficult to apply. For instance, the cost of food produced by large-scale agriculture using fertilizers and pesticides does not include the destructive impact these can have on the soil. Nor does it include the pollution coming from the shipping that carries them around the world. True prices are very difficult to assess, as in many other areas, given the complex nature of modern manufacturing processes.

Taxes on the use of resources should be as near to the point of production as possible, in order to apply to all relevant aspects of manufacturing processes. Such taxes should promote efficiency in energy use and innovation at the beginning of the production cycle, limiting the need for repair and recycling later. There should be trade-offs where carbon taxes are introduced *de novo*. In other words, citizens should be offered tax swaps, basically trading environmental taxes against reductions elsewhere. Sometimes, such a strategy can create a 'double dividend' – limiting pollution but at the same time producing other benefits elsewhere.

It is a well-established theorem that, as far as possible, we should tax the 'bads' (the sources of emissions) rather than the 'goods' (such as human labour, in the form of income tax). This notion fits neatly with 'the polluter pays' principle. However, once again the distinction is not as clear-cut as one might assume, since, through taxation, we also want actively (via incentives) to encourage 'goods' in respect of climate change – such as investment in renewable technologies. Taxing the 'bads' implies that these will be replaced more and more by 'goods', in so far as taxation produces social or economic changes; hence revenue from such sources will inevitably decline, even if taxation takes the form of incentives. Hence, once more we must bear in mind the overall tax system, since compensatory changes will need to be introduced elsewhere.

The pioneers of carbon taxes have been the Nordic countries. They were introduced in the early 1990s, so there has been some time to assess their level of success. The task is complicated, however, by the fact that taxes vary from country to country and all have evolved over time. In the early 1990s the Danes introduced taxes on electricity, energy consumption and fossil fuels. These were later complemented by a household CO_2 tax. In Finland, what is generally seen as the first CO_2 tax in the world was established in 1990 and applied across industry, transport and private households. Initially, the tax was relatively low, but it was later expanded. Sweden, Norway and Iceland have followed somewhat different paths again.

The level of ambition of such taxes, at least initially, was modest and, judged against that base-line, the results have been significant.[26] In Finland, without the CO_2 tax, emissions would probably have been 2–3 per cent higher by the year 2000 than they turned out to be; in Sweden, Norway and Iceland the figure was 3–4 per cent. The absolute level of emissions, however, increased across the 1990s in all these countries. Only in Denmark did the absolute volume of CO_2 emissions fall. The reason is that the Danes directed the tax revenue to environmental ends – it was used to subsidize energy-saving practices.

Given that these are the most advanced countries in respect of carbon taxes, it is obvious that there is a long way to go before such taxes make the contributions we (rightly) expect of them. Most current discussions remain at the level of what 'could be achieved' – that is, they are hypothetical. The possibilities of tax swaps, for example, have been explored in detail in various national contexts. Thus a study in the US analysed a swap in which a tax of $15 per metric ton of carbon would be balanced against a reduction in the federal payroll tax on the first $3,660 that workers earn.[27] Payroll tax in the US is a flat-rate tax up to a limit (in 2005) of $90,000 and is a regressive tax, hitting lower earners disproportionately. In fact, for more than 60 per cent of households it is the largest single federal tax they pay. A 'double dividend' comes into play, since taxes on labour supply can discourage workers from increasing their productivity, or even from entering the workforce at all.

The study's author suggests a tax on the carbon content of fuels at source, set at $55 per metric ton of carbon. Allowing for the short-term demand adjustments that are likely to occur, the tax would have raised $78 billion if it had been in effect in 2005, which could have lowered payroll tax by almost 11 per cent. It would have the greatest benefit for low-paid workers, who would save some three-quarters of their payroll taxes. Those at the top rate of earnings covered by the payroll tax would save about 4 per cent. The tax could be raised at a later point to compensate for its positive effects in reducing emissions and therefore creating falling revenue. Of course, the 'double dividend' could be largely lost as producers pass on the extra costs to consumers in the shape of price increases. However, the research shows that poorer households would still gain disproportionately.

Since the potentially regressive impact of carbon taxes is a worry to many, it is worth looking at some of the strategies that have been put forward to counter it. A research study carried out in the UK by the Rowntree Foundation studied four sectors where such taxes either have been established or are under active consideration.[28] These were in energy, water and transport use by households, together with the household generation of waste. The point was to see what ways could be devised to make such taxes at least neutral in terms of how they affect the less well-off.

The study confirmed that, if nothing else changed, in these areas environmental taxes would have a significant adverse impact upon poorer households. People on low incomes may already be inclined to stint on energy consumption, perhaps even to the detriment of their own health, especially where heating is concerned.

A reason why the UK has not followed the Nordic states and other countries in introducing household carbon or energy taxes is that fuel poverty in Britain reflects the peculiarly inadequate thermal characteristics of the country's housing stock. The Rowntree Foundation study mentioned above shows an enormous variation in energy use even among households within the same income band. Within each of 10 income bands used in the research, some households consumed as much as six times more energy than others. There were also large variations in emissions. The research showed that the poorest households pay significantly more per unit of energy than the most affluent ones. Hence if a uniform carbon tax were imposed, it would be even more regressive than might appear at first sight.

Tax and benefits packages aimed at the poorer households can help reduce this effect. However, some among the fuel poor would become actively worse off, which would be likely to sink such proposals politically.

There is an approach that could work. It involves a combination of incentives and sanctions. By means of incentives, households would be persuaded to implement energy-efficient measures; a 'climate change surcharge' would be imposed on all households which, after a certain time, had not taken steps to carry out these measures. A nationwide energy audit would identify cost-effective measures that would need to be implemented by every household in order to avoid the climate change surcharge. The scheme would be put into practice over a given time period – say, 10 years – beginning with those living in the most affluent homes, as measured by existing property tax categories. Those in the highest tax bands would be obliged to carry out the work first, with others following in sequence and the poorest left to last. The latter group would be able to get low-cost loans, paid for from the surcharge levied on households that failed to get the necessary improvements done on time. For rented accommodation, the property-owners would pay.

The researchers argue that a minimum of 10 per cent of household CO_2 emissions would be saved over the 10-year period. While the cost to householders would be £6.4 billion, they would be saved a net sum of £19.4 billion. The average return to householders would be 23 per cent, with the poorest gaining more than the affluent, resulting in a sharp drop in fuel poverty. The report concludes that 'the fact that such a scheme currently seems not to be considered suggests the public and political will to mitigate climate change is not yet very powerful'.[29]

The report suggests that similar results can be achieved in other areas too – household water use, transport and waste management. As far as the first of these is concerned, the study argues that water metering under any scenario would have more positive results for poorer households than the current situation, where households pay a bill partly based on a standing charge and partly on the value of their properties. Taxes on fuel for cars are not regressive, since over 30 per cent of households do not own a car and most of such households are poor. Ways can be found of compensating low-income motorists for fuel duties, for example by abolishing licence duty for those groups. However, for purposes of political legitimacy, it would be crucial to spend the revenue on environmental purposes.

Finally, it would be possible to increase the level of waste recycling without adversely affecting the poor. At the moment, the poor pay more for waste collection in relative terms than do the more affluent. The researchers argue for a reduction in council taxes by the same amount for all households, and the addition of a weight-based charge for waste disposal. The charge would vary according to how far waste material was recyclable.

The Rowntree Study is important, because it goes some way to providing a carbon audit of the tax system, at least in the areas covered. It takes into account existing fiscal instruments and tries to spot the unintended consequences of reforms. All the proposed strategies are fairly complex, suggesting that it is difficult to reach the holy grail of reconciling carbon taxes with greater tax simplicity while still protecting the under-privileged. At present, it seems that no country has attempted a full-scale carbon tax audit, but such appraisals are surely necessary, since virtually all individual taxes will have knock-on consequences.

Do we need carbon taxes at all if and when oil and gas prices rise again, as they are certain to do when the recession eases? Won't they act like taxes anyway? Won't poorer people have to be given subsidies as the price of energy to the con-sumer rises? These questions do not admit of straightforward answers, for reasons given earlier. High prices will act as the equivalent of taxes, when compared to previous price levels, and undoubtedly will prompt changes in behaviour in the direction of greater frugality and efficiency in energy use, as well as adding a powerful stimulus to the development of new energy technologies.

The difference from carbon taxes, however, is that they create no stream of revenue to the state, but instead generate large new costs, and hence inflationary consequences, that somehow have to be absorbed; moreover, oil and gas prices are essentially unpredictable. And there is the danger that they will result in a return to the use of coal. So we will need carbon taxes anyway, but in which areas, and how far they take the form of incentives rather than punitive taxes, will certainly be very strongly influenced by whatever happens in world energy markets.

Carbon rationing

Carbon rationing has some fervent advocates and some equally vociferous opponents. Supporters like the idea because of its apparent simplicity, its universal character and its radical nature. Each member of the population would have an annual carbon allowance for energy use in respect of domestic con-sumption and travel, including air travel. The allowance would be the same for all adults, with a smaller quota for children. The scheme would be mandatory. Once more, the role of government would be crucial, for it would have not only to determine at what level the quotas would be fixed, but also to be responsible for monitoring its operation.

Each year, the allowance would be reduced by an amount, specified well in advance, tracking the trajectory of national targets for emissions reductions. Individuals who live low-carbon lifestyles could trade their surplus emissions at a market price to those who consume more. Organizations as well as individual citizens could in principle be included. The quotas would be divided into carbon units. Everyone would have a smart card containing their allowance for the year, which would be used every time domestic bills were paid or travel services used. Carbon rationing, it is argued, would do away with many of the more specific government programmes designed to encourage energy conservation; people would be able to choose for themselves how best to meet the quota.

Three different versions have been proposed – involving what their originators call, variously, Tradable Energy Quotas, Domestic Tradable Quotas and Personal Carbon Allowances. The first of these was proposed by David Fleming.[30] It would cover organizations (including the government) as well as individuals. A cap would be set based upon national emissions reductions targets. A 20-year rolling budget would be set up at the start of the scheme. For the first five years the quotas would be binding and for the second five years they would be 'firm'; the final ten years would be a 'forecast', to allow individuals and companies to prepare over time. Of the overall ration, 40 per cent would be allocated to adult citizens free of charge; the other 60 per cent would be issued to 'primary dealers' who would sell on to organizations in a secondary market. The scheme would cover oil, gas, electricity and coal. Individuals could choose to sell their units as soon as they received them, and then buy back from the market as they made energy-relevant purchases. In other words, they could opt for a pay-as-you-go procedure. Those outside the system (such as overseas visitors) would have to use such a means.

Domestic tradable quotas are the currency units in a comparable scheme suggested by researchers at the Tyndall Centre.[31] The principal difference between the two is that the Tyndall scheme includes aviation. The third approach, proposed by Mayer Hillman and Tina Fawcett, involves the allocation of what they call Personal Carbon Allowances, which would cover individuals only.[32] It would apply to all household energy use and personal travel, including flying. Like the other two, it would involve yearly reductions in allocated quotas with early warning given.

The authors of a government-sponsored survey of the feasibility of carbon rationing note that the state of the debate at the moment is a somewhat unhappy one. Those who propose such schemes see them as something of a panacea. Others oppose them as being impractical, expensive, open to widespread fraud and likely to favour the affluent over the poor. Both sides base their arguments upon largely untested assumptions about political feasibility, operational feasibility and cost. 'Practical understanding and analysis', the authors – Simon Roberts and Joshua Thumin – argue, are being undermined by 'confrontational debate', in which they 'take second place to the preservation of increasingly entrenched positions'. [33]

As Roberts and Thumin point out, the introduction of carbon rationing will not immediately make it easier for people to alter their activities. It may well motivate them to act, but will not enable them to do so. Carbon rationing is not therefore a substitute for other policies needed to curb greenhouse gas emissions. Roberts and Thumin set out to provide what they say is lacking – a careful analysis of the pros and cons of the approach.

In brief, their conclusions are as follows. Would carbon rationing lead to large-scale fraud? Not necessarily, but to prevent it such a scheme would probably have to be linked to biometric ID cards – themselves highly controversial and likely to be very costly. Even then, it might be hard or impossible to prevent a widespread black market from developing. Would people be able to manage their budgets effectively, or would some founder? Research on ordinary household budgeting has shown that most are good at living within their budgets and keeping track of their finances. However a significant minority are not good at either. What would happen to them if they mismanaged their carbon budgets is not clear. Would they face fines, or possible imprisonment?

Would carbon rationing favour the affluent at the expense of the poor? Not in every way, because affluent people create more emissions than the poor, especially if aviation is included – they will therefore need to buy from poorer groups. However, just as the better-off have found ways of exploiting welfare systems to their advantage, much the same would be very likely to happen in the case of carbon credits.

Would the public be prepared to accept carbon rationing? According to Roberts and Thumin, we simply do not know – virtually no research seems to have been carried out to assess public response to the idea. Among proponents 'there is a widespread assumption that [a carbon rationing scheme] will trigger significant change in behaviour . . . but [there is] no evidence of this'.[34] It would not be possible to test carbon rationing proposals through pilot studies. The main reason is that in order to work, a scheme has to be compulsory.

Roberts and Thumin do not reach any hard and fast conclusions, but on the basis of their observations, my own view is that carbon rationing is impractical and unfeasible. Its apparent attractions are blunted once the idea is carefully scrutinized. I would reaffirm my case made earlier: we will not be able to bludgeon people into submission when it comes to responding to climate change.

The re-emergence of utopia

Let us return for a brief visit to Sweden. In the Western Harbour area of Malmö, a new housing development is under way. Buildings sporting massive glass panels sit alongside modest timber structures, all surrounded by parks and walkways. Parking space is limited to 0.7 cars per apartment, and the area is connected to the rest of the city by a dense public transport network. Electricity is provided by wind turbines, solar panels and thermal heating. Solar window shades not only help generate electricity, but also reduce direct sunlight, lowering the need for air-conditioning in the summer. The energy-saving dwellings cost no more to build than conventional homes, but use only a third of the energy required by the average domestic dwelling in the rest of Malmö. Waste separation units positioned close to each home, coupled to a system of vacuum waste chutes, provide for recycling.

We don't know at present how far such communities can be generalized, or what some of their drawbacks might be. They are an example of the opportunities created by the twin problems of climate change and energy security. Could they be the outliers for broader processes of social transformation? I believe so, because now is surely the time for us to try to come more to terms with what I have earlier called the problems of over-development – put another way, the downside of affluence.

Consider that emblem of modernity, the car. The fate of the car will have a profound impact upon our struggle to limit global warming. Cars and other motor vehicles account for 14 per cent of total world CO_2 emissions – more if one includes those produced during the course of their manufacture. More than a billion cars have been made since the earliest models were introduced. If car ownership and use follow their current trajectory, in little over a decade there will be a billion cars on the roads at the same time.[35] In the US, car use plus car manufacture account for fully 60 per cent of the country's emissions; the US produces 45 per cent of all CO_2 emissions generated by cars worldwide. What is the definition of a 'pedestrian' in America? Answer: someone who has just parked his car.[36]

We don't know the extent to which, or how quickly, new forms of propulsion for vehicles, such as electricity from renewable sources, or hydrogen, can come into use on a large scale. Yet, whatever happens to fuel sources, we can already catch a glimpse of the possibility of 'life beyond the car'.

The attraction of cars has always been that they offer freedom, mobility and speed. Yet the proliferation of cars on the roads negates these very qualities. What meaning do they have when drivers are endlessly stuck in traffic jams? We say 'stuck in a traffic jam' as though it came from external sources – in fact, every individual driver *is* the traffic jam. Part of the logic of eco-towns is to break dependence on the motor-car, and numerous experiments are being tried within orthodox city environments. For instance, local authorities have introduced congestion charging and traffic calming, and have banned cars altogether from some areas, thereby encouraging people to put a positive value on walking or cycling.

As French economic historian Jean Gimpel has shown, technological 'progress' is sometimes achieved through reversals.[37] For instance, nylon was once touted as the material of the future for clothing. Yet the 'traditional' cloths of wool and cotton made a dramatic comeback. A possible future (brought about by planning) is certainly likely to be a return to localism, involving networks of small, self-reliant communities (the future that many greens envisage). James Kunstler has remarked that city life will be marked by 'a return to smaller scales of operation in virtually every respect of travel and transport'.[38]

Much more likely, and desirable, is that such a tendency will interact with its opposite – a further expansion of mobility, but where transport will change its nature.[39] There could be a return to cityscapes that existed before the invention of the car, but which could nevertheless be integrated with a world of high mobility. The driverless car is already here, with its robot driver proven as being more capable and safer than even the most skilled and careful human counterpart. In cars now on sale high-tech devices already exist that help prevent collisions on fast-moving roads without the intervention of the driver.

A digital system of transport could follow, perhaps combining driverless with driven cars, all composed of small, ultra-light vehicles. The transportation device would be a 'personal multimodal pod in which passengers can stay in comfort throughout a journey leaving all the hassle of switching between different transport modes and network levels to the pod'.[40] Smart cards would be used to pay and control access. Such a system would rewrite the relationship between the 'public' and the 'private'. Real-life travel could be integrated with virtual access within 'tele-immersion environments'.

Utopian? Well, yes, but also actually at some point quite probable. The division between 'private' vehicles – the car – and 'public' transport has already begun to break down. Thus car clubs, where members don't own the vehicles they drive, but have privileged access to them, have sprung up in numerous cities in the US and Europe. It is not difficult to see that such systems could be liberating, as well as add significantly to

TECHNOLOGIES AND TAXES   161

quality of life. One should also remember that the car is a lethal instrument. The freedom it confers, and the love it can inspire, comes at a terrible price – it has been estimated that some 40 million people have been killed on the roads since the car first made its appearance, greater than the number that died in the two world wars combined.

Whatever happens from now on, climate change is going to affect our lives and we will have to adapt to its consequences. Politics intrudes here just as much as everywhere else and how processes of adaptation will be managed is an issue of prime importance. Just as in the case of controlling emissions, the developed countries have responsibilities towards the rest of the world as far as adaptation is concerned, and in the following chapter I shall discuss what these are.

7

THE POLITICS OF ADAPTATION

Initially borrowed from evolutionary biology, the term 'adaptation' has come into widespread use in the climate change literature. In a way, it is a misleading term, because it implies reacting to the consequences of climate change once it has occurred. However, just like our efforts to limit the warming of the world's climate, adaptation as far as possible has to be anticipatory and preventative.

Adaptation has been described as the 'poor and derided cousin of emissions reduction'.[1] For some while, discussing adaptation was taboo among environmentalists, on the grounds that it would adversely affect efforts directed at combating climate change itself. Times have definitely changed, however. In the discussions at Bali (see below, pp. 186–92), as much time was devoted to discussion of adaptation as to mitigation. It is one of the four 'building blocks' from which, to mix metaphors somewhat, the roadmap proposed at the Bali meetings is to be constructed. An Adaptation Fund, set up by the UN some years before, has had some flesh put on its bare bones. The fund had been widely criticized for being too difficult for countries to qualify for and for being seriously underfinanced. In future, developing countries will have direct access to it and it will have significantly greater resources to dispense.

In some ways the issues surrounding adaptation are even more complex than those to do with mitigation. For in preparing to adapt before climatic changes have actually taken place, or when they are in their early stages, we have to specify what the effects of global warming will be, in the many contexts in which they will have an impact. Providing some concepts to help guide our efforts at adaptation is important, because such concepts can help give shape and direction to policy. Let me first underline the relevance of the distinction already made, between adaptation after the event and adaptation oriented to possible futures. I shall speak of *pro-active adaptation* (PA) to refer to the second of these categories. Within the limits of our knowledge – and in any real-life context, of funding – PA should be the prime focus of our attention whenever we think about adaptation, although reactive adaptation will certainly be necessary.

PA is about diagnosing and responding to *vulnerabilities*. Vulnerability is once again all about risk – the risk of suffering damage to a valued activity, way of life or resource. Vulnerability is plainly an economic and social phenomenon, not just one concerned with the physical environment. We can't discuss vulnerability without also focusing on its opposite, *resilience*. Resilience can be defined as *adaptive capacity*, the capacity not only to cope in the face of external changes or shocks, but, wherever possible, to respond actively and positively to them. It can be a property of the physical environment, of an individual or of a group. In the first case it is about the capability of the built environment to withstand shocks of one kind or another. It could take the form, for example, of strengthening dykes, or building new ones, in advance of expected increases in vulnerability to flooding. In the second, it refers to qualities of character – the ability to make the best of adverse circumstances, or actively to triumph over them. Defined as a quality of a group, it concerns factors such as the capacity of members of a community to act together rather than to become divided and fragmented; and to be able to modify, or even transform, existing ways of life should it become necessary so to do. Smallholders who grow a variety of crops, for example, will be more resilient than those dependent upon a single cash crop.

Most of the concepts introduced earlier in this book are directly relevant to adaptation. In deciding what forms of resilience to invest in and cultivate, we always have to bear in mind a balance of risks. Adaptation sounds like a version of the precautionary principle, because (as PA) it is a pre-emptive doctrine – it is intervention taken to prevent or contain future risks. Yet, as in all risk situations, when deciding on a particular strategy, we have to weigh different risks and opportunities against each other. The percentage principle applies.

Political and economic convergence are as important to the politics of adaptation as they are to mitigation – they are likely to influence how far citizens accept whatever policies are proposed. The limitations of the politics of fear and anxiety are just as pronounced here as elsewhere. 'The polluter pays' principle is also just as relevant as in the case of mitigation, both within nations and among them. The richer countries must shoulder the lion's share of responsibility for adaptation, as far as the developing world is concerned, just as they have to do in limiting the progress of global warming. The developing countries are much more vulnerable to the effects of climate change than the industrial ones, partly because many are located in climatically volatile regions and partly because they haven't got the resources that the developed countries have to prepare.

As with mitigation, the state will have to play a lead role in policy formation and enactment. However, all the points made earlier in the book apply. To promote adaptation, governments must help stimulate innovation and creativity in the diverse worlds of business and civil society. Citizen involvement is necessary, with a distribution of rights and responsibilities across the different levels of governance. A major political problem is the fact that funding for adaptation projects will inevitably compete, to some degree, with investment needed for mitigation.

What a country needs to do in order to adapt will vary greatly depending on its existing climate patterns and geographical location. The US has one of the most volatile climates in the world; extreme weather events will become even more pronounced and frequent. In countries with more temperate climates, such as in Northern Europe, climate change may initially produce some positive effects. The edge will go off winter, while the other seasons will, by definition, be warmer, although with greater day-to-day temperature fluctuations than before.

However, if global warming proceeds unchecked, the adverse effects will quickly overwhelm these temporary benefits.

In the UK, as the frequency and intensity of storms increase, large volumes of rain will fall quite suddenly, resulting in flash floods. Yet, at the same time, summer droughts will put pressure on water supplies. As temperatures rise, there will also be wider implications for health; existing ailments, such as skin cancer or cataracts, will increase, and subtropical diseases previously unknown in the country could also make an appearance.

The first premise of adaptation policy for any country is to do a detailed mapping of vulnerabilities, local and national. Adaptation could promote innovation in much the same way as mitigation strategies can do. At least some such changes could be valuable in and of themselves, whatever happens to the climate – for instance, actions to promote more efficient use of water, improved systems of weather prediction, or the introduction of crops hardy enough to thrive under adverse circumstances.[2] Adaptation brings us back to the issue of planning, since it involves thinking ahead in a systematic way. It should be understood not only as looking for vulnerabilities and blocking them off, but as investigating also what the knock-on consequences of mitigation strategies are likely to be.

In the rest of this chapter I shall look at issues of adaptation in Europe and then consider in some detail a case study from the UK – adaptation to risks of flooding. I will then switch gear to consider the formidable problems that adaptation poses in the developing world. The role of insurance is likely to be crucial in adaptation – although most current discussions seem to ignore it – and I shall consider it in some detail. The insurance industry has done a great deal of work on climate change, as well it might; yet that work does not seem, thus far, to have been integrated with the rest of the climate change literature.

Adaptation in the context of Europe

Europe is diverse climatically and geographically. Adaptation will rarely be straightforward because of the combination of that diversity with the inherent complexity of the effects of climate change. This observation is even more apposite if one accepts that 'Europe' doesn't end at the boundaries of the EU, but stretches over to central Asia. The average temperature in Europe defined in this way rose by a full 1 per cent over the course of the twentieth century, more than that for the world as a whole.[3] I shall concentrate here on effects that are either being felt now, or are almost certain to happen regardless of how far climate change is successfully controlled from here on in.

A warmer atmosphere contains a higher proportion of moisture, and means more rainfall, but new patterns of precipitation will vary from one region to another in their frequency and intensity. Rainfall and snowfall have increased in Northern Europe, while in the south droughts are becoming more common. There are several main areas of especial vulnerability as global warming takes hold. Not just Southern Europe, but the whole of the Mediterranean basin will suffer from the combined impact of high temperature increase and reduced rainfall in areas already facing water shortages.

The effects of rising temperatures are more marked at higher altitudes than lower down and will affect the Alps in particular, leading to melting of the snow and changing river flows. Coastal regions will suffer from more storms, and in some areas increased erosion. Floodplains holding large populations will be at greater risk of flash floods. In Scandinavia, much more rainfall is expected than in the past, most of which will actually take the form of rain rather than snow – major changes will occur in particular in climatic patterns in the Arctic Circle, where temperatures are rising more rapidly than anywhere else.

A very large range of activities will be influenced in some way by these changes. They will affect businesses of all shapes and descriptions. Agriculture, forestry, fishery and tourist industries will be in the front line. In parts of the subcontinent, where rainfall will decrease, water flow for thermal and nuclear power plants, as well as for hydroelectricity, might be affected.

Possible adaptation measures are many, as are the levels of governance at which they would take effect. Inexpensive measures could make a significant contribution – for example improving water conservation, making changes in crop rotation, changing the dates at which seeds are sown and introducing crops that are able to survive periods of drought. Other sorts of strategies that could be contemplated are much more demanding and expensive. New early warning systems could be introduced, perhaps on a pan-European level, such as flood and forest fire warning systems. Whole communities could be relocated away from low-lying coastal areas and flood plains. Poorer groups will be most vulnerable and systematic policy innovation will be needed to ensure their protection.

Flexibility in most cases is the key to resilience, since it isn't normally possible to predict in detail what will have to be confronted and when. Wherever possible, mitigation and adaptation should be combined. For example, insulation for buildings could be provided in such a way as to make them sturdier.

The principles of no risk without opportunity and looking for climate change positives apply. For instance, tourism in some areas may decline – rising heat, coupled to water shortages, is likely to affect summer resorts in the south. Yet as a result of the same changes other coastal areas could be opened up as tourist destinations. New economic opportunities could be created as a result of technological innovation, such as in the case of building techniques, materials and products. The need to rethink health systems could be a driving force of new forms of preventative medicine or healthcare.

The EU principle of subsidiarity – that decisions should be taken and policies applied at the lowest appropriate level, and the closest to the citizen – should come fully into play. Many policies will be best forged and delivered primarily in local communities. Local knowledge will be important in how best to proceed. There are examples already to hand. For instance, in southern Spain, farmers have got together with local municipalities to create initiatives to save water through electronic management and distribution systems for the irrigation of crops.

At the same time, coordination necessarily will have to be pursued at an EU level. Climate change will have effects everywhere and these will not follow administrative boundaries. This theorem applies to the EU itself, which must concern itself also with 'wider Europe' – the North African side of the Mediterranean, and the Caucasus region – since coordination across these areas will certainly be desirable. Some sectors within the EU are already closely integrated – such as those covering agriculture, water, biodiversity, fisheries and energy networks – and adaptation policies will have to be tailored to this fact.

The European Commission is developing a range of programmes designed to apply to widely shared problems. In 2008 it set out a framework to tackle the impact of global warming upon human and animal health. The programme will consider different aspects of the effects of climate change on mortality and morbidity, including likely changes in the means of transmission of certain infectious diseases. The Water Framework Directive provides the opportunity for an EU-wide programme for water management that could incorporate adaptation objectives.

The directive includes measures for the prediction and management of floods that apply across all member-states. There are EU Action Plans on the safeguarding and restoration of biodiversity; Forest Focus programmes, which are concerned with tree stocks and soil monitoring across the EU; a forthcoming Sustainable Consumption and Production Action Plan; an Integrated Coastal Zone Management Programme; a Disaster Risk Reduction Programme and more. The European Social Fund will be drawn upon to help raise consciousness about issues of adaptation and oversee other initiatives.

The EU is also funding adaptation policies and programmes in developing countries and has set up partnerships with many already. The Commission has published proposals aimed at sharing Europe's experience in creating adaptation measures with the developing world. It is examining the possibility of building a Global Climate Change Alliance that will promote dialogue and cooperation between the EU and developing countries.

Lots of impressive-sounding programmes: will they add up to much? Many pro-Europeans hope that such initiatives, as with tackling climate change more generally, will help provide a new beginning for the EU, which of late has been foundering. The thesis that mitigation of, and adaptation to, climate change for some purposes should be dealt with on a European rather than a purely national level is incontestable. Yet how effective the EU will be, as in climate change policy, is likely to depend on how far it can bring its member-states into line.

Floods in the UK

As a type case of issues about adaptation within countries, I shall take the example of flooding, storms and coastal erosion in Britain. Flooding in the UK involves a diversity of hazards. The value of property in the London floodplain alone is some £160 billion. The Thames Barrier has proved effective protection so far, but is coming into use with increasing frequency. Most of the times it has had to be closed have been over the past 10 years. During the winter of 2001–2 it was closed a record 24 times, as a result of historic highs in the freshwater levels of the river. Of the total stock of domestic dwellings in the UK, 10 per cent is currently at risk of flooding. In the summer of 2007, the UK experienced the most intense rainfall known since records began, giving rise to widespread floods.

The strongest storm to hit Western Europe so far occurred in Shetland in the early 1990s. It was as violent as a category five hurricane, and continued on and off for more than three weeks. Because of the normal rigours of life in Shetland, buildings there are constructed to a higher standard than in other parts of the UK. Were such a storm to occur in densely populated areas further south, there could be massive property damage and widespread loss of life.[4] Another major worry concerns dams, likely to be affected if intense downpours increase. Dam failures have become more frequent in recent years. About two million properties in the UK are potentially vulnerable to flooding alongside rivers, estuaries and coasts; and a further 80,000 from flooding resulting from heavy rains with which urban drains cannot cope.[5]

For some 40 years, from 1961 onwards, the UK insurance industry had an agreement with the government that cheap flood cover would be provided for all homes without regard to risk.[6] The result was large-scale moral hazard. State projects proceeded as though flood insurance could be taken for granted. Governments felt able to proceed with large-scale building programmes in areas of flood risk – such as the Thames Gateway – without reference to insurability.

The agreement was abandoned by the insurance industry in 2002, and a new partnership between government and the industry was introduced in its stead. Private insurers agreed to provide cover to home-owners and businesses where the annual risk of flooding is put at no more than a 100:1 chance. Beyond that level, the state has to pick up the costs. The insurance companies agreed to the plan on condition that the government reciprocated by taking on board a range of preventative measures for the future. These include, for example, new investment to counter flooding, especially in areas of high vulnerability; placing restrictions on new building in areas without adequate flood protection; and improving programmes providing information to the public about local flooding hazards.

For future building to be covered under the agreement, areas vulnerable to extreme weather and rising sea levels must be avoided, or arrangements set up to incorporate insurance costs into home and business pricing. Solar panels should be installed on the roofs and façades of all new buildings, since the relative cost is insignificant. Roofs should offer a surface that gives a good reflective signal for radar satellites, allowing the buildings to be monitored for movement. A high standard of insulation for walls and roofs is necessary. Low-energy electrical fittings must be installed, which also reduce fire risk. Buildings must be constructed of materials that are robust in the face of floods and storms.[7]

The rise in the number and intensity of flooding incidents in the early 2000s in shoreline areas led the government to alter its pre-existing coastal management policy. A key necessity was to develop a more integrated approach to planning, since, until recently, coastal management was in the hands of a heterogeneous assortment of different authorities and groups.[8] There was little coordinated thinking about what forms of coastal management would best serve current and future citizens.

A new policy was introduced which ruled that coastal protection should be guided by the relationship between risks and costs. Not everywhere can or should be protected – for instance, low-lying and sparsely populated areas will no longer necessarily be defended. The policy was introduced without consultation with local interests. Property prices immediately dropped in areas where protection was to be withdrawn. The result was huge protest in those areas. In response to these difficulties, some local authorities established funds to protect parts of the coastline under threat, even where national policy had opted for no intervention. The idea was to provide time for the local communities to develop adaptive policies of their own, or find ways of coming to terms with the fact that there would be no more state aid. Local community workshops were set up to discuss the future of the coastline.

The whole system of coastal management is in a transitional state. A number of major issues remain to be resolved.[9] Even with recent changes, planning regulations are not strong enough to stop houses and business premises from being built in areas of substantial risk of coastal erosion and flooding. Buildings are still being constructed in potentially hazardous areas. Since the state no longer recognizes an obligation to defend all people and property along the coastline, some property owners are providing their own protection, even though it might be inappropriate and out of line with wider policy – a further recipe for conflict. The situation where neither the state nor private insurance provides cover, which applies in some coastal areas, is inherently unstable.

So far, national policy is well ahead of local and regional thinking, at least on most such issues. At the same time, a new system of governance is emerging, albeit one marked by struggle and divisions of interest. Research shows a growing realization among local groups that the coastline cannot stay unchanged. It is necessary to plan ahead for a period of at least half a century, against a background of uncertainty, not just calculable risk. Neither perspective has been part of coastal policy and thinking until quite recently.

No risk without opportunity: this theorem applies to the evolution of coastal governance as in so many other areas. Rather than defending the status quo, it is far better to think creatively about what sustainable and resilient coastal communities should be like. The practical difficulties that stand in the way of such a transformation in outlook, however, are considerable. For instance, properties have to be protected from major flood risks in the here-and-now, even though the measures may not be sustainable in the longer term – such as building 'hard defences' by increasing the height of the flood walls.

Insurance, hurricanes and typhoons

Innovations in insurance are going to be of key importance as far as adaptation is concerned. These will have to span the state and the private sector, since the state's role as insurer of last resort will come under great strain. However, once more, innovations pioneered here could prove to be of wider application than only in the field of climate change.

The most difficult forms of adaptation to manage will inevitably be those related to weather changes that take a catastrophic form. When one looks on a world level, the number of 'natural' catastrophes has risen significantly over the past 30 years. Most catastrophes are weather-related, implying that there is a connection between this increase and rising world temperatures. One way of indexing the increase is via levels of insurance claims.[10] Such analysis suggests that a sharp increase in the number of natural catastrophes has taken place over the past 10 years in particular. Since 1970, of the largest catastrophes, 34 occurred between 1988 and 2006. For understandable reasons, the insurance industry has been very active in promoting research into such trends.

In one study, some 16,000 natural catastrophes over the period from 1980 to 2005 were analysed.[11] They were grouped into six categories, depending upon the degree of insurance losses they led to. The categories were:

1 Small losses (up to $10 million).
2 Medium-sized losses ($10–$60 million).
3 Medium-sized to serious losses ($60–$200 million).
4 Serious losses ($200–$500 million).
5 Devastating losses ($500 million–$1 billion).
6 Extreme losses (more than $1 billion).

The smaller categories were fairly stable over the dates in question, but there was a steep rise in each of the three larger ones. The research showed that fully 85 per cent of claims in all categories were for weather-related natural catastrophes.

The insurance claims made in any specific year are mainly determined by the number of catastrophes that occur – those in categories 5 and 6. The record for claims thus far is 2005, the year in which three damaging hurricanes occurred: Katrina, Wilma and Rita. In terms of insurance claims, Katrina produced the highest level ever, while the others were the sixth and seventh highest recorded. Over the period 1970–88, total damage amounted to more than $10 billion in just one year. Since 1989, however, totals of more than $15 billion have been submitted in 10 separate years.

Insurance claims are skewed towards the richer countries, since the insurance industry there is more developed and hence has more liabilities. Looked at in terms of death rates, the highest levels of catastrophic damage occur in Asia, but not because of the intrinsic frequency of natural disasters; rather, because that continent has the highest number of large population centres. Between 1980 and 2005, some 800,000 people died in Asian countries as a result of such disasters, 90 per cent of them as a result of category 5 and 6 events. North America and Europe experienced more or less the same proportion of natural disasters, but the amount of damage suffered was three times as great in the former as in the latter.

The above studies do not by any means cover all insurance claims and losses. They do not include, for example, the consequences for liability insurance and life insurance; or damage to roads, railways and other forms of public infrastructure, which are hardly ever insured. Real losses more generally may be many times higher than insured losses. The insured losses in hurricane Katrina amounted to about $49 billion, compared to estimated total losses of $144 billion. The difference in the less developed parts of the world is greater, since insurance cover is much less advanced. In the two major cases of flooding that happened in China in the 1990s, the cost of the damage, in one case, was 30 times higher than the sum covered by insurance and, in the other, nearly 50 times higher.

Weather-related risks create enormous problems both for private insurers and for the state. Progress with adaptation will depend a great deal on how far both parties can come up with feasible new policies. It is crucial that the insurance industry pioneers new ways of dealing with the rising scale and frequency of catastrophic risks, since otherwise the burden on government will be insupportable. The option that private insurers have of simply pulling back from insuring certain hazards is not available to governments, which will have to pick up the pieces. It is therefore in the interests of both parties to cooperate.

Risks associated with climate change, as I have often stressed in this book, shade so far over into uncertainty that they often cannot be calculated with any precision. A single episode can cause large-scale damage, but the extent of likely damage is not readily predictable, since so much depends upon context. The damage done by a storm or hurricane, for example, depends vitally upon the path it takes, not only on its strength. It is hard to even up premiums over a period of time, since the level of damage varies greatly from year to year.

The capital requirements are large, since, in a year of high losses, the pay-out all has to come in or close to that period. This fact means that the insurer must constantly have liquid capital to hand. The amount of money needed to cover the costs of a catastrophe can be as high as 100 times the premium income in the year in which it takes place. The insurer therefore has to look for a way of spreading risk through reinsurance – against a backdrop of the probability that natural catastrophe risks will lead to much greater damage in the future. Moreover, the reinsurers face much the same risks as the original insurers, because of the high element of uncertainty.

New thinking will be needed to push back the boundaries of insurability. Until recently, catastrophic insurance was based upon somewhat traditional models of risk management. That is to say, it depended upon calculations derived from previous catastrophic events. Such a practice was no longer possible after hurricane Andrew, the predecessor to Katrina, which caused a level of damage greater than had previously been thought conceivable.

Work has begun on the construction of sophisticated catastrophe models, with the objective of reducing areas of uncertainty. These make use of some of the same techniques of computer modelling involved in attempts to predict the likely progress of climate change. For a hurricane of a given strength, 1,000 or more different potential paths through a specific area can be mapped. The point is to make the models sufficiently detailed to distinguish probabilities and hence, again, to be able to calculate premiums.

Catastrophe bonds have also been introduced to spread risk across capital markets. They are complex financial instruments, which aim at neutralizing risk for the original insurer, but also contain safeguards for those who purchase them. Allianz issued a pioneering catastrophe bond in 2007, which provided cover against large-scale losses occurring from earthquakes in Canada and the US (although excluding California) and river flooding in Britain.

Given that the level and extent of catastrophes will continue to mount, perhaps sharply, it is a matter of urgency to re-examine the relative roles of private insurers and the state. The cost to the US federal government of hurricane Katrina alone was in the order of $100 billion, given as direct assistance and as tax benefits. Even then, it covered no more than part of the losses incurred, especially if one includes secondary economic effects (forgone employment, for example). There is also an issue of moral hazard, when the state is known to be the insurer of last resort. Those who are vulnerable to risk have less of an incentive to deal with it themselves in advance, since they (believe they can) fall back on the state when necessary. Especial care will have to be taken to ensure that a situation does not emerge in which only the affluent can get adequate insurance cover.

The state should aim to create financial and fiscal conditions in which disaster and catastrophe cover can be expanded under the aegis of the insurance industry. It will not lose its role as insurer of last resort, but that role can be brought more within the bounds of realism. Ideally, insurance provided by the state should only kick in above a certain level, set according to the bounds of coverage by private insurance. The industry must not retreat in the face of an increasing preponderance of disasters and catastrophes, but must continue to explore ways of expanding insurability.

Adaptation: the developing world

Hurricane Jeanne made many people in the US homeless when it struck in 2004. However, it caused 1,500 deaths when it hit Haiti a short while earlier. During the hurricane, heavy rain fell on the island non-stop for 30 hours. Haiti is 98 per cent deforested, the result of the fact that the poor on the island harvest the trees for charcoal. As a consequence, the rain cascaded down the hillsides, inundating the capital city and other areas. Many survivors became homeless, rice and fruit harvests were obliterated and diseases spread.

The Dominican Republic shares half the island with Haiti. It is not as poor and much of the rainforest remains intact. Only 25 people died there as a result of the hurricane. An aid agency funded by the US had planted numerous trees in Haiti over a period of some two decades in order to replenish that which had been lost. Yet they were almost all cut down, mostly by people living in extreme poverty, for whom making charcoal was their only source of livelihood.

J. Timmons Roberts and Bradley Parks carried out research into a large number of weather-related disasters in poor countries over the period between 1980 and 1992.[12] They made use of the Emergency Events Database, developed by the US Geological Survey. This survey contains data on 12,800 disasters happening over that period. They included disasters coming from many sources, but the researchers were able to identify those where the major cause was weather events, which made up about half the total. They judged the evidence sound and detailed enough to make effective comparisons in some 4,000 of these cases.

The weather events included cyclones, droughts, floods, heat waves, hurricanes, tidal waves, tornadoes, tropical storms, typhoons, winter storms, hailstorms, dust storms, rainstorms, thunderstorms and waves of cold weather – the list itself is a potent reminder of the power that climatic fluctuations have over people's lives. Roberts and Parks made tallies of the numbers of people killed, rendered homeless or otherwise seriously affected by the weather events. A single total was created for each nation covered, providing an indicator for the whole period. The aim was to help understand why some countries and regions suffer more profoundly and consistently as a result of extreme weather events than others do. Put the other way around, they studied why some seemed more resilient than others.

They found an overall connection between the level of income of a country and its capacity to withstand weather-related shocks. The most damaging human disaster of the closing decades of the twentieth century was the result of the drought in East Africa in 1984. It was concentrated in three particularly impoverished countries: Ethiopia, Sudan and Chad. About 500,000 people died, while far more suffered from malnutrition and lost their homes. The totals of those made homeless as a result of weather-related disasters over the period make sobering reading, as the authors observe. They include 62 million in Bangladesh and 50 million in China. More than 25 million people became homeless in Laos, India, Sri Lanka, Vietnam, the Philippines and Pakistan combined.

Comparison between the severity of the weather events and their consequences showed clearly that vulnerability correlates closely with economic and political weakness, with a steep rise for the very poorest countries – those comprising the 'bottom billion' in terms of population numbers (see below, pp. 212–16). Ineffective and corrupt government, dependence on low-value tropical crops, the existence of sprawling shanty towns and poor communications and transport links all play a part. It isn't poverty as such that heightens vulnerability. Where countries remain very poor, but have overcome some of these problems, their resilience in the face of disasters is much greater.

The world has moved on from the time at which many leaders and citizens in the South believed that talk of climate change was a tactic used by the rich countries to stop others from developing. Such an attitude has been replaced by a more sober realization of just how threatened by the effects of global warming the less developed countries are. There is, in principle, the possibility of closer collaboration between North and South, not only in terms of contraction and convergence, but especially as concerns adaptation.

Aid and financial assistance from the rich to the poorer nations must focus much more on adaptation than has been the case up to now. At the moment, the resources needed to help the developing countries even begin to assess their vulnerabilities is lacking. The Adaptation Fund, mentioned earlier, is only just getting under way. Finance set aside for the 48 least developed countries to prepare national adaptation plans consists of about $33 million, around two-thirds of which is provided by the industrial countries. Yet how the money should be distributed remains the subject of strident debate, with the consequence that the money has not actually been forthcoming. Proper and detailed vulnerability assessments should be the first line of defence in adaptation, since practical action is hardly feasible if the extent and location of risks are not known.

Many of the mechanisms or changes needed for the developing countries to become richer are also important for adaptation to climate change. Population growth is a major influence on both, suggesting the vital importance of a renewed drive on the part of international agencies to help bring that rate down. The main means of doing so is well established – empowering women and assisting their incorporation into the labour force. Thus far, there has been little progress in linking adaptation to existing poverty-alleviation programmes. Some of the small island states in the Caribbean seem to have been the first to make some advances.

A commodity support fund that would protect cash-crop economies from the buffetings of price fluctuations in the marketplace would help promote resilience. It is a long way from local flooding and coastal erosion in Britain to the much larger disasters found elsewhere. Yet common strategies can be forged. For instance, partnerships instituted between government and business, and government and citizens' groups, in order to tackle such problems are also relevant for poorer countries.

Serious attention should be given to extending the role of insurance in the vulnerable countries of the world. Insurance is far less extensive in the deprived countries than in the richer ones, for obvious reasons, but the potential importance of insurance is huge. For instance, climatic variations are a major threat to subsistence farmers in large areas of Africa; those variations will deepen with the progress of global warming. Two new approaches have been introduced in recent years to provide assistance to the farmers and prevent crop failure.[13] One is the use of satellite and computer-based models to provide seasonal precipitation forecasts, which can help to reduce risk. Seed varieties can be adjusted, for example, to choose those most suitable for expected rainfall conditions. The other is the use of new mechanisms of insurance cover. Thus, index-based weather insurance can be developed and linked to micro-credit for agricultural inputs.

These programmes have so far remained separate from one another, but it may be possible to integrate them. A pilot insurance scheme has been introduced for smallholder farmers in Malawi. Those who tailor their crops to projected rainfall conditions will be able to get insurance coverage that should allow them greatly to expand the area of land they will sow for crops, as well as the yield they will achieve.

Even in the most deprived conditions, poor people are not normally without resources – they have assets and capabilities that can help develop resilience. Adaptation policies should as far as possible focus on strengthening that resilience. For instance, traditional systems of adapting to climate variability include switching crops, social networks of support and assistance or collective savings mechanisms. All can in principle be bolstered by high-tech means of providing information or creating more extensive support networks.

Farmers in the high Andes of Peru and Bolivia observe the Pleiades star constellations so as to get advance warning of possible weather conditions several months into the future. They look at the intensity of the brightest star in the cluster, its size, the date of its first appearance and its position. If the star appears clear in the sky just before dawn, abundant rain is indicated and a rich potato crop predicted. Planting processes are modified accordingly. Scientists have confirmed that the level of visibility of the cluster is related to the presence or otherwise of wispy cirrus clouds high in the sky; and that these are also associated with the warm phase of El Niño. The farmers have, in effect, been monitoring the phases of El Niño for centuries; but they could get a lot of further help from modern methods of weather prediction.

As the examples of disasters mentioned earlier show, Bangladesh is one of the countries most exposed to the effects of climate change, because of its geographical location. The country is low-lying and will be one of the first to suffer from rises in sea levels. If those levels rise by 45 centimetres, then 10 per cent of the country will be under water. Even with its pre-established climate, the country gets too much rainfall in the monsoon season, causing frequent floods, while during other parts of the year it is prone to drought.

The Bangladeshis are not just sitting around waiting for the rich countries to invest and help them in preventative adaptation – although this surely will be necessary. Meanwhile, the country has set up a National Adaptation Programme of Action, involving working groups from each of the main producing sectors.[14] It has developed detailed assessments of vulnerability and suggested a range of action programmes, although the implementation of some of these will have to depend upon foreign aid programmes to be forthcoming.

Even in the very poorest areas, Bangladeshis are building dykes and embankments, changing their agricultural practices and sharing their knowledge with other poor countries in Asia and Africa. Full flood protection is currently widely practised in Bangladesh, but controlled flooding looks a necessary strategy for the future. An early warning system for cyclonic disasters already exists and could be further extended. Satellite and information technology allow for the continuous monitoring of the formation of cyclones in the Bay of Bengal.

Major efforts are under way to increase the resilience of local communities in areas under particular threat, drawing upon local expertise and involvement. One study, for example, identified 600 vulnerable households, made up of poor farmers, fishermen, day labourers and single parent households. Male- and female-headed groups developed ideas and plans for how to diversify their means of livelihood, set up training groups on the likely effects of climate change and introduce new production processes. The work produced a whole series of novel proposals, some of which were immediately implemented, with considerable success.

Floating gardens – an idea now copied internationally – were first introduced in Bangladesh. A floating garden uses aquatic weeds as a base on which crops can be grown. It can be introduced where land is otherwise unavailable to expand the productive capacities of local villages and towns. Floating gardens are inexpensive to construct and can be established on a permanent basis.

In closing the gap between the attempts of the developed nations to limit climate change and those of the developing ones, assessments of vulnerability are likely to be very important. The vulnerability of the richer countries includes the knock-on effects of climate change-induced disasters in poorer states, which could greatly exacerbate the tensions already visible in world society. In chapter 9 I will consider such dangers in some detail.

8

INTERNATIONAL NEGOTIATIONS, THE EU AND CARBON MARKETS

In his State of the Union speech in 2006, President George W. Bush accepted that the US 'is addicted to oil'. He came late to a view that has now been extensively documented. As discussed earlier, the American way of life is wedded to motor transport. The automobile in the US, it has been said, 'is not just a technology or mode of transportation; it is a fundamental determinant of the entire economy'.[1] Its influence has grown over the years, even if we look only at relatively recent history. In 1950 the transportation sector (including airlines) accounted for 54 per cent of total US oil consumption. The figure was 60 per cent by 1980, and is today up to 70 per cent. Australia and Canada also have very high emissions per person, and for much the same reasons. Petrol and diesel consumption in these countries per head is some two and a half times greater than in Britain, France or Germany, and three times higher than in Japan.

These differences are not just because of miles travelled. Average energy consumption per mile in these countries is twice as high as in the European nations. In the light of such figures, it isn't surprising to see that the US accounts for 44 per cent of the greenhouse gas emissions from the industrial (OECD) countries as a whole. If the states of the US were separate countries, 25 would be in the top 60 in terms of emissions. Texas emits more greenhouse gases than France, having only just over a third of its population.[2]

The US is not, however, top of the list in terms of emissions per head. The small gulf states of Qatar, the United Arab Emirates, Kuwait, together with Brunei, are out in front, followed by Australia and Canada; the US is in seventh position. The carbon emissions per head of the latter three countries in 2007 were 26 tonnes of CO_2 for Australia, 25 for Canada and 23 in the case of the US. America's rate is vastly more consequential, of course, given its size. The average emissions of the EU15 countries are only about half that of the US. The German figure in 2007 was 12, that of the UK was 11 and that of France was 9. The trend figure is quite different. In the case of the US, the figure is rising, while in the EU the average has declined.

The large developing countries

The level of emissions from the developing countries, measured per head of population, is much lower than in the case of the rich ones. Many produce only minimal emissions per member of the population. If measured cumulatively (emissions per head since the onset of industrialization in the early nineteenth century) the proportion drops even further. For a few developing countries, the picture changes if emissions from deforestation – which often do not feature in the orthodox statistics – are included. Indonesia, to take the most prominent example, moves up to sixth in the world in terms of per capita emissions.

However, the overall pattern is shifting dramatically. China, India and Brazil are all big countries, both in terms of territory and population. As they grow economically, their absolute levels of emissions are shooting up, above all, those of China. Indeed, China has now replaced the US as the world's largest polluter, although its emissions per head are only about one-fifth of those of America. Since 1990, China's emissions have gone up by a staggering 73 per cent, reflecting not only the fact that it has a very high level of economic growth, but also its heavy

> 0.5 % Decrease per year   > 0.5 % Increase per year   Change rate below 0.5 % per year

Figure 8.1 Net change in forest area, 2000–5

Source: IPCC 2007

dependence on coal for energy. One of the most oft-quoted statistics in debates about climate change is that the Chinese are building one new coal-fired power station every week; the latest figures show that the figure is now closer to two.

Current developments in China reflect policies initiated under Mao in the 1950s. On several occasions, Mao faced the threat of international sanctions against his regime, and as a consequence he determined to make China as self-sufficient as possible. In the 1950s he took the decision that China's energy should be supplied through internal resources – coal and, to a much lesser degree, oil. A large oil field was discovered in the barren north-east part of the country, at Daqing, and smaller discoveries were made elsewhere. The Daqing field peaked some while ago, and production has been declining since 1997. Of the other largest oil-fields in the country, 10 have also peaked and production has levelled off, leaving coal as the only option.

As in the case of other socialist economies, heavy industry was seen as the key to prosperity. The giant state-controlled firms established at that point were inefficient and consumed enormous amounts of energy in relation to output. Subsequent Chinese economic growth was propelled not by these companies, but by much smaller manufacturing plants. As a consequence, although emissions grew, the level of energy efficiency in the Chinese economy in fact became higher. This process, however, later went into reverse again, because of a renewed period of investment in heavy industry. The boom, with its unfortunate environmental consequences, is not the result of market advantage. It comes from the fact that state-owned banks, flush with capital from China's overall economic success, have begun lending extensively, at cheap rates, to the state-owned manufacturers (this process began to stagnate in late 2008, as credit around the world became scarce).[3]

India was influenced by the central planning model until the economic reforms of the 1990s. Until that point, and largely for that reason, its rate of economic growth was slow. In 1994, Indian CO_2 emissions amounted to 1.2 tonnes per head of population. The overall figure for the country made up 3 per cent of total global emissions at that date. After several years of high growth in the economy, that figure rose to just under 3.5 tonnes per person by 2006, and its contribution to total emissions rose by 50 per cent compared to 10 years earlier.

Brazil is historically a more developed country than either China or India. The country's present-day figure for emissions, at 6.2 tonnes per head, however, is less than it otherwise would be because of its response to the oil crisis of the 1970. Besides developing the widespread use of biofuels, at that time Brazil initiated a range of hydroelectric programmes to cut down on its oil dependence. The country is unusual among developing nations for having been an environmental pioneer – fully 40 per cent of its energy comes from renewables, which is, by quite a margin, the highest proportion of any country in the world. However, the doubts surrounding the use of biofuels, and the fact that some parts of the country's forests have been cut down to make way for their production, limit their impact as far as climate change is concerned. Brazil is well aware of its acute vulnerability to the consequences of climate change. Successive governments have struggled to contain deforestation. If this factor is added in to the equation, then Brazil's per capita emissions figure rises steeply, to 12.3 tonnes per head.

'Why should we do anything – it's your problem!' Until recently, this was the attitude of the leaders of the developing countries in relation to the developed ones, with the exception of Brazil and a few others, notably Costa Rica. The industrial countries have created the dangers, the leaders of the developing world tend to say; let them be responsible for reducing them – especially where measures taken might inhibit economic growth.

Rio, Kyoto and after

The history of international negotiations aimed at mitigating climate change goes back some 15 years. From small beginnings, the enterprise has mushroomed fast. The IPCC itself grew out of a previous environmental endeavour, the Montreal Protocol, initiated by the UN in 1987, which was concerned with eliminating the industrial chemicals that produced the hole in the ozone layer over the Antarctic. The initiative, mainly preoccupied with ensuring that the harmful chemicals, chlorofluorocarbons (or CFCs), were replaced by substitutes, seems to have been successful in beginning to reverse the harm done.

The IPCC's first assessment of where the world stands in relation to climate change was offered in 1990, as part of the run-up to the Rio Earth Summit which followed two years later. The Summit introduced the UN Framework Convention on climate change, which was signed by 166 nations at that point (today there are 188 signatories). The US and some other countries were strongly opposed to binding emissions targets, as a result of which no such targets were included. All participating nations agreed to calculate their emissions and report the levels annually. It was accepted that there should be 'common but differentiated responsibilities' among nations for stabilizing climate change. All should at some point accept responsibility, but the developed countries have the obligation to act first.

In spite of some foot-dragging by the US, there was widespread acceptance that mandatory cuts would be necessary for progress to be made. At meetings in 1995 it was agreed that the industrial countries would set themselves targets for emissions reductions. The then US president, Bill Clinton, eventually came round to accepting this view after some initial hesitancy. However, the US Congress voted unanimously against any agreement that didn't include cuts for the developing societies.

In 1997, at Kyoto in Japan, after tortuous negotiations, an agreement was drawn up by which the developed countries would cut their emissions by an average of 5.2 per cent over 1990 levels by the period 2008–12. The Kyoto Protocol was set up in such a way that it could come into force without complete consensus. The rule set up for the Protocol to become part of international law was that 55 of the more developed countries, accounting for at least 55 per cent of total emissions from the industrial states, would have to sign up. Russia, which accounted for 17 per cent of 1990 emissions, initially stated its opposition to Kyoto, but eventually ratified towards the end of 2004. The final agreement meant that Kyoto received support from countries that were, between them, producing 61 per cent of world emissions.

The Bush administration, inclined towards climate change scepticism anyway, and influenced strongly by industrial lobbies, was worried that China might achieve a competitive advantage over the US, given that the developing countries were not required to make any cuts. Bush believed that, if the US were to take more steps to combat global warming, even in the context of the Kyoto agreements with other nations going along, the country might damage its international competitiveness. As the world's dominant economy, the cost of taking steps to cope with climate change – since the US would have had to agree to substantial emissions reductions – might have affected the wider world economy too. In many people's eyes, Bush was one of the villains of the climate change piece, but his father, George Bush senior, had gone even further than his son, declaring at the 1992 Rio Earth Summit that 'the American way of life is not negotiable'.[4]

Apart from the US and Australia, all the other industrial countries, and a large majority of countries in the rest of the world, put their names to Kyoto.

It was the Bush administration that pressurized Russia not to participate. One of President Putin's economic advisers, Andrei Illarionov, claimed that Kyoto would destroy the world economy 'like an international Auschwitz'.[5] However, Russia at that point wanted EU support for its bid to join the World Trade Organization; while the EU, the leading force in climate change negotiations, needed Russian participation in Kyoto to salvage the whole thing. So in effect a bargain was struck.

An additional factor was that by the early 2000s Russian emissions were much lower than they had been in 1990, because of the contraction of the economy and the collapse of some of the large state-owned industrial companies. The EU countries realized that this situation could help with the carbon trading scheme that had just been established. Russia's emission 'reductions' would be available to help ease EU member-states' problems with meeting their own emissions targets. An unfortunate outcome of the whole episode was that Russia was legitimated to carry on squandering energy domestically without thought to environmental damage.

The result of compromise, the targets agreed at Kyoto bear little relationship to what is required to make a serious impact upon global warming. They are too low and they contain all kinds of anomalies. Take the case of Australia, which came out of the negotiations with the agreement that its emissions could actually be increased rather than cut. Like the Americans, the Australians initially wanted only voluntary reductions. They then argued that Australia is a special case, because it is a net energy producer with a very large transport-dependent sector. They also pointed to reductions in deforestation that had been made before 1990. Given the need to persuade Australia to sign, the country got what it was asking for (although it later opted out anyway, signing up only in 2008 after a change of government).

Because the Kyoto agreements were not adopted until 2005, most countries were slow in making any progress at all towards reaching even the modest targets that had been set. In practice so far, little has been achieved. The EU has been by far the most forceful advocate of proposals to limit emissions, but even its record is wanting. A few member-states are on track to meet their targets, but most are struggling. Emissions in Spain have gone up by over 30 per cent since 1990. In the US, emissions grew by 13 per cent during that period, overwhelming whatever progress the EU countries might make by 2008–12. And of course Kyoto does not include the developing countries at all – even though these are, as explained, now major contributors to world emissions in absolute terms.

The Kyoto agreements have been widely dismissed – with a goodly dose of irony – as 'hot air'. Apologists for them offer several arguments in their favour by way of riposte. It has been said, for instance, that they are, above all, a learning process. In the post-2012 period, the world can come up with more universal and rigorous formulae – negotiations for a post-Kyoto regime are already under way; they began in Bali in 2007. The principle of 'common but differentiated responsibility', it is argued, provides a way forward for the world community.

Contraction and convergence puts flesh on this idea. A range of schemes has been put forward to develop the notion. The Climate Action Network, for example, has proposed a three-track system. The developed countries would have emissions reduction targets, Kyoto-style. In the case of the developing world, targets would be set not in terms of emissions, but in terms of carbon intensity. Carbon intensity refers to the proportion of fossil fuel involved in producing a given economic output. The poorest countries would be concerned only with adaptation, and would receive financial assistance so to do.[6]

The Kyoto Protocol also initiated the Clean Development Mechanism (CDM). The CDM allows industrial countries to get credits to put towards their Kyoto targets by funding clean energy projects in developing states. The scheme took off slowly, since few countries were willing to act until Kyoto had finally been ratified. Some 700 projects had been approved by the middle of 2007, most of them located in the four biggest developing countries: China, India, Brazil and South Africa.[7] The CDM is not quite the win–win framework it seems, since it allows developed countries to relax their own emissions reduction efforts. An important influence upon the emergence of the CDM was what has been described as 'Europe's desperation'.[8] On current trajectories, the EU is unlikely to reach its overall Kyoto target, an outcome that would seriously threaten the EU's claim to be far ahead of the rest of the pack. The CDM is one means of helping to save face and hence investors queued up to develop projects, since they were almost certain to meet with approval.

It is uncertain how far the CDM has actually helped to introduce renewable energy projects into the developing countries. Marginal projects dominate, such as the containment of industrial gases by bolting on filters to already existing pipes. It has been said that perhaps half the reductions claimed are the result of 'accounting tricks' and are empty of content. In one case, the projects in a specific country were all concerned with emissions of HFC-23, a by-product of the manufacture of refrigerants. The total cost of the parts amounted to $70 million, while the value of the subsidy provided through the CDM was some $1 billion. Emissions reductions were achieved, but in a cumbersome and highly inefficient way, with much of the money being swallowed up as a result of corrupt practices.[9]

Not much has been done to focus the CDM more effectively, mainly because of the political stakes involved. Environmentalists are reluctant to criticize the only means that exists for directly helping the developing countries. As just pointed out, the EU needs the credit mechanism to help meet its targets. The developing countries, or some of them,

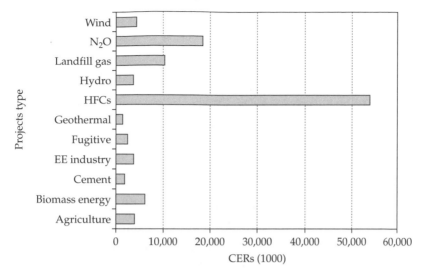

Figure 8.2 Currently registered Kyoto projects by type

Source: 'Europe's Dirty Secret: Why the EU Emissions Trading Scheme Isn't Working', *Open Europe*, August 2007, p. 29, graph 5.

especially China, the leading recipient, do get investment. A report from the World Bank estimates that the CDM has stimulated investments of $59 billion since it was first established. However, the same report states that the value of such investments will halve in 2009 and reach almost zero by 2010; the reason is the looming expiry of the Kyoto Protocol.[10]

Kyoto will have to be replaced by 2012, and the further round of meetings held at Bali in 2007 sought to get the ball rolling. Some 12,000 delegates attended. Following arduous negotiations, the President of the conference, Rachmat Witoelar, announced: 'We have finally achieved the breakthrough the world has been waiting for: the Bali roadmap!'[11] The roadmap is a new negotiation process to replace Kyoto, beginning with more meetings in Poznan, held in December 2008, and Copenhagen.

However, probably the best one can say about Bali is that the negotiations did not collapse. The roadmap is little more than a vague sketch. The agreements do not contain a single specific commitment. They offer no recognition of the problems inherent in the Kyoto framework, or any acknowledgement of the minimal impact it has had on world emissions. As one commentator put it: 'If this is success, give me failure.'[12] He has a point. International negotiations of this sort do have clear positives. They mark the recognition of common dangers and could be said to symbolize the world community coming together. Perhaps more concrete measures can be agreed in due course. However, the negatives are large. The splits between key players, the divergent interests and perceptions that exist between nations and blocs of nations, are all still there. Even if common and specific commitments could be forged, there are no effective mechanisms of enforcement.

The great danger of the Kyoto-style approach to climate change is that an elaborate, detailed and nuanced architecture may be created, but no buildings actually get constructed. David Victor has convincingly argued that the four basic elements of Kyoto (and the 'roadmap') almost ensure just such an outcome. These elements are universal participation, binding emissions targets, integrated emissions trading and compensation to poorer countries to get their cooperation.[13]

Binding targets are only ever likely to work at a national or local level, with the partial exceptional case of the European Union. Such targets function best where a clear and known mechanism exists for reaching the desired outcome – as in the case, for example, of the agreements on halting the depletion of the ozone layer. In the instance of climate change, there are many factors that can influence the level of emissions; there are significant unknowns as far as the processes needed to reach the targets are concerned (for example, technological change – where it will happen and how fast – is essentially unpredictable); and even governments have only limited control over those processes. These observations suggest that it will not be through Kyoto-style agreements that most progress will be made. Moreover, energy security does not figure at all in those agreements.

The role of the EU

The European Union first set out an integrated strategy for dealing with climate change issues at summit meetings in

Cardiff and Vienna in 1998. The objective at that time was to discuss common modes of response on the part of the member-states and to assist them in meeting Kyoto targets. Climate change became one of the priorities in the 6th Framework Programme for Research, lasting from 2002 to 2006. The EU from the beginning recognized its obligations to help poorer countries, not just to concentrate upon its component nations. It has also emphasized that climate change policy must march in tandem with that concerning energy.

In January 2007 the European Commission announced an upgraded strategy to combat global warming, endorsing its long-standing policy that world temperature increase should be limited to 2 per cent over pre-industrial levels. The core proposal is that the developed countries should reduce their emissions of greenhouse gases by an average of 30 per cent below 1990 levels by 2020. The EU will take the lead by cutting emissions by 20 per cent. That cut will rise to 30 per cent if and when the other industrial countries come on board. Renewable energy will form 20 per cent of the energy mix by then, with (controversially) a binding minimum 10 per cent use of bio-fuels in motor transport. Given that renewables currently account for only 8.5 per cent of EU energy consumption, the goal is an extremely ambitious one.

For the next 10 years, the developing countries, the EU proposes, should make every effort to lower their emissions and should start to reduce them in absolute terms from 2020/5. As envisaged in the Bali 'roadmap', action must be taken urgently in the here and now against deforestation. The European Emissions Trading Scheme (ETS), on which more below, is envisaged as a crucial means of allowing the EU countries to meet their commitments – the Commission anticipates that means may be found to link different trading schemes into a single worldwide one.

In early 2008 the Commission put forward a new directive, setting out a framework for the EU in terms of the 2020 targets that member-states will be expected to achieve. The directive recognizes that they start from different positions as far as renewable energy is concerned. Moreover, some have made much greater efforts than others in the past to get their emissions down. Differences in GDP and GDP growth are also taken into account. Member-states that have a relatively low GDP and need high economic growth will be able to increase their greenhouse gas emissions compared to the baseline year of 2005.

Under the plans, Denmark, Ireland and Luxembourg will be required to achieve a 20 per cent reduction in emissions over a 1990 deadline by 2020, Britain and Sweden 16 per cent, Germany and France 14 per cent. Bulgaria can increase its emissions by 20 per cent and Romania by 19 per cent. The new plan is estimated to cost on average no more than .05 per cent of GDP, although one might legitimately doubt whether the cost can be calculated at this point, given the complexity of the factors involved. In principle, it should deliver the overall target of a 20 per cent reduction in emissions over 1990 levels with quite a bit to spare.

Only the 10 per cent target for the use of biofuels is a constant across the EU. However, it is very unlikely to stay intact in the light of the environmental problems caused by most biofuels at the moment, above all the loss of agricultural land. The Commission recognizes the criticisms that have been made of biofuels, but argues that it is possible to produce them without incurring environmental damage, and, indeed, says that stringent criteria will be deployed to ensure that this is so. Most, however, will have to be imported.

Several leading scientists, as well as numerous NGOs, have expressed their doubts about biofuels and have criticized the EU's plan. They say it is a mistake to introduce quotas for biofuels before their effects have been fully assessed. The chief scientific adviser to the British government, John Beddington, has commented that rising demand for biofuels in the US has delivered a 'major shock' to world agriculture, producing elevated world food prices. Moreover, if biofuel production were to come at the expense of further deforestation, the outcome would be 'profoundly stupid'.[14]

Some major countries, including France and Germany, initially expressed concern over their quotas. Nicolas Sarkozy, the French President, at one point argued that France should not be subject to emissions targets at all because the widespread use of nuclear power has already lowered its emissions levels. Business leaders from various states have been critical of the

EU acting on its own in relation to climate change. Higher energy costs, they say, will make European companies less competitive in the wider world, and may lead them to decamp elsewhere. The Germans have been especially worried about the competitiveness of their car, chemicals and steel industries. One in every seven jobs in Germany depends in some way upon the car industry.

The Commission President, José Manuel Barroso, has admitted the validity of these concerns. 'We all know', he stated, 'that there are sectors where the cost of cutting emissions could have a real impact on their competitiveness against companies in countries that do nothing.'[15] There is no point in Europe setting up demanding regulations if the result is simply that production shifts to countries where there is an emissions free-for-all. International agreements, Barroso argued, would be one way to handle the difficulty, but if these cannot be reached, then the EU should look at compensation for the energy industries. Others have suggested a mechanism such as a carbon tax on imports. Nevertheless, in the current proposals such ideas have been left on hold.

As the crisis in financial markets started to bite, a rebellious group of member-states in October 2008 pressed for a deferment of the date at which the EU's plans for emissions targets were supposed to be accepted as binding. Eight countries led the insurrection, including Italy and a cluster of ex-East European nations. The Italian Prime Minister, Silvio Berlusconi, commented that the targets would devastate Italian industry. Berlusconi and his Polish counterpart, Donald Tusk, both used the argument that they didn't have to stick to a deal that had been struck while they were not in office. Besides Italy and Poland, the governments of Bulgaria, Hungary, Latvia, Lithuania, Romania and Slovakia all said they would resist attempts to railroad the targets through.

At the point at which agreement needed to be reached, late in 2008, France held the presidency of the European Council. Reversing his previous stance, Sarkozy pulled out all the stops to gain a consensus, and was successful. A summit of European leaders held in September 2008 agreed to the Commission's plan. A substantial price was paid, however. The EU is pinning much of its hopes for reaching its targets on its emissions trading schemes, discussed below. To gain an agreement, the terms of the scheme were weakened. Most companies in the processing industries, such as steel and cement, will be exempt from paying for carbon permits, while coal-fired power stations were allocated large discounts on the price of carbon.

The EU has instituted a Strategic Energy Review that has important implications for its climate change programme. National Energy Efficiency Action Plans (NEEAPs) for each member-state are a major part of the strategy to reach the emissions reduction targets. The Energy Savings Directive requires member-states to reduce energy end-use by 9 per cent by 2016. In the 17 NEEAPs submitted to the Commission by late 2007, many states say they will adopt higher targets than the 9 per cent one.

The public sector figures large in most of these plans, as the section of the economy over which governments have the most direct leverage. Ireland has adopted a target of a 33 per cent reduction in public sector energy use by 2020, with Germany aiming almost as high. The Irish Power of One campaign is very comprehensive, promoting best practices in different spheres through a targeted multi-media campaign. Malta is appointing Green Leaders in each ministry to champion energy efficiency and the use of renewables. In the UK, all new homes built with government funding will have to comply with the Code for Sustainable Homes. Such dwellings will have an energy saving of 26 per cent compared to the previous building code.

Will the EU be able to meet the demanding aims it has set for itself? There is plenty of room for doubt. The fate of the Lisbon Agenda, set up in 2000 to improve the EU's economic competitiveness, is a salutary one so far as climate change policies are concerned. The Lisbon Agenda was about competitiveness. It was aimed at creating a common framework of labour market reform, welfare reform and investment in IT across the EU. Yet the EU lacks the capacity to intervene in these issues directly, since the member-states retain power over the most important areas involved, such as taxation, labour market and welfare policy. The best it has been able to come up with is the 'open method of coordination', which essentially uses peer pressure to drive the non-performing countries along.

The Lisbon agenda has only had limited success and the EU lags well behind schedule. If the experience has taught us anything, one commentator observes, 'it is the real and true limitations of academic reports, high-level conferences and expert testimony to drive forward social and economic change'.[16] In other words, too much talk, too little action. We are driven back to one of the main themes I accentuate throughout this book. The common commitments set up by the EU might help secure effective action within its member-nations, but it will be national policy-making which will in the end determine how much progress really is made.

Carbon markets

The case for carbon markets was established at Kyoto, but, like all other aspects of climate change policy, was and is heavily influenced by political considerations. The European Commission originally wanted to impose an EU-wide carbon tax as part of its climate change agenda. It was unable to do so for a familiar reason – because it lacks the capability to override the wishes of member-states concerning fiscal issues. Several member-states – most notably the UK – were fiercely resistant to any measures that implied tax harmonization. However, environmental issues within the Union can be dealt with by majority vote. Carbon trading could be introduced without such battles.

Designing markets to limit pollution had its origins in the US, where they were originally used with some success to control emissions of sulphur dioxide.[17] Such emissions, coming from coal-fired power stations, were the main cause of 'acid rain'. But instead of directly regulating the amount of sulphur dioxide, a market in emissions credits was created. The original proposal of Robert Stavins, the scheme's principal architect, to auction credits to the emitters, thereby establishing a market price, was blocked in Congress. It would have meant that the utility companies would have to pay large sums of money for the permits, money which would have gone to the federal government.[18] Permits were in fact issued free to virtually all companies, with a maximum total that could be issued in any one year of 8.9 million tonnes.

In spite of its limitations, the scheme produced significant cuts in emissions and at a much lower overall cost than the industry lobbyists who had opposed it had claimed it would incur. They had argued it would cost the industry $10 billion or more annually. The actual yearly sum turned out to be about $1 billion. The market forces generated helped produce quick and effective technological innovations in key parts of the industry. The scheme thus achieved a fair degree of success, sufficient to inspire some environmentalists, including Vice-President Al Gore. The Clinton administration commissioned a detailed economic modelling exercise on how it could be extended to cover carbon.

The outline of a possible international carbon market was drawn up at Kyoto. It was agreed that the industrial countries could sell 'emissions reductions units' to one another, and could also trade them with developing countries to count towards their reduction targets. In spite of the fact that the US did not sign up to the Kyoto agreements, the idea of carbon trading did not go away. It was taken up first by business. British Petroleum set up an internal trading scheme committing the company to reduce its greenhouse gas emissions by one-tenth by 2010 as compared to 2000. It achieved this target very rapidly, in fact within a single year. The European Emissions Trading Scheme (ETS) started operation early in 2005. It covered about half of the EU's CO_2 emissions – those coming from fixed sources of power production, especially electricity and from certain energy-intensive industries. It did not extend to other greenhouse gases.

The European Commission initially proposed to auction the emissions credits. As in the US, lobbying from industry sank the proposal. A hybrid creature arose from the negotiations between the Commission and member-states. An auction would have established an open market with a single price for carbon. The system that was introduced in its place allowed member-states the right to set up their own national allocation plans. These were supposed to be developed on the basis of criteria established at Kyoto, but they were vague; moreover, some states had no precise measures of their emissions in place. The result was an over-generous allocation of allowances, since it was in every member-state's interest to get the most favourable conditions it could, or at a minimum get a certain amount of wriggle room. A market was created, but one that produced very mixed consequences.

A lot of money has changed hands within the ETS, but the scheme has been ineffective for the purposes for which it was set up. Early on in its history, the carbon price reached as much as 31 euros per tonne. Later it dropped so dramatically that it was worth .001 per cent of that sum. It lost its value completely as it became clear that there was a large surplus of allowances because of the slack built into the national allocation plans. In addition, some power-generating companies had made windfall profits by passing onto consumers the price of carbon credits, even though they were allocated free of charge.

The ETS has probably had some effect on emissions. Studies indicate that emissions in 2005 were around 7 per cent lower than they would have been had the scheme not been in place.[19] Yet some of that gain probably comes from member-states' tactical exaggerations of their emissions in the build-up to the scheme. The Clean Development Mechanism is up and running, which would not have been possible without the ETS. Moreover, the ETS has served to prompt the emergence of carbon trading markets elsewhere in the world, and these can in principle learn from the problems that emerged in the European experience.

The Commission has stated that Phase 1 of the ETS was a 'learning phase', and that ways will be found to apply a tighter cap to the market as it evolves. In January 2008 the Commission proposed a more rigorous version of the ETS, designed to overcome its earlier limitations. Allocation of allowances is to be done centrally rather than left to member nations. In the lead-up to Phase 2, national allocation plans will be scrutinized much more intensively than before. More than 60 per cent of allowances will be auctioned and other greenhouse gases will be included besides CO_2. Aviation emissions, left out from the original scheme, are due to be incorporated by 2010. Post-2012 the Commission wants maritime transport and forestry to be covered too.

Several projects for establishing carbon markets exist in the US, the most advanced being that developed by the state of California. Governor Arnold Schwarzenegger signed bill AB32 in California towards the end of 2006. As discussed in chapter 5, the state has committed itself to a 25 per cent reduction in greenhouse gases by 2020 and 80 per cent by 2050, although only part is slated to be achieved through the carbon market. A multi-state emissions market has been proposed by George Pataki of New York State, which the government of California says it wishes to join. The Chicago Climate Exchange market, a voluntary scheme, has been in existence for some while. Unlike most other voluntary carbon markets, it is allowance-based rather than project-based – in other words, there is an agreed-upon market cap.[20] It has been successful in the sense that a lot of money flows through it. Its impact on emissions is harder to assess, but is at best very limited.

As measured in terms of turnover, carbon markets were advancing rapidly over the period from 2003 to 2008. According to the Carbon Finance Unit of the World Bank, 337 metric tonnes of carbon dioxide equivalent were exchanged through projects in 2008, more than twice as much as the previous year, which itself saw trading rise by 40 per cent over the preceding one. The Bank estimated the size of the world carbon market at $64 billion in 2007.

Whether these figures will be maintained in a more adverse world economic situation, and where faith in markets has diminished, is a matter of conjecture. Carbon emissions trading markets are certainly here to stay, although at the moment it is an open question how well the ETS – by far the largest – will function in revised form. Large amounts of money are flowing through the trading markets. Yet they still exist only in the form of experiments whose capability to deliver the goods remains uncertain. We should guard against the possibility that they take on a life of their own and are therefore seen as 'successful' simply because a lot of trading goes on. As has been shown by the experience of the ETS so far, it will not be easy to assess the impact they have on limiting emissions, even though this is their sole rationale. Although many pin high hopes on them, at the moment they are in an experimental stage. We do not know how well they will work, or how far they can be introduced on an international, let alone a global, level.

The prime author of the Stern Review has recently proposed a 'new global deal on climate change'.[21] Stern's purpose is to help shape negotiations for a post-2012 global treaty, with the aim of limiting greenhouse gas concentrations to between 450 and 500 ppm CO_2e. Given the level of greenhouse gases already in the atmosphere, he says, this objective is so demanding that there is little scope for any major country or group of countries to fall behind in achieving the necessary emissions cuts. 'All countries must play their part. . . . Once the basic arithmetic has been recognised, governments across the world ought to commit to credibly coordinated policies.'[22]

Carbon emissions trading will allow for global targets to be attained most efficiently and at least cost, although markets will have to be carefully designed and applied, since the wrong policies can produce market distortions, perverse incentives and promote protectionism. Stern envisages a worldwide cap and trade system in place by 2020, which would cover all the industrial countries and also the more affluent developing nations.

When he says 'all countries must play their part', Stern means the developing countries too. The developing societies now account for some 50 per cent of all emissions currently going into the air, although China is responsible for the bulk of the total. Without policy adjustments, that proportion will probably rise to 70 per cent by 2030. The rich countries have to accept that emissions from the less well-off countries will grow for some time, as development proceeds, and therefore must cut their own emissions sharply. However, the large majority of all countries will have to show a fall in emissions before 2030. Carbon markets, Stern says, are likely to stimulate the technological innovation that will be needed to reduce emissions.

Extraordinarily, there is no mention of politics in Stern's discussion, no analysis of power, or of the tense nature of international relations. It is as if the 'global deal' will be reached as soon as the nations of the world see reason. 'All must play their part' – yes, but who is there to implement the 'must'? Stern places an enormous amount of faith in carbon markets, yet they depend upon prior political support.

My overall conclusions from the points discussed in this chapter are straightforward. Don't hold your breath for the success of the post-Bali negotiations. They aren't likely to help much in containing global warming. The scale of the enterprise is truly impressive, given the very high proportion of the world's nations involved. Yet the very fact of near-universal involvement means that agreements will tend to gravitate to the lowest common denominator – producing anodyne results. Action on the part of the European Union, within a much more limited arena, has more chance of achieving a worthwhile outcome, and the EU must be commended for the vanguard role it has taken in responding to climate change; but since it is not clear how it will hold its member-states to their targets, the reality may fall well short of the aspiration. To put it another way, most will depend upon what the member-states choose to do.

As for carbon markets, we will have to wait and see. If the second phase of the ETS is indeed more rigorous than its predecessor, it will offer a model for others to follow. The incoming US administration is committed to introducing a national emissions market, whose design can avoid the mistakes made in the European system. A global carbon market still looks a long way off. Moreover, the financial crisis has shown that international markets must have more effective economic governance, which will itself take some time to achieve.

9

THE GEOPOLITICS OF CLIMATE CHANGE

Discussions of international relations and climate change tend to be of two kinds. On the one hand, there are many works about the mechanics of reaching international agreements to contain emissions. On the other, a growing number of studies seek to analyse the implications of climate change for geopolitics. I argue in this chapter that we have to bring these two sets of concerns much closer together than they are at the moment. Once more, energy – especially oil and struggles centred upon it – supplies one of the main points of connection.

It might seem that responding to climate change will intrinsically contribute to international collaboration. Yet the processes and interests promoting division are strong.[1] The melting of the Arctic ice provides a good example. When the area was just an ice field, there was considerable international cooperation over the activities carried out there, which were mainly of a scientific nature. The fact that navigation across the Arctic is becoming increasingly possible, and that major new oil, gas and mineral resources might become available, has led to divisions of interest and to international friction, fortunately so far of a confined nature.

Climate change issues – especially in conjunction with developing scarcities of energy – could become both militarized and dominated by security risks. The result could be a progressive deterioration of international cooperation, where security is

Figure 9.1 The Arctic: the interaction of climate change and geopolitics

Source: Sunday Times, 29 June 2008, p. 17.

increasingly seen as divisible. What should be an overriding goal of reducing emissions could fall prey to a competitive struggle for resources, exacerbating already existing tensions and divisions. The leaders of states, or groups of states, could exploit climate change to their own sectional ends. Several different paths to violent conflict are imaginable. For instance, political leaders might use climate change-induced strains to gain or retain power in internal struggles – for example, migrants might be used as scapegoats in such power bids. In volatile areas of the world, a country weakened by the consequences of climate change might be attacked by its neighbours seeking to gain advantage from the country's problems.

A further possibility is that armed conflicts could occur as states try to gain a hold over resources where demand is outstripping supply – the most likely path if worst-case scenarios of climate change were to prevail. This could happen if the world economy becomes 'renationalized' with a widespread return to protectionism. Yet another possibility is that 'subsistence conflicts' – of the sort that has devastated Dafur – might become commonplace. Groups living on a level close to bare subsistence could clash as their means of livelihood start to evaporate, drawing in military 'protectors' of one sort or another. Each of the above paths could overlap or intertwine.[2]

Although the sources of the bloodshed, starvation and homelessness provoked by the conflict in Dafur are complex, the situation there has been called the 'first climate change war', since the drying up of Lake Chad is one of the factors that contributed to the migration which led to it.[3] Given this influence, we see again a situation in which climate change intersects with energy resources. China is actively involved in Sudan because of the oil and minerals the country possesses. The Chinese have supplied arms and training to the government forces and for some while refused to join the UN and other major nations in condemning the role of the Sudanese government in the sorry events.

It has become commonplace to point out that most conflicts today, in contrast to the struggles of the twentieth century, derive from weak rather than strong states. However, much will also depend on how robust the links, connections and mutual interests of core regional states and groups of states prove to be. 'Pivotal states' are nations which have a significant influence on a region as a whole. If they are stable and economically successful, they tend to have a mollifying effect on that region. Conversely, if they run into difficulties, these might spill over to affect the whole surrounding area. Such countries include Brazil and Mexico, South Africa and Nigeria, Egypt, Pakistan and South Korea. Of course, if major setbacks were to occur in very large countries such as China or India, the reverberations would be that much more disruptive.

The US is already starting to see the world through the prism of a struggle for energy resources against the backdrop of damage inflicted by climate change. The main focus of US strategic and military planning, according to a recent official report, will henceforth be on a competition for resources, a competition the Pentagon sees as already under way. The global reach that China is seeking to establish, it argues, is driven by the demands of its economy for raw materials rather than by any specific ideological outlook. China's growing influence in the Middle East and Africa is a matter of particular concern.[4] Russia's return to geopolitical prominence has been driven almost entirely by the rise prior to 2008 in the prices of oil, gas and industrial minerals. The attention now devoted to resource scarcity, Michael Klare has observed, 'represents a qualitative shift in US thinking', prompted 'not by an optimistic faith in America's capacity to dominate the world economy but by a largely pessimistic outlook regarding the future availability of vital resources'.[5]

This concern has impelled a return to investment in seapower. The US, the Defense Department emphasizes, must be able to patrol the main sea routes of the world in order to ensure its national security.[6] Overall, 75 per cent of the world's oil and 90 per cent of traded manufactured goods are transported by sea. In its budget proposal for 2009, the US government outlined a comprehensive new programme for investment in nuclear-power aircraft carriers, destroyers carrying heavy anti-missile capability, submarines and other combat ships. The existing fleet is to be redeployed with greater emphasis on the prime routes through which most raw materials pass.

Not long ago, most US military bases were located in Western Europe, South Korea and Japan. Over the past few years, a transfer from such areas to East-Central Europe, Central and Southwest Asia, and parts of Africa has begun. These regions contain states deemed to be supporting terrorism, but they are also home to more than three-quarters of the oil and gas reserves in the world and a large percentage of those of uranium, copper and cobalt.[7] At least some of the bases earmarked to have a permanent presence in Iraq are there in order to protect oil installations, as well as to provide training for police and army units acting against insurgents.

China and Russia are building their own security networks, in a self-conscious challenge to US dominance. As already mentioned, China's involvement in Sudan has arguably contributed to the bloodshed in that country. The country is also involved in North Africa, Angola, Chad and Nigeria. It has become one of the main suppliers of military equipment to some of these states. Its development and military advisers compete with those coming from the US. In Central and East Asia, Russia and China have formed a counterpart to NATO, in the shape of the Shanghai Cooperation Organization, a large military alliance. Its component states have made a strong push to assert influence over resource-rich countries. One of those countries, Kazakhstan, is a member of the alliance, together with Kyrgyzstan, Tajikistan and Uzbekistan.

An illusory world community?

Just at the time when the world needs more effective governance, international institutions look weaker than they have been for some years. The United Nations has played a vital role in the struggle against climate change, particularly in the shape of the IPCC, which has been the major influence propelling international concern about global warming. Yet the UN has few resources of its own, and can be paralysed by the actions of blocs of nations, or even single nations, especially on the Security Council. A more multipolar world could, of course, provide a better balance for cooperation, but it could just as easily produce serious divisions and conflicts with no arbiter to resolve them.

We seem to be seeing a return to a form of authoritarian nationalism, prominent among some of the key players on the world scene, most notably China and Russia, but including many smaller oil-rich nations too. Together with the policies of the Bush administration – which to some extent sparked that return – the international system has been redefined in terms of power and military capability. The burst of enthusiasm at the turn of the century that heralded a new world order based on international agencies rather than nations, and upon collaboration between nations rather than traditional sovereignty, seems already to have gone into reverse.

Discussing such changes, the influential writer on global politics, Robert Kagan, speaks of a 'return to normality'.[8] The title of his most recent book is *The Return of History and the End of Dreams*. The dreams he is talking about were those of creating a new kind of international order following the end of the Cold War, and, more generally, with the advance of globalization. They were about the shrinking importance of the nation-state, the deepening of international collaboration, the disappearance of ideological conflicts and the freeing up of commerce and communications. The European Union seemed in the forefront of these transformations, pioneering a mode of organization that is not just international but genuinely transnational.

'It was all a mirage', he says.[9] The nation-state remains as strong as ever, while competition between the great powers has returned. The major nations are struggling with one another for influence and prestige. China and Russia, in particular, are seeking to assert themselves, and both see international relations through the prism of great power rivalries. In each case there is a strong connection with energy. Russia's quest to return to great power status is based on its large oil and gas resources, while China is searching for energy supplies to sustain and fuel its continuing growth.

The long-standing conflict between liberalism and autocracy has re-emerged, coupled with 'an even older struggle', between radical Islam and modernity. Two of the largest developing countries, India and Brazil, are democracies. However, China and Russia are not, and are explicitly marked by a belief in authoritarian leadership as the condition of effective growth, as well as of containing the possibilities of division and fragmentation which each society faces. Prime Minister Putin's notion of 'sovereign democracy' is all about creating popular support for decisive leadership while expanding the sphere of Russia's international influence from the low point it reached in the 1990s.

The member-states of the EU, Kagan says, placed a gigantic bet at that period, that economic interdependence and the collaboration of nations would triumph over traditional concepts of sovereignty. They cut down on military spending, in the belief that the power of example would win out over the power of armed force. The EU, its leaders reasoned, has served as a vehicle for the integration of a growing number of states in Western – and now Central and Eastern – Europe into a transnational system. Why shouldn't the same model be successfully applied elsewhere?

For a brief while, the chances of success looked good. Regional associations were formed in several different parts of the world. The North American Free Trade Agreement (NAFTA) spanned the US, Canada and Mexico; a counterpart, MERCOSUR, emerged in South America; in Asia, several nations got together to form ASEAN. Yet these organizations have remained no more than loose trading groups. The EU, Kagan concludes, has lost its bet. Russia has responded with traditional forms of power to blunt EU influence in the ex-Soviet states that border it. Heavily dependent upon Russia for its oil and gas supplies – as discussed in chapter 2 – the Union has proved an easy target for a resurgent Russia, which has had no problems dividing its member-states and concluding bilateral energy deals with some of them.

According to Kagan, the decline of the United Nations and other such international organizations is terminal: he speaks of the 'demise of the international community'. The UN Security Council, which had a brief moment of cogency just after the Cold War, 'is slipping back into its long coma'.[10] It has been undermined by the division between the democracies and the autocracies. The scramble for energy is one of the driving forces of this division.

Kagan suggests that a 'Concert of Democracies' should be set up, bringing together the democratic nations from the developed and developing worlds. Its role would be an interventionist one. The strength of the autocratic countries, he says, is in some ways more apparent than real. Unlike in the nineteenth and early twentieth centuries, when democracy was the exception, China, Russia and other authoritarian states live in a world where it is preponderant. Hence they face problems of legitimacy that cannot simply be ignored, or not for long. Yet the democratic countries cannot expect to exert an influence just because of the values and ideas they represent. Quoting Hans Morgenthau, Kagan concludes that we should not imagine that at some juncture 'the final curtain would fall and the game of power politics would no longer be played'.

How far this type of analysis is correct will make an enormous difference to the world's chances of resolving the issues of climate change and energy security. Great powers acting in the traditional way treat resources in terms of a zero-sum game. If Kagan is right in his portrayal of the current state of international affairs, there is little likelihood of avoiding a battle for resources. As it deepens, it could very well lead to armed conflict, a potentially terrible prospect if nuclear states become involved. The UN would be powerless to intervene, since it would be rendered impotent by the very conflicts it was supposed to help overcome.

Thankfully, what Kagan says is valid only to a limited degree. Take the case of the United Nations first. It would be difficult to deny that the record of the UN since 1989 has been distinctly patchy, as even its strongest supporters concede. David Hannay, formerly Britain's permanent representative at the body, has spoken of the early 1990s as 'the crest of the wave' in terms of the UN's successes, 'the moment when it was possible to hope that the organization was set on a new path, destined to become an effective component of the system of collective security'. [11]

During those years, the UN led a number of successful humanitarian interventions – and the Rio Summit got a new and serious environmental agenda under way. From 1993 onwards, however, the UN's performance began to tip in the other direction, as the organization became bogged down in key missions in Bosnia and elsewhere. Supporters of the UN fear that it has become marginal and discredited, while its critics actively hope that such is indeed the case. Yet, as

Hannay quite rightly observes, states continue to turn to the UN for help in facing common problems. It has an 'underlying indispensability' because there is no obvious alternative.[12]

The international community is not 'illusory'. It was wrong when US Foreign Secretary Condoleezza Rice said it originally and it is wrong when Kagan repeats it now.[13] If we concentrate only on the Security Council, which does indeed tend to be a place of power-brokering, we get a quite misleading view of the progression of world interdependence and the UN's role in furthering it. The world is far more interdependent than ever was the case before, and the UN and other international agencies are playing a fundamental role in nurturing it. Take as an example telecommunications, which are now truly globalized, but depend upon vast networks ranging across a multiplicity of national contexts. The UN and other international organizations play an essential role in such coordination, because binding international agreements are involved.

Even in more contentious areas of humanitarian intervention and the management of health and disease, the role of the UN has been, and is, central. As far as the management of conflicts go, the UN has been more important than would appear on the surface – and more successful. The failures, such as in Bosnia or Rwanda, tend to be very visible, but successes – preventing conflicts from developing in the first place – receive much less attention and publicity.

Kagan says the world has reverted to what it was before the 'dreams' of the early post-1989 period – an arena for nation-states to pursue their power struggles. Yet this conclusion is eminently disputable. The nation-state has obstinately refused to go away, yes. I have argued for its continuing importance throughout this book. However, the world context in which nations stake their claims to sovereignty has changed massively over the past two or three decades. It is simply not the case that there is a 'return to normality' – to patterns of the past. Sovereignty does not have the same meaning as it did. This is surely obvious on an economic level, where states, no matter how large, cannot govern their economic affairs in the way in which they were able to earlier in the post-war period.

Interdependence is a part of our lives in the twenty-first century, and states which act in denial of that situation will quickly be brought to heel in one way or another. The fate of the attempt of the Bush administration to ignore the new realities is instructive. Bush wanted to reintroduce exactly the kind of world Kagan sketches out – one in which power is what counts, and where the US is pre-eminent in wielding such power. Such a world-view went along with a contemptuous attitude towards climate change.

The abrogation of international agreements which followed undoubtedly influenced the actions of other nations, including China, Russia and Iran, which, in opposing the attitudes of the US, in fact mimicked them. But look what happened to those US ambitions. The United States, the world's greatest military power, was unable to pacify a single medium-sized country, Iraq, in spite of an easy initial military victory. It was not able to fight two wars at the same time, even with the help of allies, and as a consequence the project to bring stability to Afghanistan is meeting with, at best, limited success. The US has the world's largest economy, but the country, acting alone, has very limited capacities to influence the world marketplace – as the financial crisis has shown all too clearly.

Where Kagan must be listened to is when he says that the curtain will not fall on power politics. It is quite futile to analyse what might happen as a result of international collaboration to halt climate change without setting it in the context of the rivalries that cross-cut efforts at international collaboration. For those rivalries will determine the real opportunities that exist, the points at which real purchase can be achieved. Let us consider how this point bears on the relation between the developed and under-developed worlds.

The bottom billion

The bulk of the emissions causing climate change have been generated by the industrial countries, yet its impact will be felt most strongly in the poorer regions of the world. A basic sense of social justice should help drive attempts to reduce that impact, but there are more selfish reasons for the more affluent countries to help the more deprived too. Extreme poverty is potentially very destabilizing indeed in world society. The level of risk it produces for the more favoured countries and regions, even if global warming didn't exist, would still be formidable. Among other harmful effects, poverty is one of the main influences leading to population growth; population pressures ease as countries become richer.

The Millennium Declaration of the United Nations pledged 'to spare no effort to free our fellow men, women and children from the abject and dehumanizing conditions of extreme poverty'. Halfway to the date set for reaching the millennium goals, 2015, progress has certainly been made. The most important one, that of reducing absolute poverty by half, looks set to be reached. The same is true of those concerning education, reducing the impact of some of the worst killer diseases, and improving gender equality, employment and sanitation.

In geopolitical terms, it is essential to recognize, as Paul Collier has puts it: 'The third world has shrunk.'[14] For much of the past half-century the question of 'development' was one of a gulf between one billion affluent and four billion impoverished people in the world. The millennium goals were established with such figures in mind. Yet about 80 per cent of the five billion now live in countries that are developing, some of them at extraordinary speed. These countries have experienced rapid growth in income per capita. They have recorded an average GDP growth rate of over 4 per cent during the 1980s and 1990s. Over the early period of the current century, that rate has risen to over 4.5 per cent, although of course the fast pace of China's development alone over the period accounts for a substantial proportion of this.

These statistics drive home the importance of what I have earlier called the development imperative. Economic growth on the large scale is the only way out of poverty for the mass of the world's poor, and for many people in the world it has worked. Yet at least a billion people – located in about 60 different countries – have been left out. Most of these societies are small and their combined population does not approach that of either China or India. As Collier says, they 'are falling behind, and often falling apart'.[15] Their economies have not grown; on the contrary, their level of income has declined. It was, on average, lower in absolute terms by the year 2000 than it had been in 1970. Since then it has increased by just over 1 per cent, not enough to make any significant difference to their fortunes – they are marked not only by poverty, but by epidemics, ignorance and despair.

These societies lag behind the rest of the world because they are caught in what Collier calls four 'traps'. One is that of civil war. Over 70 per cent of the societies that contain the bottom billion have either recently experienced civil war or are still caught up in one. Susceptibility to civil war both causes economic stagnation and is caused by it. These countries face a 14 per cent possibility of experiencing a civil war over any given five-year period. Every percentage point increase in growth knocks 1 per cent off this risk. Conflict almost always affects neighbouring countries – and, as mentioned earlier, can spread to whole regions, to some extent dragging them down too.

One of the four traps is actually the possession of natural resources, especially oil and gas. Some 30 per cent of the world's poor live in countries where the economy is dominated by resource wealth. The reasons for this situation are well known. There are a few rentier states which, to some degree, have been able to escape the 'resource curse' – such as Kuwait or Saudi Arabia – mainly because their oil and gas revenues are enormous. For others, however, revenue from such sources only provides a livelihood for a tiny elite. At the same time, that revenue discourages investment in other industries, and renders the country's exports uncompetitive. Moreover, as in the past, the prices of oil and gas have been unstable, and that instability is imported into the economy.

The other two traps are, first, being a land-locked country with dysfunctional neighbours and, second, bad governance. Almost 40 per cent of the people in the bottom billion live in countries that are land-locked. The case of Switzerland shows that it is possible to be both land-locked and wealthy; but Switzerland has friendly neighbours, whose countries have excellent communications. In countries such as Uganda, Sudan and Somalia it is a different story. The economies of the land-locked societies in Africa are not integrated with those of their neighbours, but are either turned inwards or open to the vagaries of the world market.

Together with Chad, Bangladesh comes last in Transparency International's ratings of corruption. Yet it has managed to put in place fairly effective economic policies and has achieved a significant measure of economic growth. It has done well because it has few natural resources of its own and because it has an extensive coastline – (although, as discussed in chapter 7, one which puts it at high risk as sea levels rise as a result of global warming). No doubt the country would have fared even better if it had been less corrupt.

Bad governance, a matter that extends well beyond corruption as such, compounds each of the other sets of problems – producing societies in which governments are either paralysed by divisions or where there is, in effect, no government at all. One study equated failed states with countries comparable in other respects. The results showed the average cost of being a failed state, over the period during which it could be classified as such, to be £100 billion.[16]

Political reform is always, in principle, possible, and achieving it is normally the key to progress in other areas. Some of the world's poorest countries have managed such reform in the past, most importantly China. In the 1960s the country faced ruin as a result of the policies of Chairman Mao. The subsequent leadership took the decision to change direction, resulting in the economic success that is such a feature of world society today.

On the face of things, the nations that make up the 'bottom billion' are threatening to drop off the edge of world history, since they are locked into a deteriorating cycle from which most other nations have, in large degree, escaped. Ethical reasons alone demand that the rest of the world community cannot sit by while local tragedies unfold. But in the context of climate change, there are important material reasons why the more affluent nations cannot remain uninvolved. The pressures created by climate change and increasing energy scarcity, sketched out at the beginning of the chapter and throughout this book, could cause the problems of the bottom billion to be dispersed around the world as a whole. What has happened in Sudan is an awful reminder of how global struggles may play out if ways are not found to contain and reshape them.

Oil and geopolitics

The fate of the bottom billion is likely to have a major influence on how far international terrorism will continue to be a prominent feature on the world scene. The states where the poorest live frequently display a lethal combination of terrorism, international crime, drugs and money-laundering.

Where these states are also oil-producers, their history tends to be even more blighted. It would be difficult to overemphasize how important oil and gas have been in shaping world politics in the decades since the end of the Second World War. As Thomas Friedman says, when historians look back at our era, they might well conclude that one of the most important geopolitical trends was the influence of oil wealth over the changing centre of gravity of Islam.[17] In the early post-war years, that centre of gravity was located in Cairo, Istanbul, Beirut, Casablanca and Damascus, all in their way cosmopolitan cities offering the hope of progressive modernization. At that time, many Muslim nations were relatively liberal and there was widespread talk of the need to separate church and state on the Turkish model.

Yet because of the growing importance of oil, and the dominant position which the Gulf states and Saudi Arabia hold in its production, conservative interpretations of Islam have become much more prominent than they used to be. Saudi Arabia is the guardian of two of the holiest mosques of Islam, in Mecca and Medina. 'Desert Islam', aggressive and reactionary, was originally shaped by poverty; now it is in possession of untold wealth. The half-century-old pact with the US kept the ruling family in place and, in turn, helped conservatism to flourish.

'Oil is the enemy of freedom' – is it possible to make such an apparently absurd theorem stick? Without too much oversimplification, the blunt answer is 'yes', and the reasons why are well known. What Friedman calls the First Law of Petropolitics brings an impressive range of cases together.[18] The tiny kingdom of Bahrain, he observes, led the way among states in the Gulf in holding free parliamentary elections, ones in which women could vote and stand as candidates. Bahrain was the first such state in which oil was discovered, about three-quarters of a century ago – but much more recently, it was also the first in which it started to run out. The leaders of the country began to think in terms of diversifying the economy, which in turn led to the beginnings of political reform.

Friedman has undertaken a systematic study of the relationship between the fluctuating price of oil and political change. His 'Law' states that the higher the price of oil, the more likely an oil-producing country is to turn autocratic. Political leaders get popular support from the rentier income flowing into the country and feel free to ignore what opposition groups may say, and indeed, to some large degree, what the rest of the world thinks too. Oil-rich governments use their revenues to by-pass the need for taxation, thereby avoiding the pressures that come from tax-payers, who normally demand accountability.

Oil money promotes the use of patronage, creating an inner group of rulers; that self-same revenue makes possible the creation of an elaborate system of police, security services and surveillance. Michael Ross argues that it is not only conservative Islam which produces the subordination of women; it is the dominance of oil money as such. Since there is little economic diversification, there is no chance for women to join the non-agricultural workforce, which in turn has the effect of keeping the birth rate high.[19] There are 23 countries in the world which get the large part of their income from oil and gas; not one of them is a democracy in anything but name.

Russia is among the most important of such countries, now in the grip of a small elite drawing its power almost wholly from revenue provided by oil, gas and mineral reserves. The symbiotic, yet tense, relationship between the EU and Russia has attracted a great deal of recent commentary. Some 40 per cent of the EU's gas supplies, 30 per cent of its oil and about a quarter of its coal come from Russia. EU–Russia relationships need to be normalized, a task that is routinely spoken about but, so far, not realized. From a climate change point of view, a major concern of a continuing EU–Russia dialogue should be a reopening of Russia's oil and gas industry to European, and then to other foreign, investment.

Large-scale new investment is needed to reduce the profligate way in which energy is produced (and used) in Russia.

It has been estimated that the volume of gas flared off in the country each year is equivalent to a quarter of total Russian gas exports to Europe.[20] Leaky pipelines add substantially to this total. In the meantime Russia won such a liberal deal at Kyoto that there is no motivation to control emissions. Recent Russian commitments to reduce leakage should receive international support and encouragement, as should moves to raise energy prices for consumers, although neither is motivated by climate change considerations. On the back of high oil prices, Russia adopted a forceful stance in international relations.

Vladimir Putin's notion of sovereign democracy has nothing to do with democracy as ordinarily understood and everything to do with sovereignty – with the assertion of Russia's right and capability to act as a great power. The EU is rightly encouraging its former East European member-states to diversify their sources of energy supply and move towards full-cost pricing for consumers (although EU leaders objected when Russia tried to force the Ukraine to make such a move overnight), but with little impact so far. The sole exception is the Czech Republic, which has built an oil pipeline to Germany and has concluded a long-term gas deal with Norway.

These considerations show just how much there is to play for, should the industrial countries be able simultaneously to reduce their dependence on oil and lower their carbon emissions. The famous 'curse of oil' does not only apply within nations, but to the world system as a whole, since the need to sustain a steady flow of oil plays such a large part in contemporary geopolitics. If the industrial countries could break away from their wholesale dependency on oil and natural gas; it would be a major benefit not only for them but, perversely, also for the producer nations. It would help bring about one of the most far-reaching realignments of international relations in history.

One does not have to envisage a future in which the developed countries will become autonomous in respect of their energy supplies, which for most is neither practicable nor desirable. Interdependence – for example, in the shape of large-scale smart energy grids powered by renewable technologies – will continue to be a fact of life and has a clear positive side, in terms of the pooling of resources. But it will become far more possible than it is now for them to be protected from system breakdown by the capacity for significant energy self-provision.

The US and China

Following the toxic years of the Bush administration, terminating in an economic crisis brought on by America's habit of living beyond its means, many think the US will have to adopt a humbler role in the world than hitherto. The 'unipolar moment' seemed to pass in a flash. The US went from being spoken of as the centre of a global empire to being something of a world pariah.

The rest of the world community has become so used to regarding the US as the climate change laggard that it might be difficult to shift gear if and when it becomes an environmental leader. Yet with the election of President Obama, the US has again demonstrated its capacity for renewal. That capacity will be needed on a political level, but perhaps even more importantly on an economic one. The US was the driving force of the last great wave of technological innovation, in the shape of the internet, and the same is likely to be true of innovation in renewable technologies.

The world needs enlightened American leadership – as long as it is based on a reassertion of the Wilsonian tradition that was so influential for a lengthy period of the twentieth century. We can foresee a new rapprochement between the US and Europe, although not one that signals a reinvention of 'the West'. Combating climate change could be one means of building that rapprochement. The formal, bureaucratic approach favoured by the European Commission is unlikely to be duplicated by the US leadership. I quoted survey results earlier (chapter 5) which showed that the American public was simultaneously less persuaded of the dangers of climate change than the public in other nations and, at the same time, more optimistic about dealing with it. US inventiveness and optimism, so often mistaken for naivety, might stand the rest of the world in good stead at the moment.

It is essential to reform the Clean Development Mechanism (CDM; see chapter 8), but more important will be the promotion of economic convergence with the developing countries. The two processes are not quite the same, since technology transfer does not necessarily promote increased competitiveness for the recipient country. We should move away from simple technology transfers to a situation where such transfers are accompanied by investment in the means of mobilizing and extending them – through the provision of technical education and the funding of R&D capacity within the developing nations. The relaxing of normal patent protections will be highly important for such a process. Wherever possible, instead of merely importing high-tech machinery or products, connections should be forged between high-tech and low-tech – that is, local – knowledge. In chapter 7, I gave examples from the field of adaptation, but the same applies to mitigation policy.

As far as the second of these issues is concerned, it would make sense to adopt a different approach from that of the CDM. We should look for policies which coordinate with the interests of developing countries, while still having the effect of cutting back emissions. An instance in point is the possibility of supplying latest-generation natural gas technology to China, which would help reduce local pollution as well as cutting greenhouse gas emissions.

The large bulk of greenhouse gas emissions is produced by only a limited number of countries – as far as mitigation is concerned, what the majority of states do pales in significance compared to the activities of the large polluters. Only a limited number of states have the capability seriously to pioneer technological innovation relevant to climate change – rules governing knowledge transfer and investment from these countries to others will be more important than universal accords.

To be able to exploit this situation, we need quite a different perspective from those that emerged from Kyoto and Bali. An approach based on agreements or partnerships between individual nations, groups of countries and regions makes more sense – and could eventually act to strengthen more universal measures. The Kyoto agreements already recognize several different clusters of countries, incorporating varying provisions for them.[21] As one author has remarked: 'It is increasingly becoming clear [that] the Kyoto Protocol is less a global agreement than a set of differing regional approaches.'[22]

The experience of the World Trade Organization offers a possible parallel. It has proved impossible to reach agreement on the Doha round of negotiations within the WTO, but progress on trade negotiation has been made through regional and bilateral agreements. More than 200 such agreements are currently in operation. Studies have shown that such deals can support the overall objectives of the WTO's multilateral trading system rather than, as might seem to be the case on the surface, act to undermine them. Regional agreements have allowed countries to go beyond what has been possible to achieve universally; but these concordats have subsequently paved the way for progress made at the level of the WTO.

The Group of Eight (G8) – the seven most influential industrial countries in the world, plus Russia – is too much of a talking-shop to play a significant role. At a meeting held in July 2008, the G8 countries sought to achieve a consensus over climate change targets. The leaders announced a plan to cut greenhouse gas emissions globally by 50 per cent by 2050. For the first time the US made a public commitment to pursuing such a target. A joint statement said there is a 'need for deep cuts', but suggested no means for achieving them. Invited to put their views to G8, the leaders of the world's largest developing economies argued that the proposals made were too vague to help. A group comprising representatives from G8 plus eight developing countries has been meeting since early in 2007 to help find a replacement for Kyoto, without any concrete result. The Chinese President, Hu Jintao said that his country would not accept binding targets of any sort, since Chinese per capita emissions are relatively low and because 'China's central task now is to develop the economy and make life better for the people'.[23]

A body representing the major polluters should be established post-haste. If we include the EU as a single entity, then 70 per cent of cumulative world emissions of greenhouse gases have been produced by just six countries. They should be meeting regularly with one another. The 20 most polluting countries have been responsible for 88 per cent of total emissions since the start of the industrial age. They should be getting together too. Countries could propose how they would contribute to a collective effort to control emissions, a process that could proceed at least in some part separately from whatever other international endeavours in which members were involved.

Means of review and scrutiny would have to be set up, perhaps with a rotating leadership. The body would look at packages proposed by governments in order to make sure that they reflected an equitable distribution of effort in terms of differential contribution to world emissions. In addition, it would review progress, both in terms of country commitments and overall outcomes, and also monitor involvements of the group with the developing world.

The industrial countries will be primarily responsible for making the case for economic convergence count. It would be hard to exaggerate how important economic convergence is. A crucial lever in world politics will be supplied if it can be shown that those countries, regions or localities that follow a progressive programme gain economic advantage by so doing. Such a programme can be both technological and social. It will apply among the industrial societies, giving them a basis for both fruitful competition and cooperation. But it will also help break the deadlock that exists at the moment, in which the developing countries see development and climate change policy as an either/or.

It will also be vital to show the economic significance of gains in energy efficiency, whether these be produced by technology or another means. Such gains form a crucial positive link between energy security and climate change, since on this issue they point in the same direction. If energy efficiency provides a competitive edge, then it will have an effect upon how the developing countries react. Anything that contributes to widening the area of convergent interest between reducing emissions and improving competitiveness will be valuable. The same applies to corporate behaviour. Companies are becoming more conscious of environmental issues because their leaders can see how central they are. Much will depend upon those companies demonstrating that progressive environmental policies can generate competitive advantage, since what they achieve will influence business practice everywhere. A similar theorem could apply to state institutions if improvements in performance flow from environmental policies.

The social basis of advantage will be as important as its economic or technological bases, especially in so far as it rests upon areas of political convergence. Pioneering social policies (for example, in the field of health) will be important. Assessment of vulnerability will play a large part in stimulating both industrial and developing societies to action – vulnerability not only to climate change itself, but also to other threats that climate change will accentuate. Wherever there are clear avenues of convergent interests, they should become focal points of cooperation.

The US and China surely need to get together, since, where climate change and energy security are concerned, they hold the future of the world in their hands. They could be rivals, and hasten the scenario in which a struggle for resources dominates world politics and where, at the same time, climate change proceeds apace. Yet it doesn't need much foresight to grasp that such an outcome would not be in the interests of either. From an initial position of denial, the Chinese leaders have become well aware of the fact that their country can't follow the same path as the West did in its development. That is, it can't continue to pump emissions into the air on a grand scale and hope to repair the damage later. In spite of a refusal to accept mandatory targets, the Climate Change Plan issued by the Chinese government in 2006 is comprehensive and anticipates a major switch-over to renewable energy sources, along something like the timescale anticipated by the developed countries. For instance, it sets out a goal of increasing the proportion of electricity coming from renewables to 16 per cent by 2020.

A series of earlier reports commissioned by the Chinese government made it clear that the country is vulnerable to the effects of climate change, a fact now wholly accepted within official circles. Millions of people in China depend on its major rivers for their livelihoods. Yet there has been a shrinkage of over 20 per cent in the glaciers that are the source of these rivers – a change that also threatens the hydroelectric plants in which China has vested a good deal of hope for energy generation. Some parts of the country are likely to experience extreme weather, given the fact that the country's climate is naturally volatile. A foretaste of the future may have been experienced in the unusually heavy snowfalls that paralysed much of the country late in 2007.

It might be thought improbable that the US and China could collaborate in a serious way on energy and climate change issues, but there is a precedent.[24] During the Cold War period there appeared to be no chance that the main adversaries, the US and the Soviet Union, could negotiate fruitfully with one another. Yet, as Senator Joseph Lieberman has observed, such collaboration did develop, and it met with some success.[25] At the outset of the arms control talks between the two protagonists, each was extremely wary of the other. Yet an effective interchange was achieved, with concrete results in terms of arms reductions. Lieberman points out that there is something of a parallel between the arms race of the Cold War and the competition for energy resources that is getting under way now.

Michael Klare argues that a starting-point could be the setting up of an annual top-level US–China energy summit, led by the president of each country. It could be modelled on comparable meetings held at the height of the Cold War. The main aims would be to minimize possible conflicts in the hunt for resources and to work out shared energy initiatives for the future, based on the fostering of low-carbon technologies. The initial meetings could lead to the elaboration of a full bilateral infrastructure, where officials, scientists and business leaders form joint committees and working-groups. In fact, a preliminary 'memorandum of understanding' for the creation of an energy dialogue between the two nations was already signed in 2004.

In October 2008 it was announced that three Chinese companies, including the country's biggest state-controlled company, China Mobile, will join the non-profit Climate Group, which is backed by some leading Western businesses. The other two Chinese corporations are Suntech, the third largest solar energy manufacturer in the world, and a privately owned firm, Broad Air Conditioning. Western businesses involved include BP, BSkyB, Nike and Tesco. China Mobile aims to reduce the energy intensity of its activities by 40 per cent by 2020. Other Chinese companies have also enquired about joining the group, whose goal is to cover more than 100 of the world's biggest firms.

The two countries could work together on a full range of technologies, with specific arrangements worked out to suspend normal patent rights. Carbon sequestration and storage could well be a centrepiece of such efforts, since coal consumption brooks so large in the energy practices of both countries. The US and China combined already account for almost half the coal consumption of the world as a whole. Of course, such bilateral connections shouldn't preclude similar arrangements with other states, especially those of the European Union. An EU–China climate change partnership already exists, aimed at speeding up technology transfers to China.

Finally, regional and bilateral policies are also likely to be crucial in respect of halting the loss of the world's rainforests. According to some estimates, about 25 per cent of CO_2 emissions over the past two centuries have come from changes in land use, of which deforestation is by far the biggest contributor. The forests that remain store some 638 gigatonnes of carbon, 280 gigatonnes of which are in biomass. 'Deforestation' sounds like a unitary activity, which therefore admits of a unitary solution, but such is not the case. We are back to the issue of the truly impoverished societies versus the rest. In these societies, the cutting back of the forest tends to be an enforced outcome of absolute poverty. The same is not always true in other countries where deforestation is taking place on a widespread level. Indonesia and Brazil, for instance, are both developing quite rapidly, even if they cannot match the pace set by the Chinese. In these cases, development is itself a source of deforestation, because of the growing demand for timber and timber-related products.

A range of strategies will be needed, rather than a single mechanism, depending upon differing local motivations for the practice. Subsidies, or emissions-reduction credits, unless they are very large, will not work for people living at the margins of subsistence. Investment in job-creation opportunities and local community interventions, for example, to empower women and reduce family sizes, will be of key importance.

The need to reduce deforestation, and quickly, may be one area where wide-ranging international cooperation could work.[26] Yet, once more, what key nations do is going to be crucial. Countries such as Brazil and Indonesia should get together to take proposals to the rest of the world. The Brazilian government has committed itself to a comprehensive national plan aimed at putting a complete stop to deforestation in the Amazon area within its territory by 2015. It is the kind of ambitious thinking that might well be pursued in collaboration with other nations whose own national programmes at the moment are far too limited in scope to address the scale of the problem.

In looking beyond international agreements of a universal sort, I am not signalling the demise of multilateralism, but its return. Multilateralism does not have to be the whole international community acting in concert – if it did, its purchase would be strictly limited. It means any form of collaboration in which several or more states are involved. Former Vice-President Dick Cheney's notion that countries would often have to act as 'coalitions of the willing' got a bad press, because it was used in the context of the war in Iraq. It was widely equated with taking a unilateral approach – not an unreasonable belief given the context in which it was used – which involved ignoring majority views in the UN and elsewhere. Yet there is no reason why coalitions of the willing shouldn't be formed to pursue activities approved or condoned by most of the world community, but where a small proportion of states need to be in the vanguard.

AFTERWORD

Notwithstanding the comparisons sometimes made, industrial civilization differs from all previous types of civilization that have gone before. Even the most advanced, such as Rome or traditional China, were regional – they were only able to extend their influence over a specific corner of the world. They made use of inanimate energy, such as water or wind, but only in a relatively marginal way. Their impact on the natural world was considerable, but mainly confined to modifications of the landscape.

Our civilization is truly global in scope; and it couldn't exist without the inanimate energy sources that fuel it. For better or worse, modern industry has unleashed a sheer volume of *power* into the world vastly beyond anything witnessed before. I mean here inanimate power, but also the power of human organization – the complex social, economic and political systems upon which our individual lives now depend. Power cuts two ways. The Enlightenment thinkers saw such capabilities as essentially benign. Thus Marx wrote in a celebrated phrase: 'Human beings only set themselves such problems as they can resolve.' Yet from the early days of industrial development there were those who saw the new powers as destructive or as threatening to escape the control of their creators.

In the shape of the controversy between the optimists and the doomsday thinkers, the debate continues today and is unresolved. Our civilization could self-destruct – no doubt about it – and with awesome consequences, given its global reach. Doomsday is no longer a religious concept, a day of spiritual reckoning, but a possibility imminent in our society and economy. If unchecked, climate change alone could produce enormous human suffering. So also could the drying up of the energy resources upon which so many of our capacities are built. There remains the possibility of large-scale conflicts, perhaps involving the use of weapons of mass destruction. Each could intersect with the others, as analysed in the previous chapter.

No wonder many take fright. Let's go back! Let's return to a simpler world! They are entirely understandable sentiments and have practical application in some contexts. Yet there can be no overall 'going back' – the very expansion of human power that has created such deep problems is the only means of resolving them, with science and technology at the forefront. There will probably be nine billion people in the world by 2050 – after which world population hopefully will stabilize, especially if the least developed countries make significant economic and social progress. Ways will have to be found of providing those nine billion people with a decent way of life.

What hope is there that, as collective humanity, we will be able to control the forces we have unleashed? The question is more or less unanswerable, since there are so many contingencies, unknowns – and, yes, unknown unknowns – involved. I'm not wholly sympathetic to those I have called the optimists, because they say that all the risks we face today have been exaggerated, which is false. I do side with them in the sense that risk and opportunity belong together; from the biggest risks can also flow the greatest opportunities, if collectively we can mobilize to meet them.

To some considerable degree we are in the hands of our political leaders. It has become customary to be cynical about politics, but the political field retains its capacity to inspire. The use of political capacity, national and international, will be essential to coping with the dilemmas that confront us. As I have said, two countries, the United States and China, have the ability to make or break our chances of success. Of course, bilateral cooperation, even in this unique case, can only get us so far. If ever a problem called for multilateral cooperation, with every country in the world on board, climate change is it. As with the internal policies of states, the 'how' matters more than the 'what'. Target-setting isn't going to have much impact, but many other forms of collaboration can do so. The sharing of scientific findings, technology transfer, direct aid coming from some nations to others, and a host of other collaborative activities are the way forward.

In spite of the divisions and power struggles that exist, coping with climate change could be a springboard for creating a more cooperative world. It might be a means of reinvigorating the UN and other institutions of global governance. I am cautious about these possibilities, partly because I want to skirt what I earlier called a bandwagon effect – the tendency to claim climate change as a vehicle for what one wanted to achieve anyway. Yet clearly it could happen, and, if so, it would be enormously consequential for world society as a whole.

Much will ride upon how successful over the next few years the European Union will be in reducing its average emissions. It starts with an advantage over the US in one sense, since some of its member-states have already made substantial progress in emissions reductions. They are pointing the way, both within the EU and as far as the rest of the world are concerned. The EU now comprises some 495 million citizens, so its impact in any case will be large. I have pointed to some of the difficulties that might restrain its ambitions. As far as its geopolitical influence is concerned, a great deal will depend upon two issues – how far it can sort out its relationship with Russia and how far, in the absence of the Lisbon Treaty, it can develop sufficient leadership capability to speak with one voice on the world stage.

Within the industrial countries there are many political battles to be fought and won. The US is once more in a prime position because of its large-scale contribution to greenhouse gas emissions and its gargantuan appetite for oil. It will be a colossal task to turn around a society whose whole way of life is constructed around mobility and a 'natural right' to consume energy in a profligate way. Yet it isn't as hopeless an endeavour as it looks. Numerous states, cities and organizations within the country have not only been pressing for change but are leading the way in introducing it.

The shaky condition of the US automobile industry is itself indicative of the pressure for a break with the past. The car manufacturers have in large degree been the authors of their own troubles. They actively lobbied the federal government under President George W. Bush to block any moves towards enlightened environmental policy, and they found a receptive audience in the White House. Their profit strategy was based on the gas-guzzlers they produced with such abandon. Now there is row upon row of unwanted SUVs.

All governments face deep dilemmas in reconciling climate change and energy policy with sustaining popular support, especially in times of economic difficulty. Public support is likely to wax and wane, for reasons I have discussed. In order to cope, governments will have to resort to a range of strategies while at the same time trying to foster a more widespread consciousness of the need for action. The habits and routines of everyday life stand in the way, but the key problem is the difficulty of getting people to accept that the risks are real and pressing.

Technological innovation is one of the several major jokers in the pack – the more so given the diversity of technologies vying for attention as we seek to shake free from our dependency on fossil fuels. Much can be done to reduce emissions without further advance. Yet the realm of technology is the most important domain where the theorem applies that the quantum leap in power that has created dangers for us can allow us to meet them. A new Dark Ages, a new age of enlightenment, or perhaps a confusing mixture of the two – which will it be? Probably the third possibility is the most likely. In that case, we all have to hope that the balance will be tilted towards the enlightenment side of the equation.

NOTES

Introduction

1. See, for example: Robert Henson, *The Rough Guide to Climate Change* (London: Rough Guides, 2008); Andrew Dessler and Edward Parson, *The Science and Politics of Climate Change* (Cambridge: Cambridge University Press, 2006); David King and Gabrielle Walker, *The Hot Topic* (London: Bloomsbury, 2008); Elizabeth Kolbert, *Field Notes from a Catastrophe* (London: Bloomsbury, 2006).

Chapter 1: Climate Change, Risk and Danger

1. Scott Borgerson, 'Arctic Meltdown', *Foreign Affairs*, March/April, 2008.
2. Intergovernmental Panel on Climate Change (IPCC), Fourth Assessment Report, 3 vols. and summary (Cambridge, Cambridge University Press, 2007).
3. IPCC Working Group 2, *Climate Change Impacts, Adaptation and Vulnerability* (Cambridge: Cambridge University Press, 2007).
4. S. Fred Singer and Dennis T. Avery, *Unstoppable Global Warming* (New York: Rowman and Littlefield, 2007).
5. Ibid., p. xi.
6. Patrick J Michaels, *Meltdown* (Washington, DC: Cato Institute, 2004).
7. See Bjørn Lomborg, *The Skeptical Environmentalist* (Cambridge: Cambridge University Press, 2001). Also see the writings of the scientist Richard Lindzen – for example, 'Climate of Fear', *Wall Street Journal*, 12 April 2006; 'There is no "Consensus" on Global Warming', *Wall Street Journal*, 26 June 2006; 'Debunking the Myth',

Business Today 43 (2006). A critical examination of Lomborg's claims is available at www.lomborg-errors.dk.

8. Bjørn Lomborg, *Cool It* (New York: Alfred A. Knopf, 2007), p. ix.
9. Christopher Booker and Richard North, *Scared to Death* (London: Continuum, 2007), p. 454. For a recent addition to the ranks of the sceptics, see Nigel Lawson, *An Appeal to Reason* (London: Duckworth, 2008). His conclusion is: 'We appear to have entered a new age of unreason, which threatens to be as economically harmful as it is profoundly disquieting. It is from this, above all, that we really do need to save the planet' (p. 2). Similar ideas are presented, in somewhat less florid fashion, in Colin Robinson, *Climate Change Policy* (London: Institute of Economic Affairs, 2008).
10. Booker and North, *Scared to Death*, p. 388.
11. See also James Lovelock, *The Revenge of Gaia* (London: Penguin, 2007).
12. David King and Gabrielle Walker, *The Hot Topic* (London: Bloomsbury, 2008), p. 80.
13. See Michael Glantz, *Currents of Change* (Cambridge: Cambridge University Press, 1996). Over the past decade, new weather forecasting methods have been developed to give advance warning of El Niño some two years ahead, making it possible for countries affected to prepare in advance.
14. James Hansen et al., 'Target atmospheric CO_2, where should humanity aim?', NASA/Goddard Institute for Space Studies, New York, 2007, available online.
15. King and Walker, *The Hot Topic*, ch. 5. See also John D. Cox, *Climate Crash* (Washington, DC: Joseph Henry, 2005).
16. Fred Pearce, *The Last Generation* (London: Eden, 2007), p. 26.
17. Jared Diamond, *Collapse* (London: Allen Lane, 2005).
18. Ibid., p.107. See also the important earlier work by Joseph Tainter, *The Collapse of Complex Societies* (Cambridge: Cambridge University Press, 1988).
19. Diamond, *Collapse*, p. 119.
20. See Joel Levy, *The Doomsday Book* (London: Vision, 2005).
21. Martin Rees, *Our Final Century* (London: Arrow, 2004).
22. Bill McGuire, *Surviving Armageddon* (Oxford: Oxford University Press, 2005), p. 16.
23. Ibid., pp. 27–32.
24. Frank Furedi, *Invitation to Terror* (London: Continuum, 2007), p. 112. Anyone interested in risk should begin with two of the leading books on the subject, worth reading together. These are Ulrich Beck, *Risk Society* (London, Sage, 1992), one of the classics of sociology, which treats risk mainly from a negative point of view, as danger to be avoided; and Peter Bernstein, *Against the Gods* (New York: Wiley, 1996), which is mainly about the energizing, positive aspects of risk and risk management. Beck's latest thinking is outlined in his *World at Risk* (Cambridge: Polity, 2008).

25. Dan Gardner, *Risk: The Science and Politics of Fear* (London: Virgin, 2008), p. 302.
26. Ibid., p. 3
27. Ibid., pp. 188–95
28. See Barbara Combs and Paul Slovic, 'Newspaper Coverage of Causes of Death', *Journalism Quarterly* 56 (1979).
29. Gardner, *Risk*, pp. 166–70
30. See note 21, above
31. See note 16 above.

Chapter 2: Running Out, Running Down?

1. Richard Heinberg, *The Party's Over* (Gabriola Island: New Society Publishers, 2003), p. 31.
2. Paul Middleton, *A Brief Guide to the End of Oil* (London: Robinson, 2007), ch. 3.
3. David Strahan, *The Last Oil Shock* (London: Murray, 2007), p. 40.
4. David Howell and Carole Nakhle, *Out of the Energy Labyrinth* (London: Tauris, 2007), pp. 88–92.
5. International Energy Agency, *World Energy Outlook 2007* (Paris: OECD/IEA, 2007).
6. Stephen Leeb, *The Coming Economic Collapse* (New York: Warner, 2007), p. 1.
7. See, for example, Kenneth Deffeyes, *Hubbert's Peak: The Impending World Oil Shortage* (Princeton: Princeton University Press, 2001); Paul Roberts, *The End of Oil* (London: Bloomsbury, 2004); Michael T. Klare, *Resource Wars* (New York: Holt, 2002); Matthew R. Simmons, *Twilight in the Desert* (New York: Wiley, 2005); Strahan, *The Last Oil Shock*. Strahan's title unconsciously echoes that of Fred Pearce on global warming, quoted in chapter 1: *The Last Generation*.
8. Strahan, *The Last Oil Shock*, p.60
9. Carola Hoyos and Javier Blas, 'Investment is the Key to Meeting Oil Needs', *Financial Times*, 29 October 2008.
10. David Victor et al., *Natural Gas and Geopolitics* (Cambridge: Cambridge University Press, 2006).
11. Julian Darley, *High Noon for Natural Gas* (White River Junction: Chelsea Green, 2004).
12. Ibid. p. 5
13. David Strahan, 'Lump Sums', *Guardian*, 5 March 2008.
14. Quoted in Dieter Helm, *The New Energy Paradigm* (Oxford: Oxford University Press, 2007), p. 19.
15. Ibid., p.21
16. Speech of then-President Vladimir Putin, quoted in Edward Lucas, *The New Cold War* (London: Bloomsbury, 2008), p. 212.
17. Adele Airoldi, *The European Union and the Arctic* (Copenhagen: Nordic Council of Ministers, 2008).
18. Strahan, *The Last Oil Shock*, p. 180.

19. Reported in Times Online, 11 January 2008.
20. Leeb, *The Coming Economic Collapse*, p. 77.

Chapter 3: The Greens and After

1. Nicholas Stern, *The Economics of Climate Change* (Cambridge: Cambridge University Press, 2007), p. xviii. The quote actually appears in the Review in several slightly different formulations.
2. William Morris, *News from Nowhere* (London: Longmans, p. 280.
3. Ralph Waldo Emerson, *Nature – Conduct of Life* (New York: Read, 2006). Originally published in 1836.
4. Bradford Torrey, *The Writings of Henry David Thoreau: Journal*, vol. 14 (Boston: Houghton Mifflin and Company), p. 205.
5. Janet Biehl and Peter Staudenmaier, *Ecofascism* (Edinburgh: AK Press, 1995). See also Franz-Joseph Bruggemeier et al., *How Green Were the Nazis?* (Ohio: Ohio University Press, 2005).
6. Quoted in Robert Goodin, *Green Political Theory* (Cambridge: Polity, 1992), p. 30.
7. Ibid., pp. 50ff.
8. William Rees, 'Ecological Footprints and Appropriated Carrying Capacity', *Environment and Urbanisation* 4 (1992).
9. See, for example, Ted Mosquin and Stan Rowe, 'A Manifesto for Earth', *Biodiversity* 5 (2004).
10. Peter Bernstein, *Against the Gods* (New York: Wiley, 1996).
11. Cass R. Sunstein, *Laws of Fear* (New York: Cambridge University Press, 2005), p. 4.
12. Ibid., p. 18.
13. Donella H. Meadows et al., *Limits to Growth: A Report for the Club of Rome's Project on the Predicament of Mankind* (New York: New American Library, 1972). See also Donella H. Meadows et al., *Limits to Growth – The 30-Year Update* (London: Macmillan, 2004), and many other publications by the same group of authors.
14. World Commission on Environment and Development, *Our Common Future* (Oxford: Oxford University Press, 1987).
15. Ibid., p. 326
16. Richard North; 'Sustainable Development: A Concept with a Future?' Liberales Institute Occasional Paper (2005), p. 6.
17. William Baue, 'Rio+10 Series', *Sustainability Investment News*, 23 August 2002. Simon Dresner puts the matter forcefully: '[Sustainable development] is a concept which combines post-modern pessimism about the domination of nature with almost Enlightenment optimism about the possibility to reform human institutions': *The Principles of Sustainability* (London: Earthscan, 2002), p. 164.
18. W. M. Lafferty and J. Meadowcroft, *Implementing Sustainable Development* (Oxford: Oxford University Press, 2000), p. 19.
19. Wilfred Beckerman, 'The Chimera of "Sustainable Development"', *Electronic Journal of Sustainable Development* 1 (2008).

20. Daniel Esty et al., *The Environmental Sustainability Index* (Davos: Global Leaders of Tomorrow Environmental Task Force, 2001).

21. The website of the Global Commons Institute, led by Aubrey Meyer, provides detailed background information.

22. See Avner Offer, *The Challenge of Affluence* (Oxford: Oxford University Press, 2006).

23. Both quotes from John Talberth and Clifford Cobb, *The Genuine Progress Indicator 2006* (Oakland: Redefining Progess, 2006), p. 1.

24. Offner, *The Challenge of Affluence*, p. 19.

25. Sustainable Society Index, 2008, available online from the Sustainable Society Foundation.

26. John Dryzek, *The Politics of the Earth* (Oxford: Oxford University Press, 1997), p. 145.

27. See Arthur Mol and David Sonnenfeld, *Ecological Modernisation Around the World* (London: Cass, 2000).

Chapter 4: The Track Record So Far

1. See Marcel Wissenburg, *Green Liberalism* (London: UCL Press, 1998), p. 7.

2. David Shearman and Joseph Wayne Smith, *The Climate Change Challenge and the Failure of Democracy* (London: Praeger, 2007), p. 133.

3. Robyn Eckersley, *The Green State*. (Cambridge, MA: MIT Press, 2004), ch. 4 and passim.

4. Yale Center for Environmental Law and Policy and Center for International Earth Science Information Network, Columbia University: 2008 Environmental Performance Index.

5. Germanwatch, *Climate Change Performance Index* (Bonn, 2008), pp. 4–5. For the best survey of climate change policy in the industrial countries, see Hugh Compston and Ian Bailey, *Turning Down the Heat* (London: Palgrave Macmillan, 2008).

6. Semida Silveira, 'Sustainability in the Energy Sector – the Swedish Experience', available from the Swedish Energy Agency, 2006.

7. Paul Harris, *Europe and Global Climate Change* (London: Elgar, 2007).

8. See Axel Michaelowa, 'German Climate Policy Between Global Leadership and Muddling Through', in Compston, *Turning Down the Heat*.

9. Federal Ministry for the Environment, *Nature Conservation and Nuclear Safety: Investments for a climate-friendly Germany* (Synthesis Report, Potsdam, July 2008), available online.

10. I am grateful to Olaf Corry for his help in providing the statistics that follow.

11. For a comprehensive analysis, see Irene Lorenzoni, Tim O'Riordan and Nick Pidgeon, 'Hot Air and Cold Feet', in Compston, *Turning Down the Heat*.

12. Hilary Benn: 'Climate Change Bill: Update Following Passage Through the Lords', DEFRA (2 June 2008).

13. For a heavily critical view, see Paul Brown, *Voodoo Economics and the Doomed Nuclear Renaissance* (London: Friends of the Earth, 2008).
14. Quoted in Ruth Sutherland: 'Comment', *Observer* (25 May 2008), p. 3.
15. 'Heathrow expansion', available on the Sustainable Development Commission website.
16. Quoted in Ian Jack, 'When It Comes to Railways, the Government is on the Wrong Track', *Guardian* (14 June 2008), p. 34.
17. Michael Pitt, *Learning Lessons from the 2007 Floods* (London: Cabinet Office, 2008).
18. James Randerson, 'Cut in Coal Brings UK Emissions Down by 2 per cent', *Guardian* (28 May 2008).
19. Committee on Climate Change, *Building a Low-Carbon Economy* (London, 2008), available online

Chapter 5: A Return to Planning?

1. John Dryzek, 'Ecology and Discursive Democracy', in Martin O'Connor, *Is Capitalism Sustainable?* (New York: Guilford Press, 1994), pp. 176–7.
2. Evan Durbin, *Problems of Economic Planning*. London: Routledge, 1949, p. 41.
3. Friedrich von Hayek, *The Constitution of Liberty* (Chicago: University of Chicago Press, 1960).
4. See, for example, David Orrell, *The Future of Everything* (New York: Thunders Mouth Press, 2006). For a critique of environmental prediction, see Orrin Pilkey and Linda Pilkey Jarvis, *Useless Arithmetic* (New York: Columbia University Press, 2007).
5. Jaco Quist and Philip Vergragt, 'Backcasting for Industrial Transformations', in Klaus Jacob et al., *Governance for Industrial Transformation* (Berlin: Environmental Policy Research Centre, 2003), pp. 423–5. Many other examples are discussed in this text.
6. Cynthia Mitchell and Stuart White, 'Forecasting and Backasting for Sustainable Urban Water Futures', *Water* 30 (2003).
7. R. Bord et al., 'Public Perceptions of Global Warming', *Climate Research* 11 (1998).
8. Ipsos MORI, 'Public Attitudes to Climate Change 2008', available on the Ipsos MORI website.
9. Irene Lorenzoni and Nick Pidgeon, *Defining the Dangers of Climate Change and Individual Behaviour* (Norwich: Centre for Environmental Risk, University of East Anglia, 2006).
10. Quoted in Martin Patchen, *Public Attitudes and Behaviour About Climate Change* (Purdue University Outreach Publication, 2006), p. 16. See also Sheldon Ungar, 'Knowledge, Ignorance and the Popular Culture', *Public Understanding of Science* 9 (2000); and John Sterman, 'Risk Communication on Climate', *Science* 322 (2008).
11. Patchen, *Public Attitudes*, p. 16.

12. Pew Research Center for the People and the Press, *Little Consensus on Global Warming* (2006), available on the Pew website.
13. HSBC, 'International Survey of Public Attitudes Towards Climate Change', reported on the HSBC website.
14. Patchen, *Public Attitudes*, p. 14.
15. Department for Environment, Food and Rural Affairs, *A Framework for Pro-Environmental Behaviours* (London: HMSO, 2008).
16. Ron Pernick and Clint Wilder, *The Clean Tech Revolution* (New York: Collins, 2007), pp. 263-73.
17. See Ithiel de Sola Pool, *The Social Uses of the Telephone* (Cambridge, MA: MIT Press, 1977).
18. Richard Florida, *The Rise of the Creative Class* (New York: Basic Books, 2004), pp. 34–5.
19. Malcolm Gladwell, *The Tipping Point* (London: Little, Brown, 2000).
20. For a discussion of some of these practices, see Richard Thaler and Cass Sunstein (yes, the self-same destroyer of the precautionary principle), *Nudge* (New Haven: Yale University Press, 2008).
21. For this section I am heavily indebted to the work of Sarah Pralle, *Branching Out, Digging In* (Washington, DC: Georgetown University Press, 2006), which was drawn to my attention by Hugh Compston. See also Sarah Pralle, 'Agenda-setting and Climate Change', in Hugh Compston, *The Politics of Climate Policy*, special book issue of *Environmental Politics*, forthcoming, 2009. As I do, Pralle draws heavily upon John Kingdon's book, *Agendas, Alternatives and Public Policies* (New York: Longman, 1995).
22. Kingdon, *Agendas*.
23. D. Wood and A. Velditz, 'Issue Definition, Information Processing and the Politics of Global Warming', *American Journal of Political Science* 51 (2007).
24. Helen Clayton et al., Report of the First Inquiry of the All Parliamentary Climate Change Group: *Is a Cross-Party Consensus on Climate Change Possible – or Desirable?* (London: HMSO, 2006), p. 3.
25. Quoted in ibid., p. 13.
26. Robin Eckersley, *The Green State* (Cambridge, MA: MIT Press, 2004), pp. 243–5. However, she adopts the precautionary principle, which I avoid and I have somewhat modified her list while, I hope, still maintaining its spirit.
27. Edelman Trust Barometer 2008 (London: Edelman, 2008).
28. For an account going up to the late 1990s, see Peter Newell, *Climate for Change* (Cambridge: Cambridge University Press, 2000), ch. 5. The quotation is from p. 98.
29. Quoted in ibid., p. 104.
30. Quoted in Peter Senge, *The Necessary Revolution* (London: Brealey, 2008), p. 77.
31. Quoted in ibid., p. 77.
32. Christine MacDonald, *Green Inc* (London: Lyons Press, 2008).

33. Senge, *The Necessary Revolution*, ch. 13.
34. Details of the company's '2020 Strategic Framework for Sustainability' is available on its website.
35. Available on Citigroup's website.
36. Charles Prince, CEO of the company, quoted on the Citigroup website in the press release of the $50 billion programme, 8 May 2007.
37. Senge, *The Necessary Revolution*, ch. 5.
38. Tommy Linstroth and Ryan Bell, *Local Action* (Burlington: University of Vermont Press, 2007), ch. 3.

Chapter 6: Technologies and Taxes

1. Jeremy Rifkin, *The Hydrogen Economy* (New York: Tarcher, 2002).
2. Ibid., p. 9.
3. For a caustic survey of hydrogen and other renewable technologies, see James Lovelock, *The Revenge of Gaia* (London: Perseus, 2007
4. IPCC, Mitigation. Contribution of Working Group III to the Fourth Assessment Report (Cambridge: Cambridge University Press, 2007), p. 269
5. (No author): 'Going underground', *New Scientist* (11 October 2008).
6. Ron Pernick and Clint Wilder, *The Clean Tech Revolution* (New York: HarperCollins, 2007).
7. 'Dig Deep', *The Economist* (June 21 2008).
8. Wallace Broecker and Robert Kunzig, *Fixing Climate* (New York: Hill & Wang, 2008).
9. Paul Hawken et al., *Natural Capitalism* (London: Little, Brown, 1999).
10. Robert Socolow and Stephen Pacala, 'Stabilization Wedges', *Science* 305 (2004), pp. 968–72.
11. Christopher Freeman, *The Economics of Hope* (New York: Pinter, 1992).
12. Nicholas Stern, *The Economics of Climate Change* (Cambridge: Cambridge University Press, 2007), ch. 16.
13. See Bethany McLean and Peter Elkind, *The Smartest Guys in the Room* (New York: Penguin, 2003).
14. John Scott and Gareth Evans, 'Electricity Networks', in Dieter Helm (ed.), *The New Energy Paradigm* (Oxford: Oxford University Press, 2007).
15. Stern, *The Economics of Climate Change*, p. 403.
16. Ibid., p. 402.
17. Amory B. Lovins et al., 'A Roadmap for Natural Capitalism', *Harvard Business Review* 77 (May/June 1999), pp. 78–81.
18. Scott and Evans, 'Electricity Networks', pp. 51–62.
19. Swanbarton Limited, *Status of Electrical Energy Storage Systems* (London: Department of Trade and Industry, 2004).
20. European Commission, *European Union Technology Platform Smartgrids* (Luxembourg: Office of Official Publications, 2006).

21. UNEP, *Green Jobs* (Washington, DC: Worldwatch Institute, 2008).
22. Green New Deal Group, *A Green New Deal* (London: New Economics Foundation, 2008).
23. Michael Shellenberger and Ted Nordhaus, *The Death of Environmentalism*, 2005, p. 26; available at http://thebreakthrough. org/images/Death_of_Environmentalism.pdf. They coined the quip 'I have a nightmare!' that I quoted in the Introduction. In their subsequent book *Break Through* (Boston: Houghton Mifflin, 2007) they say this line was the most quoted part of their earlier essay and, indeed, it does stick in the mind.
24. Van Jones, *The Green Economy* (Center for American Progress, September, 2008).
25. Robert Pollin et al., *Green Recovery* (Center for American Progress, September 2008).
26. Mikael Skou Andersen et al., *An Evaluation of the Impact of Green Taxes in the Nordic Countries* (Copenhagen: TemaNord, 2000). See also Runar Brannlund and Ing-Marie Gren, *Green taxes, Economic Theory and Empirical Evidence from Scandinavia* (Cheltenham: Elgar, 1999).
27. Gilbert Metcalf, *A Green Employment Tax Swap* (Washington: The Brookings Institution, 2007).
28. Paul Ekins and Simon Dresner, *Green Taxes and Charges* (York: Rowntree Foundation, 2004).
29. Ibid., p. 14.
30. David Fleming, *Energy and the Common Purpose* (London: Lean Economy Connection, 2006).
31. Richard Starkey and Kevin Anderson, *Investigating Domestic Tradable Quotas* (Norwich: Tyndall Centre, 2005).
32. Mayer Hillman and Tina Fawcett, *How We can Save the Planet* (London: Penguin, 2004).
33. Simon Roberts and Joshua Thumin, *A Rough Guide to Individual Carbon Trading* (London: Centre for Sustainable Energy, 2006), p. 3.
34. Roberts and Thumin, *A Rough Guide*, p. 31.
35. See John Urry, *Mobilities* (Cambridge: Polity, 2007).
36. Tom Vanderbilt, *Traffic* (London: Allen Lane, 2008).
37. Jean Gimpel, *The Medieval Machine* (New York: Penguin, 1977).
38. J. Kunstler, *The Long Emergency* (London: Atlantic, 2006), p. 270.
39. I am greatly indebted to John Urry's *Mobilities*, referenced above, for this analysis.
40. John Tiffin and Chris Kissling, *Transport Communications* (London: Kogan Page, 2007), p. 204

Chapter 7: The Politics of Adaptation

1. European Commission: *Adapting to Climate Change in Europe* (Brussels: Commission of the European Communities, 2007).

2. Gwyn Prins and Steve Raynor, *The Wrong Trousers* (Oxford: James Martin Institute, 2007), pp. 33-4.

3. European Commission, *Adapting to Climate Change in Europe*. Green paper of the European Commission, Brussels, 2007.

4. David Crichton, 'Insurance and Climate Change': paper presented at conference on Climate Change, Extreme Events and Coastal Cities, Houston, 9 February 2005, p. 17.

5. Tim O'Riordan et al., 'Designing Sustainable Coastal Futures', *21st Century Society* 3 (2008).

6. Crichton, 'Insurance and Climate Change'.

7. Sue Roaf et al., *Adapting Buildings and Cities for Climate Change* (Oxford: Elsevier, 2005).

8. See DEFRA, 'Making Space for Water', available at www.defra.gov.uk/environ/fcd/policy/strategy.htm

9. O'Riordan et al., 'Designing Sustainable Coastal Futures', pp. 152-5.

10. Helmut Kesting, *Hedging Climate Change* (Munich: Allianz Economic Research, 2007).

11. Ibid., p. 202.

12. J. Timmons Roberts and Bradley C. Parks: *A Climate of Injustice* (Cambridge, MA: MIT, 2007).

13. Daniel Osgood et al., 'Integrating Seasonal Forecasts and Insurance for Adaptation Among Subsistence Farmers' (Washington, DC: World Bank Policy Research Working Paper, 2008).

14. UNDP Human Development Report, *Risk, Vulnerability and Adaptation in Bangladesh* (Bangladesh Centre for Advanced Studies, 2007).

Chapter 8: International Negotiations, the EU and Carbon Markets

1. Quoted in Ian Rutledge, *Addicted to Oil* (London: Tauris, 2006), p. 121.

2. Bill McGuire, *Surviving Armageddon* (Oxford: Oxford University Press, 2005), p. 54.

3. 'A Ravenous dragon', *The Economist*, 15 March 2008, pp. 17-18.

4. Quoted in Rutledge, *Addicted to Oil*, p. 10.

5. John Carey, 'Russia's Path to Kyoto', *Business Week* (1 October 2004).

6. Aubrey Meyer, *Contraction and Convergence* (Bristol: Green Books, 2001).

7. Robert Henson, *The Rough Guide to Climate Change* (London: Rough Guides, 2008), pp. 292-3.

8. David G. Victor, 'Fragmented Carbon Markets and Reluctant Nations', in Joseph E. Aldy and Robert N. Stavins, *Architectures for Agreement* (Cambridge: Cambridge University Press, 2007), p. 148.

9. Victor, 'Fragmented Carbon Markets', p. 149.

10. Reported in 'A moment of Truth', *The Economist* (17 May 2008), pp. 77–8.
11. Rachmat Witoelar: 'Address to Closing Plenary', UN Climate Change Conference, Bali, 2007, available online.
12. Oliver Tickell 'The "Bali Roadmap"', in *Was Bali a Success? Open Democracy* (online), 18 December 2007.
13. For an excellent analysis, see David G. Victor, 'Fragmented Carbon Markets'.
14. Quoted in James Randerson: 'Top Scientists Warn Against Rush to Biofuel', *Guardian* (25 March 2008).
15. Quoted in 'EU Emissions Trading Scheme', EurActiv.com (February 2008), p. 3.
16. Anne Mettler, *From Why to How* (Brussels: Lisbon Council, 2008), p. 1.
17. See Donald MacKenzie, *Making Things the Same* (Edinburgh: School of Social and Political Studies, 2008); and 'Constructing Emissions Markets', in *Material Markets* (Oxford: Oxford University Press, 2009), ch. 7. I draw extensively upon his excellent discussion in what follows.
18. Denny Ellerman et al., *Markets for Clean Air* (Cambridge: Cambridge University Press, 2000).
19. Danny Ellerman and Barbara Buchner, *Over-allocation or Abatement*, Report no 141 (Cambridge, MA: MIT Joint Program on the Science and Policy of Global Change, 2006).
20. For a useful survey, see Ricardo Bayon et al., *Voluntary Carbon Markets* (London: Earthscan, 2008).
21. Nicholas Stern, 'Key Elements of a Global Deal on Climate Change', 2008. Available on the website of the London School of Economics.
22. Ibid., p.10.

Chapter 9: The Geopolitics of Climate Change

1. Peter Halden, *The Geopolitics of Climate Change* (Stockholm: Swedish Defence Research Agency, 2007).
2. Ibid., pp. 150–8.
3. See Gerard Prunier, *Dafur, the Ambiguous Genocide* (London: Hurst, 2005).
4. US Department of Defense, *Military Power of the People's Republic of China* (Washington, DC: Office of the Secretary of Defense, 2006).
5. Michael Klare, 'The New Geopolitics of Energy', *The Nation* (19 May 2008), p. 3. See also the same author's *Rising Powers, Shrinking Planet* (New York: Holt, 2008).
6. Department of the Navy, *A Cooperative Strategy for 21st Century Seapower* (Washington, DC: Department of the Navy, 2007).
7. Klare, 'The New Geopolitics of Energy'.

8. Robert Kagan, *The Return of History and the End of Dreams* (London: Atlantic, 2008).
9. Ibid., p. 3.
10. Ibid., p. 77.
11. David Hannay: *New world Disorder* (London: Tauris, 2008), p. 75.
12. Ibid., p. 300.
13. When Condoleezza Rice was set to replace Colin Powell as US Secretary of State, she remarked that the foreign policy of the Bush administration would 'proceed from the firm ground of national interest, not from the interests of an illusory international community'. Quoted in Louis Klarevas, 'Political Realism', *Harvard International Review* 26 (2004), p. 2.
14. Paul Collier, *The Bottom Billion* (Oxford: Oxford University Press, 2007), p. 3.
15. Ibid., p.3
16. Ibid., pp. 74–5.
17. Thomas Friedman, *Hot, Flat and Crowded* (London: Allen Lane, 2008), pp. 82–110.
18. Ibid., pp. 94–5.
19. Michael Ross, 'Oil, Islam and Women', *American Political Science Review* 43 (2008).
20. Pavel Baev et al., *Pipelines, Politics and Power* (London: Centre for European Reform, 2008).
21. Carlo Carraro, 'Incentives and Institutions', in Joseph E. Aldy and Robert N. Stavins, *Architectures for Agreement* (Cambridge: Cambridge University Press, 2007), pp. 164–5.
22. C. Egenhofer et al., quoted in ibid., p. 165.
23. Phil Waugh: 'Deal on Climate Change at Risk', *Evening Standard* (9 July 2008), p. 27.
24. Klare, *Rising Powers*, pp. 244–61.
25. Remarks of Senator Joseph Lieberman to the Council on Foreign Relations: 'China/US Energy Policies: A Choice of Cooperation or Collision', Washington, DC (2 December 2005); quoted in Klare, *Rising Powers*, p. 245.
26. See Charlotte Streck et al., *Climate Change and Forests* (London: Chatham House, 2008).

REFERENCES

'A Moment of Truth': *The Economist*, 15 May 2008.

Airoldi, Adele: *The European Union and the Arctic*. Copenhagen: Nordic Council of Ministers, 2008.

Andersen, M. S., N. Dengsøe and A. B. Pedersen: *An Evaluation of the Impact of Green Taxes in the Nordic Countries*. Copenhagen: Nordic Council of Ministers, 2001.

'A Ravenous Dragon': *The Economist*, 13 March 2008.

Baev, Pavel, et al.: *Pipelines, Politics and Power: The Future of EU–Russia Energy Relations*. London: Centre for European Reform, 2008.

Baue, William: 'Rio+10 Series'. *Sustainability Investment News*, 23 August 2002; available at: www.socialfunds.com/news/article.cgi/913.html.

Bayon, Ricardo, Amanda Hawn and Katherine Hamilton: *Voluntary Carbon Markets*. London: Earthscan, 2007.

Beck, Ulrich: *Risk Society*. London: Sage, 1992.

Beckerman, Wilfred: 'The Chimera of "Sustainable Development"'. *Electronic Journal of Sustainable Development* 1, 2008.

Benn, Hilary: 'Climate Change Bill: Update Following Passage Through the Lords'. DEFRA, 2 June 2008.

Bernstein, Peter L.: *Against the Gods*. New York: Wiley, 1996.

Biehl, Janet and Peter Staudenmaier: *Ecofascism*. Edinburgh: AK Press, 1995.

Bobbitt, Philip: *Terror and Consent*. New York: Knopf, 2008.

Booker, Christopher and Richard North: *Scared to Death*. London: Continuum, 2007.

Bord, R. et al.: 'Public Perceptions of Global Warming'. *Climate Research* 11, 1998.

Borgerson, Scott G.: 'Arctic Meltdown'. *Foreign Affairs* 87/2, March/April 2008, pp. 63–77.

Brannlund, Runar and Ing-Marie Gren: *Green Taxes, Economic Theory and Empirical Evidence from Scandanavia*. Cheltenham: Edward Elgar, 1999.

British Antarctic Survey: 'Climate Change – Our View'. December 2007; available at: www.antarctica.ac.uk//bas_research/our_views/climate_change.php.

Broecker, Wallace and Robert Kunzig: *Fixing Climate*. New York: Hill & Wang, 2008.

Brown, Paul: *Voodoo Economics and the Doomed Nuclear Renaissance*. London: Friends of the Earth, 2008.

Bruggemeier, Franz-Josef, Mark Cioc and Thomas Zeller (eds): *How Green Were the Nazis?* Ohio: Ohio University Press, 2005.

Capoor, Karan and Philippe Ambrosi: *State and Trends of the Carbon Market*. Washington, DC: The World Bank, 2007.

Carey, John: 'Russia's Path to Kyoto'. *Business Week*, 1 October 2004.

Carraro, Carlo: 'Incentives and Institutions', in Joseph E. Aldy and Robert N. Stavins, *Architectures for Agreement*. Cambridge: Cambridge University Press, 2007.

Clayton, Helen et al.: *Report of the First Inquiry of the All-Parliamentary Climate Change Group: Is a Cross-Party Consensus on Climate Change Possible – or Desirable?* London: HMSO, 2006.

Collier, Paul: *The Bottom Billion*. Oxford: Oxford University Press, 2007.

Combs, Barbara and Paul Slovic: 'Newspaper Coverage of Causes of Death'. *Journalism Quarterly* 56, Winter 1979.

Commission on Growth and Development: *The Growth Report*. Washington, DC: World Bank, 2008.

Compston, Hugh and Ian Bailey (eds): *Turning Down the Heat: The Politics of Climate Policy in Affluent Democracies*. London: Palgrave Macmillan, 2008.

Cox, John D.: *Climate Crash*. Washington, DC: Joseph Henry Press, 2005.

Crichton, David: 'Insurance and Climate Change'. Paper presented at conference on *Climate Change, Extreme Events and Coastal Cities: Houston and London*. Houston, 9 February 2005.

Darley, Julian: *High Noon for Natural Gas*. White River Junction: Chelsea Green, 2004.

Deffeyes, Kenneth: *Hubbert's Peak: The Impending World Oil Shortage*. Princeton: Princeton University Press, 2001.

Department for Environment, Food and Rural Affairs: *A Framework for Pro-Environmental Behaviours*. London: HMSO, 2008.

Department of the Navy: *A Cooperative Strategy for 21st Century Seapower*. Washington, DC: Department of the Navy, 2007.

de Sola Pool, Ithiel (ed.): *The Social Uses of the Telephone*. Cambridge, MA: MIT Press, 1977.

Dessler, Andrew and Edward Parson: *The Science and Politics of Climate Change*. Cambridge: Cambridge University Press, 2006.

Diamond, Jared: *Collapse: How Societies Choose or Fail to Survive*. London: Allen Lane, 2005.

'Dig Deep': *The Economist*, 19 June 2008.

Dresner, Simon: *The Principles of Sustainability*. London: Earthscan, 2002.

Dryzek, John: 'Ecology and Discursive Democracy', in Martin O'Connor, *Is Capitalism Sustainable?* New York: Guilford Press, 1994, pp. 176–7.

Dryzek, John: *The Politics of the Earth*. Oxford: Oxford University Press, 1997.

Durbin, Evan: *Problems of Economic Planning*. London: Routledge, 1949.

Eckersley, Robyn: *The Green State*. Cambridge, MA: MIT Press, 2004.

Edelman Trust Barometer. London: Edelman, 2008.

Ekins, Paul and Simon Dresner: *Green Taxes and Charges*. York: Rowntree Foundation, 2004.

Element Energy: *The Growth Potential for Microgeneration in England, Wales and Scotland*. Cambridge: Element Energy, 2008.

Ellerman, A. Denny and Barbara Buchner: *Over-Allocation or Abatement?* Report No. 141. Cambridge, MA: MIT Joint Program on the Science and Policy of Global Change, 2006.

Ellerman, A. Denny et al.: *Markets for Clean Air*. Cambridge: Cambridge University Press, 2000.

Emerson, Ralph Waldo: *Nature – Conduct of Life*. New York: Read Books, 2006.

Esty, Daniel C. et al.: *Environmental Sustainability Index*. Davos: Global Leaders of Tomorrow Environment Task Force, 2001.

'EU emissions trading scheme'. Available at: www.euractiv.com/. February 2008.

European Commission, Directorate-General for Research: *European Technology Platform Smartgrids*. Luxembourg: Office of Official Publications of the European Communities, 2006.

European Commission: *Adapting to Climate Change in Europe – Options for EU Action*. Green Paper from the Commission to the Council, the European Parliament, the European Economic and Social Committee and the Committee of the Regions. Brussels: Commission of the European Communities, 2007.

European Environment Agency: *Greenhouse Gas Emission Trends and Projections in Europe*. Copenhagen: EEA, 2006.

European Union: *Climate Change and International Security*. Paper from the High Representative and the European Commission to the European Council. S113/08, March 2008. Available at: www.consilium.europa. eu/euDocs/cms_Data/docs/pressData/en/reports/99387.pdf.

Fleming, David: *Energy and the Common Purpose*. London: Lean Economy Connection, 2006.

Florida, Richard: *The Rise of the Creative Class*. New York: Basic Books, 2004.

Freeman, Christopher: *The Economics of Hope*. New York: Pinter, 1992.

Furedi, Frank: *Invitation to Terror*. London: Continuum, 2007.

Thomas Friedman: *Hot, Flat and Crowded*. London: Allen Lane, 2008.

Gardner, Dan: *Risk: The Science and Politics of Fear*. London: Virgin, 2008.

Germanwatch: *Climate Change Performance Index*. Bonn, 2007.
Germanwatch: *Climate Change Performance Index*. Bonn, 2008.
Giddens, Anthony: *Europe in the Global Age*. Cambridge, Polity, 2006.
Giddens, Anthony: *The Third Way*. Cambridge, Polity, 1998.
Gimpel, Jean: *Medieval Machine*. New York: Penguin, 1977.
Gladwell, Malcolm: *The Tipping Point*. London: Little, Brown, 2000.
Glantz, Michael H.: *Currents of Change*. Cambridge: Cambridge University Press, 1996.
Goodin, Robert: *Green Political Theory*. Cambridge: Polity, 1992.
Gore, Al: *Earth in the Balance*. New York: Plume, 1993.
Halden, Peter: *The Geopolitics of Climate Change*. Stockholm: Swedish Defence Research Agency, 2007.
Hannay, David: *New World Disorder*. London: Tauris, 2008.
Harris, Paul G. (ed.): *Europe and Global Climate Change*. Cheltenham: Edward Elgar, 2007.
Hawken, Paul et al.: *Natural Capitalism*. London: Little, Brown, 1999.
von Hayek, Friedrich: *The Constitution of Liberty*. Chicago: University of Chicago Press, 1960.
Heinberg, Richard: *The Party's Over*. Gabriola Island, British Columbia: New Society Publishers, 2003.
Helm, Dieter (ed.): *The New Energy Paradigm*. Oxford: Oxford University Press, 2007.
Helm, Dieter: 'Sins of Emission'. *Wall Street Journal*, 13 March 2008.
Henson, Robert: *The Rough Guide to Climate Change*. London: Rough Guides, 2008.
Hillman, Mayer with Tina Fawcett: *How We Can Save the Planet*. London: Penguin, 2004.
Howell, David and Carole Nakhle: *Out of the Energy Labyrinth*. London: Tauris, 2007.
Hoyos, Carola and Javier Blas, 'Investment is the Key to Meeting Oil Needs'. *Financial Times*, 29 October 2008.
HSBC: *International Climate Confidence Index*. London: HSBC Holdings, 2007.
Hughes, James: *Evidence to the Canadian Standing Committee on Environment and Sustainable Development*. Ottawa, 11 February 2008.
Intergovernmental Panel on Climate Change: *Climate Change 2007: Mitigation*. Contribution of Working Group III to the Fourth Assessment Report of the Intergovernmental Panel on Climate Change. Cambridge: Cambridge University Press, 2007.
Intergovernmental Panel on Climate Change: *Climate Change 2007: Synthesis Report*. Contribution of Working Groups I, II and III to the Fourth Assessment Report of the Intergovernmental Panel on Climate Change. Geneva: IPCC, 2007.
International Energy Agency: *World Energy Outlook*. Paris: OECD/IEA, 2007.
Ipsos MORI: *Public Attitudes to Climate Change, 2008*. London: Ipsos MORI, 2008.

Jack, Ian: 'When It Comes to Railways, the Government is on the Wrong Track'. *Guardian*, 14 June 2008.

Jones, Van: *The Green Economy*. Centre for American Progress, September 2008.

Kagan, Robert: *The Return of History and the End of Dreams*. London: Atlantic, 2008.

Kesting, Helmut: *Hedging Climate Change*. Munich: Allianz Dresdner Economic Research, 2007.

King, David and Gabrielle Walker: *The Hot Topic*. London: Bloomsbury, 2008.

Kingdon, John: *Agendas, Alternatives and Public Policies*. New York: Longman, 1995.

Klare, Michael T.: 'The New Geopolitics of Energy'. *The Nation*, 19 May 2008.

Klare, Michael T.: *Resource Wars: The New Landscape of Global Conflict*. New York: Henry Holt, 2002.

Klare, Michael T.: *Rising Powers, Shrinking Planet*. New York: Holt, 2008.

Klarevas, Louis: 'Political realism'. *Harvard International Review* 26, 2004.

Knight, Frank: *Risk, Uncertainty and Profit*. New York: Century Press, 1964.

Kolbert, Elizabeth. *Field Notes from a Catastrophe*. London: Bloomsbury, 2006.

Kunstler, James Howard: *The Long Emergency*. London: Atlantic, 2006.

Lafferty, William M. and James Meadowcroft (eds.): *Implementing Sustainable Development*. Oxford: Oxford University Press, 2000.

Lawson, Nigel: 'The REAL inconvenient truth'. *Daily Mail*, 5 April 2008.

Lawson, Nigel: *An Appeal to Reason*. London: Duckworth, 2008.

Leeb, Stephen: *The Coming Economic Collapse*. New York: Warner, 2007.

Levy, Joel: *The Doomsday Book*. London: Vision, 2005.

Lifton, Robert Jay: *Indefensible Weapons*. New York: Basic Books, 1982.

Lindzen, Richard: 'Climate of Fear'. *Wall Street Journal*, 12 April 2006.

Lindzen, Richard: 'Debunking the Myth'. *Business Today* 43, 2006, pp. 66–7.

Lindzen, Richard: 'Taking Greenhouse Warming Seriously'. *Energy & Environment* 18/7–8, 2007, pp. 937–50.

Lindzen, Richard: 'There Is No "Consensus" on Global Warming'. *Wall Street Journal*, June 26, 2006.

Linstroth, Tommy and Ryan Bell: *Local Action*. Burlington, Vermont: University of Vermont Press, 2007.

Lomborg, Bjørn: *Cool It*. New York: Alfred A. Knopf, 2007.

Lomborg, Bjørn: *The Skeptical Environmentalist*. Cambridge: Cambridge University Press, 2001.

Lorenzoni, Irene and Nick Pidgeon: *Defining the Dangers of Climate Change and Individual Behaviour*. Norwich: Centre for Environmental Risk, University of East Anglia, 2006.

Lorenzoni, Irene, Tim O'Riordan and Nick Pidgeon: 'Hot Air and Cold Feet', in Hugh Compston and Ian Bailey (eds), *Turning Down the Heat: The Politics of Climate Policy in Affluent Democracies*. London: Palgrave Macmillan, 2008.

Lovelock, James: *The Revenge of Gaia*. London: Penguin, 2007.

Lovins, Amory B.: 'Energy Strategy: The Road Not Taken'. *Foreign Affairs* 55, October 1976.

Lovins, Amory B. et al.: 'A Roadmap for Natural Capitalism'. *Harvard Business Review* 77, May/June 1999.

Lucas, Edward: *The New Cold War*. London: Bloomsbury, 2008.

MacDonald, Christine: *Green Inc*. London: Lyons Press, 2008.

MacKenzie, Donald: 'Making Things the Same'. Available at: www.sps.ed.ac.uk/__data/assets/pdf_file/0018/4860/bottom_line.pdf, February 2008.

MacKenzie, Donald: *Material Markets*. Oxford: Oxford University Press, 2009.

McGuire, Bill: *Surviving Armageddon*. Oxford: Oxford University Press, 2005.

McLean, Bethany and Peter Elkind: *The Smartest Guys in the Room*. New York: Penguin, 2003.

Meadows, Donella H. at al.: *Limits to Growth: A Report for the Club of Rome's Project on the Predicament of Mankind*. New York: New American Library, 1972.

Meadows, Donella H. et al.: *Limits to Growth – The 30-Year Update*. London: Macmillan, 2004.

Metcalf, Gilbert: *A Green Employment Tax Swap*. Washington, DC: The Brookings Institution, June 2007.

Mettler, Anne: *From Why to How*. Brussels: Lisbon Council, 2008.

Meyer, Aubrey: *Contraction and Convergence*. Bristol: Green Books, 2001.

Michaelowa, Axel: 'German Climate Policy Between Global Leadership and Muddling Through', in Hugh Compston and Ian Bailey (eds), *Turning Down the Heat: The Politics of Climate Policy in Affluent Democracies*. London: Palgrave Macmillan, 2008.

Michaels, Patrick J.: *Meltdown*. Washington, DC: Cato Institute, 2004.

Middleton, Paul: *A Brief Guide to the End of Oil*. London: Robinson Publishing, 2007.

Mitchell, Cynthia and Stuart White: 'Forecasting and Backcasting for Sustainable Urban Water Futures'. *Water* 30, August 2003, pp. 25–8.

Mol, Arthur P. J. and David A. Sonnenfeld (eds): *Ecological Modernisation around the World*. London: Cass, 2000.

Morris, William: *News from Nowhere, or, An Epoch of Rest*. London: Longmans, Green & Co., 1918.

Mosquin, Ted and J. Stan Rowe: 'A Manifesto for Earth'. *Biodiversity* 5/1, 2004, pp. 3–9.

Myers, Norman: 'Environmental Unknowns'. *Science* 269, 21 July 1995.

Newell, Peter: *Climate for Change*. Cambridge: Cambridge University Press, 2000.

North, Richard: 'Sustainable Development: A Concept with a Future?' Occasional Paper. Potsdam: Liberales Institute, 2005.

Offer, Avner: *The Challenge of Affluence*. Oxford: Oxford University Press, 2006.

O'Riordan, Tim et al.: 'Designing Sustainable Coastal Futures'. *Twenty-First Century Society* 3, 2008.

Orrell, David: *The Future of Everything*. New York: Thunders Mouth Press, 2006.

Osgood, Daniel et al.: *Integrating Seasonal Forecasts and Insurance for Adaptation Among Subsistence Farmers*. Washington, DC: World Bank Development Research Group, 2008.

Patchen, Martin: *Public Attitudes and Behaviour about Climate Change*. West Lafayette: Purdue Climate Change Research Center, Purdue University, 2006.

Pearce, Fred: *The Last Generation*. London: Eden Project Books, 2007.

Pernick, Ron and Clint Wilder: *The Clean Tech Revolution*. New York: HarperCollins, 2007.

The Pew Research Center for the People and the Press: *Little Consensus on Global Warming*, 12 July 2006.

Pilkey, Orrin and Linda Pilkey Jarvis: *Useless Arithmetic*. New York: Columbia University Press, 2007.

Pitt, Michael: *Learning Lessons from the 2007 Floods*. London: Cabinet Office, 2008.

Pollin, Robert et al.: *Green Recovery*. Center for American Progress, September 2008.

Pralle, Sarah: *Branching Out, Digging In*. Washington, DC: Georgetown University Press, 2006.

Pralle, Sarah: 'Agenda-setting and Climate Change', in Hugh Compston, *The Politics of Climate Policy*, special book issue of *Environmental Politics*, forthcoming, 2009.

Prins, Gwyn and Steve Rayner: *The Wrong Trousers*. Oxford: James Martin Institute for Science and Civilization, University of Oxford, 2007.

Prunier, Gerard: *Dafur, the Ambiguous Genocide*. London: Hurst, 2005.

Quist, Jaco and Philip Vergragt: 'Backcasting for industrial transformations and system innovations towards sustainability', in Klaus Jacob et al. (eds), *Governance for Industrial Transformation*. Proceedings of the 2003 Berlin Conference on the Human Dimensions of Global Environmental Change. Berlin: Environmental Policy Research Centre, 2004.

Rahman, A. Atiq et al.: *Risks, Vulnerability and Adaptation in Bangladesh*. UNDP Human Development Report Office Occasional Paper. Dhaka: Bangladesh Centre for Advanced Studies, 2007.

Randerson, James and Nicholas Watt: 'Top Scientists Warn Against Rush to Biofuel'. *Guardian*, 25 March 2008.

Randerson, James: 'Cut in Coal Brings UK Emissions Down by 2 per cent'. *Guardian*, 28 May 2008.

Rees, Martin: *Our Final Century*. London: Arrow, 2004.

Rees, William: 'Ecological Footprints and Appropriated Carrying Capacity: What Urban Economics Leaves Out'. *Environment and Urbanisation* 4, 1992.

Rifkin, Jeremy: *The Hydrogen Economy*. New York: Tarcher, 2003.

Roaf, Sue, David Crichton and Fergus Nicol: *Adapting Buildings and Cities for Climate Change*. Oxford: Elsevier, 2005.

Roberts, J. Timmons and Bradley C. Parks: *A Climate of Injustice*. Cambridge, MA: MIT, 2007.

Roberts, Paul: *The End of Oil*. London: Bloomsbury, 2004.

Roberts, Simon: A Rough Guide to Individual Carbon Trading. London: Centre for Sustainable Energy, 2006.

Robinson, Colin: *Climate Change Policy*. London: Institute of Economic Affairs, 2008.

Robinson, J.: 'Future Subjunctive'. *Futures* 35, 2003.

Ross, Michael: 'Oil, Islam and Women'. *American Political Science Review* 43, 2008.

Rutledge, Ian: *Addicted to Oil*. London: Tauris, 2006.

Charlotte Streck et al.: *Climate Change and Forests*. London: Chatham House, 2008.

Sanborn, F. B. (ed.): *The Writings of Henry David Thoreau: Familiar Letters*, vol. 6. Boston: Houghton Mifflin, 1906.

Scott, John and Gareth Evans: 'Electricity Networks', in Deiter Helm (ed.), *The New Energy Paradigm*. Oxford: Oxford University Press, 2007.

Senge, Peter: *The Necessary Revolution*. London: Brealey, 2008.

Shearman, David and Joseph Wayne Smith: *The Climate Change Challenge and the Failure of Democracy*. London: Praeger, 2007.

Simmons, Matthew R.: *Twilight in the Desert*. New York: Wiley, 2005.

Singer, S. Fred and Dennis T. Avery: *Unstoppable Global Warming*. New York: Rowman & Littlefield, 2007.

Smith, Julian: 'Renewable Energy: Power Beneath Our Feet'. *New Scientist*, 8 October 2008.

Socolow, Robert and Stephen Pacala: 'Stabilization Wedges'. *Science* 305, 2004.

Starkey, Richard and Kevin Anderson: *Domestic Tradable Quotas*. Norwich: Tyndall Centre, 2005.

Stern, Nicholas: *The Economics of Climate Change*. Cambridge: Cambridge University Press, 2007.

Strahan, David: 'Lump sums'. *Guardian*, 5 March 2008.

Strahan, David: *The Last Oil Shock*. London: John Murray, 2007.

Sunderland, Ruth: 'Carrots As Well As Sticks Will Help Us to Swallow Green Taxes'. *Observer*, 25 May 2008.

Sunstein, Cass R.: *Laws of Fear*. New York: Cambridge University Press, 2005.

Swanbarton Limited: *Status of Electrical Energy Storage Systems*. London: Department of Trade and Industry, 2004.

Tainter, Joseph: *The Collapse of Complex Societies*. Cambridge: Cambridge University Press, 1988.

Talberth, John and Clifford Cobb: *The Genuine Progress Indicator*. Oakland: Redefining Progess, 2006.

Thaler, Richard H. and Cass R. Sunstein: *Nudge*. New Haven: Yale University Press, 2008.

Tickell, Oliver: 'The "Bali Roadmap"', in *Was Bali a Success?* openDemocracy (online), 18 December 2007.

Tiffin, John and Chris Kissling: *Transport Communications*. London: Kogan Page, 2007.

Torrey, Bradford (ed.): *The Writings of Henry David Thoreau: Journal*, vol. 14. Boston: Houghton Mifflin, 1906.

Urry, John: *Mobilities*. Cambridge: Polity, 2007.

Urry, John and Dennis Kingsley: *After the Car*. Cambridge: Polity, 2009.

US Department of Defense: Annual Report to Congress: *Military Power of the People's Republic of China, 2006*. Washington, DC: Office of the Secretary of Defense, 2006.

Vanderbilt, Tom: *Traffic*. London: Allen Lane, 2008.

Victor, David G.: *Collapse of the Kyoto Protocol and the Struggle to Slow Global Warming*. Princeton: Princeton University Press, 2001.

Victor, David G.: 'Fragmented Carbon Markets and Reluctant Nations', in Joseph E. Aldy and Robert N. Stavins (eds), *Architectures for Agreement*. Cambridge: Cambridge University Press, 2007.

Victor, David G., Amy M. Jaffe and Mark H. Hayes (eds): *Natural Gas and Geopolitics*. Cambridge: Cambridge University Press, 2006.

Waugh, Phil: 'Deal on Climate Change at Risk'. *Evening Standard*, 9 July 2008.

von Weizsacker, Ernst, Amory B. Lovins and L. Hunter Lovins: *Factor Four: Doubling Wealth – Having Resource Use*. London: Earthscan, 1997.

Wissenburg, Marcel: *Green Liberalism*. London: UCL Press, 1998.

Witoelar, Rachmat: 'Address to Closing Plenary'. UN Climate Change Conference, Bali, 2007, available online.

Wood, D. and A. Velditz: 'Issue Definition, Information Processing and the Politics of Global Warming'. *American Journal of Political Science* 51, 2007.

World Commission on Environment and Development: *Our Common Future*. Oxford: Oxford University Press, 1987.

Yale Center for Environmental Law and Policy and Center for International Earth Science Information Network, Columbia University: *Environmental Performance Index*. New Haven: Yale Center for Environmental Law and Policy, 2009.

Young, Stephen C. (ed.): *The Emergence of Ecological Modernisation*. London: Routledge, 2000.

INDEX